KILLER CULTS

Other Books in the Profiles in Crime Series

How to Catch a Killer–Katherine Ramsland, PhD

Extreme Killers–Michael Newton

Serial Killers of the '70s–Jane Fritsch

Serial Killers of the '80s–Jane Fritsch

PROFILES IN CRIME

KILLER CULTS

STORIES OF CHARISMA, DECEIT, AND DEATH

STEPHEN SINGULAR

STERLING
New York

STERLING
New York

An Imprint of Sterling Publishing Co., Inc.
1166 Avenue of the Americas
New York, NY 10036

ISBN 978-1-4549-3939-9

Distributed in Canada by Sterling Publishing Co., Inc.
c/o Canadian Manda Group, 664 Annette Street
Toronto, Ontario M6S 2C8, Canada
Distributed in the United Kingdom by GMC Distribution Services
Castle Place, 166 High Street, Lewes, East Sussex BN7 1XU, England
Distributed in Australia by NewSouth Books
University of New South Wales, Sydney, NSW 2052, Australia

For information about custom editions, special sales, and premium and corporate purchases,
please contact Sterling Special Sales at 800-805-5489 or specialsales@sterlingpublishing.com.

Manufactured in the United States of America

2 4 6 8 10 9 7 5 3 1

sterlingpublishing.com

Cover design by David Ter-Avanesyan
Interior design by Gavin Motnyk

CONTENTS

ACKNOWLEDGMENTS

When Sterling Publishing contacted me in the summer of 2019 about writing a cult anthology, I was intrigued by the subject matter, but the offer came with a significant challenge—the deadline was short. I could meet it only on one condition: I needed the help of my partner in crime writing over the last twenty-five years—my wife, Joyce Jacques Singular. Since the early 1990s, we had worked on a dozen crime books together and she had co-authored two of them (go to www.stephensingular.com for all the books). Joyce agreed to do the research, and we got busy. She quickly put together the basic files for all the cults in this book, and I took the writing from there. She made a number of editorial suggestions, including that we end with the Columbine cult because it is ongoing and brings the book into the present. From start to finish, her help wasn't just invaluable but allowed us to meet the deadline. Finally, she wrote the introduction to the anthology. A team effort made this happen, and I'm deeply grateful for her commitment, creativity, and contributions.

INTRODUCTION

I felt myself at loose ends. I had a deep longing for connection, for overriding spirituality. I gave myself completely to this extended nuclear family. We wanted to make a better world. If I trusted in God and gave myself completely to it, what could go wrong?

—A twelve-year ex-member of
the Unification Church

Cults have been with us throughout recorded history and beyond, evolving to fit society's changing norms. When the archaeological site Göbekli Tepe was uncovered in 1994, six miles from Urfa in southeastern Turkey, scholars were startled to find that the massive structures predated Stonehenge by approximately 6,000 years and the Egyptian pyramids by 7,000 years. Göbekli Tepe is estimated to be 11,000 to 12,000 years old. One monolithic temple that is thought to have been the site of prehistoric worship is adorned with carvings of stylized humans and intricate animals as well as skulls. Fragments of three carved skulls also were found, leading some to believe that the inhabitants belonged to a "prehistoric skull cult."

Ancient Egypt had more than 2,000 gods and goddesses, all supported by cults that were critical for maintaining well-being and order. Most deities were worshipped locally, as each town had its own deity, but other gods or goddesses developed much larger followings. They could bring great wealth to a city, along with status and powerful political backing. Those cults honored Ra, Osiris, Hathor, Isis, the crocodile god Sobek, and numerous others.

In ancient Greece, the secret rituals and celebrations of the mystery schools in Eleusis, west of Athens, were centered on Demeter and Persephone, goddesses of the harvest, agriculture, life, and death. Participants drank a barley and mint mixture called *kykeon*, which some scholars think was infused with a hallucinogen that induced visions and transformation.

In Rome, the followers of Bacchus, the god of wine and ecstasy, held secret ceremonies in the surrounding mountains, dressed in animal skins and wearing crowns of ivy and oak. Often sponsored by wealthy patrons, those so-called bacchanals unleashed a frenzy of temporary madness that was intended as a rebirth and renewal initiation. Several of the cults featured in this anthology, thriving many centuries after the fall of Rome, also used alcohol and psychotropic drugs as part of their rituals.

Cults involving saints were important during late antiquity, the Middle Ages, and the European Renaissance. The use of miraculous relics, some brought back from the Holy Land, were utilized to heal the sick and convert nonbelievers. From the mid-eighteenth century through the nineteenth century, spiritualism and interest in Eastern religions began to emerge. Looser sexual attitudes and expanding freedoms gave rise to modern cults, sects, and religious movements. Some had unorthodox practices, running the gamut from celibacy to polygamy.

With the twentieth century and the coming of the new millennium, apocalyptic/doomsday cults flourished. The 1960s saw the cult of Charles Manson, the '70s the Peoples Temple of Jim Jones, the '80s the Unification Church (Moonies), and the '90s David Koresh's Branch Davidians. The majority of the cults discussed in this book functioned during the twentieth century, with some continuing into the twenty-first. With the coming of the year 2000, many became increasingly fear-based and violent in order to control their members.

Cults have flourished and evolved throughout human history, leaving us both fascinated and repelled. Why do people join cults, especially the most extreme and dangerous ones? What qualities do their charismatic leaders possess that enable them to take over a person's life or the lives of a large group of people, both educated and uneducated? What causes seemingly normal men and women to hand their power over to another who can persuade them to engage in criminal behavior? This anthology tries to answer these questions by exploring both high-profile and very obscure cults. In most instances, the answers lie in a combination of reasons, including sex, money, and violence, but all rely on the most timeless and troublesome of human emotions: fear.

—Joyce Jacques Singular

1

KEITH RANIERE AND NXIVM

Humans can be noble. The question is: Will we put forth what is necessary?

—Keith Raniere

Human beings aren't comfortable living in the unknown. We tend to fill in the spaces between what has happened already and what might happen next with projections, assumptions, frustrations, angers, and fears. If we just knew the outcomes of this impending deal or that relationship, if we could predictably increase our success, we could relax and enjoy the future we're certain is coming. But we can't—right? Over the last few decades, a number of clever businesspeople, soothsayers, gurus, visionaries, and cult leaders have emerged to sell people on the notion that they and their programs can provide absolute answers to life's uncertainties and mysteries. Join the group, pay your fees, pledge allegiance to the leaders, and good things are bound to result.

Guaranteed.

Some of those leaders probably believe that as they climb their way to success, riches, and power over others—particularly sexual power—the most notorious and salacious things they do with their followers will never be revealed to the world at large. However, that's another unpredictable thing.

When Keith Raniere and his partner, Nancy Salzman, started the business NXIVM in the late 1990s, its stated purpose was to help people with all aspects of personality development, from childhood issues to creative expression to practicing compassionate ethics. The goals were high-minded and were aimed at people with ideals, intelligence, and resources. Who among us wouldn't want to assist in constructing better personalities? The couple utilized a training program called "rational inquiry"—their key to personal and professional growth. During their seminars, Keith was referred to as "Vanguard" and Nancy, an ex-nurse and therapist, as "Prefect." For a decade, they successfully grew the company, enrolling around 16,000 people in a variety of programs. In 2009, Raniere expanded both the reputation and the reach of his business by founding the World Ethical Foundations Consortium and persuading the Dalai Lama to speak at the institute.

Raniere was creating the kind of success he had dreamed about and worked for since childhood. Born into Brooklyn's middle class in 1960, he had long wanted something more than the modest rewards his parents had earned. His father was in advertising, his mother taught ballroom dancing, and the boy was age five the year they moved to Suffern, New York. His mother died when he was sixteen, and he moved once again, this time to the area around Albany. Soon afterward he dropped out of high school, a biographical detail he liked to dismiss when telling people that he'd been a "genius student" who spoke in complete sentences at age one and by age thirteen had taught himself computer languages and college-level mathematics. An early description he had written about himself was anything but modest, stating that he was "one of the top three problem solvers in the world," with ideas and plans to bring about "the change humanity needs in order to alter the course of history."

In the late 1970s, Raniere entered Rensselaer Polytechnic Institute, which didn't require a high school graduation certificate, and majored in physics, math, and biology, with minors in psychology and philosophy. After earning a degree in 1982, he started his career in computers and consulting. Two years later a woman accused him of having sex with her underage sister, but he claimed that the girl was actually older than her physical age. Not only that: she was the reincarnation of a Buddhist goddess, he was an enlightened being, and the two of them together could establish a harmonious sexual connection that transcended the laws of New York and the United States. When he managed to convince the girl's mother that he was interested in having a serious, committed relationship with her daughter, she accepted this and charges weren't pressed. This was the first crack in the facade Raniere showed the world, but nobody paid much attention to it, and so he plowed forward with his business plans.

Approaching the age of thirty, Raniere launched Consumers Buyline, a multilevel marketing program that sold the idea of paying high commissions to established patrons for bringing in new ones. By promising discounts on hotels, dishwashers, and groceries, Raniere signed up a quarter million customers, telling people that the company was worth about $50 million. Both his claims and his business practices came under scrutiny when regulators in twenty states began probing Consumers Buyline and New York State's attorney general filed a suit charging the company with operating an elaborate profit-making pyramid scheme. After considerable legal wrangling and negotiating, Raniere settled for a penalty of $40,000, but he would renege on some of that payment, clearly demonstrating how the American justice system is heavily tilted in favor of those who commit financial fraud or white-collar crimes rather than violent offenses.

After the collapse of Consumers Buyline, Raniere launched a second multilevel business, National Health Network, to sell vitamins at a health food store with his girlfriend, Toni Natalie. That relationship became complicated when he met his future partner, Nancy Salzman, who viewed Raniere in the same glowing terms in which he had long hoped the world would see him. In promotional material that he had written, Salzman contended that "there is probably no discovery since writing as important for humankind as Mr. Raniere's technology"—a technology designed for behavior modification. To help with the National Health Network, Salzman loaned Natalie $50,000 and began treating her therapeutically.

With both women vying for Raniere's attention, the company's financial situation began to deteriorate. In 1999, the conflict went to U.S. bankruptcy court in Albany and Raniere sided with Salzman against Natalie. In the middle of their dispute, he had sent Natalie verses from *Paradise Lost* along with notes criticizing her behavior ("Commits to evil for protection—stupid/weak."). He accused her of having a "pride barrier" that could lead to a "dream death line." After listening to the testimony about their relationship, a judge said he was upset that Raniere had sent the police to Natalie's mother's house and threatened her family over their personal and financial disputes. That was the second crack in Raniere's facade, but still no one was focusing much on a small-timer like him.

A federal judge would later call Raniere's actions with Natalie "a jilted fellow's attempt at revenge," ruling that he had brainwashed her, harmed her business, and coerced her into giving up her young son to the child's father. According to Natalie, Raniere had tried to convince her that her purpose in life was to have his baby, a child who would alter the

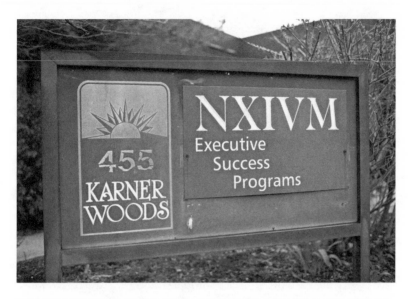

THE NXIVM EXECUTIVE SUCCESS PROGRAMS SIGN OUTSIDE OF THE OFFICE IN ALBANY, NEW YORK.

course of history—a theme running through his writings and speeches for decades.

In 1998, while knocking around New York City, Raniere had hatched the concept for NXIVM, eventually opening its headquarters in Albany. He gradually drew in hundreds and then thousands of customers with promises of everything from fulfilling one's personal potential to helping children speak a dozen languages and curing Tourette's syndrome, diabetes, and scoliosis. For the next half decade NXIVM was a success, and it received the kind of national attention that Raniere never had received before. In October 2003, *Forbes* magazine ran a cover story detailing his business practices and saying that some of NXIVM's consumers thought of him as an inspirational guru. His client list included Stephen Cooper, acting chief executive of Enron (a Houston-based energy company about to implode in spectacular ways); Antonia C. Novello, former U.S. surgeon general; Sheila Johnson, cofounder of Black Entertainment Television; Ana Cristina Fox, daughter of the Mexican president; and Emiliano

Salinas, son of a former Mexican president. The reviews of Raniere and NXIVM were basically positive.

To correct the "negative behaviors" he'd detected in high-level executives, Raniere brought in several big-name trainers—Richard Leider, Marshall Goldsmith, and Dartmouth professor Vijay Govindarajan—who charged $25,000 to $100,000 apiece for six sessions conducted over eighteen months. Other NXIVM students paid as much as $10,000 for five days of emotional processing given in thirteen-hour sessions. They were taught secret handshakes while donning colored sashes that determined one's standing in NXIVM. (Earning one's next sash was an honor akin to earning the next belt in the martial arts.) They were required to bow in front of Raniere, refer to him as "Vanguard," and attend classes such as "Face the Universe," "Money," and "Control, Freedom & Surrender." Once a day, students recited Raniere's twelve-point mission statement: "There are no ultimate victims; therefore, I will not choose to be a victim. . . ." People try to "destroy each other, steal from each other, down each other or rejoice at another's demise . . . it is essential for the survival of humankind" that wealth and resources be controlled by "successful, ethical people."

Students signed nondisclosure agreements (NDAs) about NXIVM and were encouraged to open up to teachers and reveal their negative habits, ostensibly to replace them with better ones. The object also was to render people vulnerable in front of the teacher, Vanguard, Prefect, or other students, which might lead them not only to take more classes but to repeat those previously completed.

Although it acknowledged the growth of NXIVM's "Executive Success" program, *Forbes* questioned Raniere's methods and reported on "a darker and more manipulative side" to his business with its "cult-like program aimed at breaking down his subjects psychologically" while "inducting them into a bizarre world of messianic pretensions, idiosyncratic language and ritualistic practices." It was the first time the word "cult" had been associated with Raniere at this level of exposure. To add to his aura, if not his "messianic pretensions," Raniere wore his hair long with a beard in what some interpreted as a conscious attempt to conjure historical images of Jesus Christ. He also increased the dimensions of his personal myth through some peculiar habits: he had no bank account or driver's license, drew no salary for his work, and had no bed of his own. He referred to people in need as "parasites." His fictional role models appeared to come from the Ayn Rand novels *Atlas Shrugged* and *The Fountainhead*, whose protagonists are self-serving—some would say ruthless—individualists.

In spite of the NDAs signed by NXIVM students, stories began leaking out about the seventeen-hour workshops and sleepless nights they endured. An anonymous woman claimed that they had induced hallucinations and the beginnings of her mental crack-up. After Stephanie Franco, a New Jersey social worker, spent more than $2,000 for a five-day class in Albany, she grew worried about NXIVM's rituals. Her family hired Rick A. Ross, a Jersey City cult specialist, who posted information about the organization on his website. Raniere and Salzman sued, but the case was eventually dismissed.

Sara Bronfman, the daughter of Seagram's magnate Edgar Bronfman, Sr., was twenty-six when her marriage began to crumble and she began looking for alternative ways to confront what lay ahead. Living in Belgium, she heard about NXIVM from a friend, signed up for classes, and was highly impressed with Raniere, taking a full-time job at Executive Success. Her sister, Clare, soon joined her, and they began funding the organization.

Edgar Bronfman was interviewed by *Forbes* about NXIVM and bluntly said, "I think it's a cult."

This was another crack ignored, as Raniere continued to expand his business and reputation as a success guru, opening training centers well beyond Albany. One was in Seattle.

In 2009, the first NXIVM whistleblower, Barbara Bouchey, came forward with more disturbing allegations regarding the organization. She confronted Raniere about his secret sexual relationships with clients and board members as well as other improper practices. When she decided to leave NXIVM that year, eight other women went with her, effectively closing down multiple centers, including Seattle's. Faced with harassment and lawsuits and hounded by rumors that the NXIVM brass was hatching a plot to have her thrown into a Mexican jail, Bouchey went into hiding with her son. This was another crack that essentially went unnoticed. Yet another appeared in 2010 when *Vanity Fair* ran the story "The Heiress and the Cult," which contended that Sara and Clare Bronfman had donated $150 million to NXIVM and revealed more of the organization's rituals and secrets. Raniere exploded and went on the offensive, suing the reporters behind the article. He had wriggled away from bad press and legal troubles in the past and determined that with the right strategy and advice and a positive attitude about success, he could continue playing the game and winning.

After all, although the NXIVM center had closed in Washington State, things were booming for the company in Canada. In the past, Vancouverites had commuted south of the border for NXIVM coursework in Seattle, but now the process was reversed: Americans were traveling north to the new branch that was thriving up there. Vancouver was filled with young, upwardly mobile consumers looking for innovative ways to get ahead. One woman said that her 2013 NXIVM recruitment was "like being invited to an Oscar party." The reference was appropriate because actors and aspiring actors were getting involved in the business, something Raniere had long hoped for. In Vancouver this was spearheaded by Sarah Edmonson.

In 2005, Edmondson had attended a spirituality-themed film festival and met Mark Vicente, the director of *What the Bleep Do We Know?* and a recent convert to NXIVM after his first sixteen-day "intensive" with the group. Edmonson, who was twenty-seven years old at the time, was living in a basement and scrambling for beer commercials. She was eager to get her life and career launched. She met Raniere and was charmed by him, like so many before her. He seemed to have the answers for everything: money, love, and work. Edmondson began spreading the word about NXIVM and bringing in new members, including young actors, raising her standing with Raniere.

Chad Krowchuk was one of the actors who had heard positive things from Edmondson and her husband that were backed up by acting friends Kristin Kreuk and Mark Hildreth. But it was Allison Mack who got him to attend his first five-day training in Albany. Instead of just hoping for a major gig as an actress, she'd become a TV star in the series *Smallville*, which was based on the DC Comics character Superman. Initially broadcast on The WB in 2001, *Smallville* moved to The CW after its fifth season. The show followed the story of Clark Kent in the fictional town of Smallville, Kansas, before he comes out to the world as Superman. Mack played Chloe Sullivan, a friend of Clark's who was in love with him (although he didn't feel the same way toward her). As the editor of her school's newspaper, she wants to "expose falsehoods" and "know the truth" about people, which inevitably leads her to look into Clark's past. The series was a hit and ran for ten years.

ACTRESS ALLISON MACK ARRIVES AT THE
U.S. EASTERN DISTRICT COURT AFTER A
BAIL HEARING.

Krowchuk and Mack had been child actors and were reunited in their early twenties, when he was working at Starbucks busing tables and she was on her way to stardom. Mack went to a NXIVM women's weekend retreat in 2007 and became a believer; eventually, Krowchuk joined her in Albany to meet the Raniere crowd. He wasn't as sold as Mack was on the programs and their ideas. In his view, the classes taught that everyone was responsible for his or her relationship with the external world, but if something went wrong in that world, it left students open to blame by a NXIVM coach, which to him seemed overly manipulative and judgmental. Krowchuk wasn't as committed as Mack and in time drifted away from her and NXIVM. Some of Mack's friends would later talk about how far into the group's practices and beliefs she'd gone and how much she talked about it to the point of annoyance.

Meanwhile, in downtown Vancouver, Mark Vicente and Sarah Edmondson were holding NXIVM training sessions at which recruits could earn their sashes on Wednesday evenings and weekends. Sarah had recruited more name actors, such as Nicki Clyne and Grace Park of *Battlestar Galactica*, using NXIVM as a platform for selling them on achieving more success in their careers. NXIVM also was employing Facebook and Twitter to recruit in cyberspace. Edmondson, like many others, had come into the group with high-minded goals and felt that NXIVM had helped her achieve some of them. She showed her commitment to the organization by taking part in a secret ceremony in Albany that involved having Raniere's initials branded halfway between her hip bone and her vulva.

Things went along for the next few years until problems arose from a most unlikely source. On a trip to Albany, Edmondson began witnessing activities that gradually turned her against NXIVM. In 2017, while enrolled in its Executive Success program, she came forward to accuse the group of telling the public they were conducting a skill development training session while running a sex cult. Edmondson had uncovered a secret part of NXIVM called DOS (Dominus Obsequious Sororium), a Latin phrase whose translation suggests dominating women and making them obedient to one's wishes. Edmondson said that she had seen women blindfolded, stripped naked, and asked to provide nude pictures of themselves during a submission ritual.

Edmondson's confessions were too serious and troubling to be ignored. They led to investigative reports in the media, headed by the *New York Times*, which in 2017 claimed that the group had a "secret sisterhood" in which the females were branded as "slaves." Edmonson meant "branded" literally. Others like her apparently had been marked with brands, much as ranchers do with horses and cattle. Then other women victims emerged and told the media that Raniere was a sex maniac who was running a cult devoted to satisfying his carnal desires. According to those accounts, several victims of his cravings were minors whom he manipulated into having intercourse. His accusers said that in the guise of being a healer who helped women move on from traumatic past events, including sexual assaults and rapes, he was in fact grooming them for his own pleasure. The key to a happy and enlightened life, he preached, was letting go of every boundary and attachment the world had imposed on a person—letting go of one's inhibitions. Some emotionally fragile female students did whatever he asked.

Edmondson also talked about how women in the group were encouraged to lose weight by using the NXIVM diet and eating only 800 calories or less per day for seven straight days. (Experts recommend a diet of 2,000 calories a day.) NXIVM women had to record everything they ate during a twenty-four-hour period, and if the amount exceeded 800 calories, they were punished. Some of the women privately referred to the diet as "starvation," but to say that out loud inside of NXIVM was considered dangerous. Therefore, they ate as little as possible to prove that hunger had no control or power over their lives. Making women obsess over food and weight was another way, according to some of the disenchanted students, to keep them as slaves. In her own effort to follow the approved eating regime, Allison Mack ate so much squash that her palms allegedly turned orange (a condition known as carotenemia, driven by excess beta-carotene in the blood). Along with the lack of calories, NXIVM's brass also abstained from alcohol, as a few women would learn to their shame when they tried to enliven meals with wine.

Edmondson had opened a door that no one could close. Her accusations coincided with revelations from the Me Too movement then sweeping the country, in which more and more women were stepping up with stories about how they'd been sexually abused by, in many cases, well-known men. One male celebrity after another was about to fall as reporters dug into those stories. The media assault on Raniere was unrelenting. *Forbes* and the *Albany Times* ran articles about NXIVM maintaining a group of wealthy females acting as "sex slaves." The *New York Times* published an exposé, and the FBI began working with the New York State police and the Mexican federal police to uncover more allegations about Raniere. In March 2018, he was taken into custody and appeared before a federal judge in Texas, facing charges of forced labor in New York State, along with sex trafficking and racketeering. Ex-girlfriend Toni Natalie told the court that he wasn't just a con man but also a gambling and sex addict. Other women, as is often the case, found the courage to tell their own stories about NXIVM, claiming that Raniere wasn't a healer of women but a charlatan who'd had intercourse not just with adult females in his flock but also with minors.

Further investigations into NXIVM by the Department of Justice led to more allegations that echoed Raniere's earlier failed schemes with Consumers Buyline. The DOJ's investigation was turning up evidence that NXIVM was based on a profit-making pyramid scheme of business development: the group asked participants for thousands of dollars to be used to recruit more members.

To avoid going to trial either with or separately from Raniere, five women, including Clare Bronfman, accepted plea deals with sentences of up to two years in prison. None pleaded guilty to sex trafficking per se, but they generally supported the allegations against the NXIVM leader and his threats of deportation for those who disobeyed him. Raniere pleaded not guilty and denied all the charges. His defense was essentially constructed around the argument that what occurred inside his organization was among consenting adults who were taking his classes to improve their lives. He would face his accusers in court.

As the trial opened, there was talk in the media of cults, masters, slaves, and branding at NXIVM, but the word heard again and again had only lately infiltrated the media and general population: "gaslighting." It basically had come to mean the conscious attempt to manipulate someone to undermine that person's sense of reality—to the point where that individual begins to doubt his or her feelings and perceptions, his or her thoughts and grasp of the truth. Forensic psychologist Dawn Hughes testified at the trial that cult leaders employ a wide variety of tools to impose their will on others: economic control, surveillance, threats, isolation, and other nonviolent strategies that cause people to lose their capacity to exercise free will. The state put several women on the witness stand to underscore those points.

The first prosecution witness was thirty-two-year-old "Sylvie," who at eighteen had traveled to New York from the United Kingdom and become a "slave" in the secretive part of NXIVM known as DOS. It was promoted as a way to empower women, but she described it as having the opposite effect. Every day when in the DOS program she sent a nude photo to Raniere with a note reading "good morning, grandmaster" and heart emojis. The more she did this, the more her feelings soured.

"I remember," she testified, "the thing that kind of sparked anger in me more than anything was the use of the word 'special,' actually, and that he was calling me 'brave,' because I felt so disgusting and ashamed.

I just thought—I felt like it was all lies, like it just felt disgusting, and it wasn't true."

A witness named "Daniela" told the jury how Raniere had used similar techniques to make her feel mentally and emotionally vulnerable, doubtful about her own memories. Under oath, she detailed how she and her two sisters, who were in their teens and early twenties, had had sexual relationships with Raniere—events that they claimed he'd later talk about with them in ways intended to distort their truth. Daniela knew, for example, that she'd engaged with Raniere in oral sex, yet he insisted it was vaginal.

"I feel very sure of what I felt," she testified. "I was there. It's my body so it's very confusing to have contradictory information."

The man with all the answers was now the target of his victims' collective scorn, because instead of achieving liberation from their inhibitions, they'd ended up humiliated. And that humiliation had been made public during their court appearances. Four former NXIVM members talked about a secret women's group within the organization, a "mentorship program" Raniere had created to help him engage in sexual encounters. Some of those testifying were still obviously shaken and recovering from their encounters with the cult leader. At one point, Judge Nicholas Garaufis was moved to end the cross-examination of the witness Lauren Salzman, the daughter of Nancy Salzman. "This is a broken person, as far as I can tell," the judge declared from the bench. "Whether she's telling the truth, whether the jury believes her, I think it's absolutely necessary that there be a certain level of consideration for someone's condition."

Another former NXIVM slave, "Nicole," told the court about dealing with "master" Allison Mack, who had pleaded guilty to racketeering and racketeering conspiracy. The *Smallville* actress had accused Nicole of being "weak, spoiled, entitled." When Nicole confronted Mack with Raniere's knowledge of the secret women's group, Mack, according to the witness, denied it.

"She said, 'Oh, sweetie, I'm so glad that you told me that,'" Nicole testified. "That's not true, that's not what's happening, but that's such a good sign that you can trust me enough to tell me that."

Other testimony alleged that Daniela's younger sister, Camila, was fifteen when she was led into a sexual relationship with Raniere. In a series of WhatsApp messages revealed in court, Raniere tried to persuade Camila that by her having sex with someone besides him, she had destroyed her chance to be his "spiritual successor."

"My lineage," he had told her, "is not supposed to end with my death."

In another written exchange, Raniere revealed his own obsessions by pressing Camila to compare the other man's genitals with his own. He was particularly interested in shape, size, and "fluid consistency."

"Did you like his taste better than mine?" he asked.

"I wish," she responded, "I didn't have to answer this. Yes."

"He is shorter and thinner, penis-wise?" Raniere wrote back.

"Longer but thinner," Camila replied.

Raniere then challenged Camila's recollection of events and her own experience.

"I am examining perception," he wrote her. "I know his penis is 6.75 full erect and mine is 7.5 so I'm looking at how you are slanting things."

The more he pushed her and tried to convince her that he was right and she was wrong, the more she gave in to him and accepted his view of reality. It wasn't just a matter of pleasing the man; she saw her dependence on Raniere as a way to ensure her survival.

"I feel," she revealed in one of their interactions, "like I have a gun pointed at me and I'm just trying to say what you want to hear so you won't shoot but I don't know what it is you want to hear."

Forty-two-year-old prosecution witness Lauren Salzman testified that she'd recruited six branded slaves for NXIVM and had held one person in confinement for almost two years. A "sex cult" hidden within the organization, according to this witness, had more members than previously believed and was more coercive than had been revealed so far. Salzman, who had pleaded guilty to racketeering and racketeering conspiracy, provided the jury with details about DOS, which had been activated in 2015 but had grown significantly by January 2017. To be part of DOS, women had to give up "collateral"—damning information about themselves—to prove to Raniere their lifelong commitment to his cause. Lauren had pledged her investments, two cars, and two homes to NXIVM and had vowed to resign from her positions in the organization if she ever broke her vow of secrecy.

She indicated that the material she handed over to Raniere to join DOS needed to be so bad that she would choose death over seeing it made public. Then she told the court that she'd given Raniere three nude pictures of herself and had confessed that she'd taken part in a crime that also implicated her mother, NXIVM founder Nancy Salzman. A woman in the group, according to the witness, had had a psychotic episode during a self-help program, and, under Raniere's orders, Lauren had force-fed the woman Valium and refused to take her to a hospital.

Lauren went on to identify eight women as the core of DOS, including actresses Nicki Clyne and Allison Mack. The pair, she testified, had married each other in 2017, and each had had a sexual relationship with Raniere. DOS members who failed to complete their tasks, she added, were punished by paddling or whipping, and she remembered an incident in which Raniere had kicked a DOS slave master for acting "prideful."

Some of the plans for maintaining control over members never reached fruition. About eighteen months earlier, Salzman said, the group had been working on building a basement dungeon, a "sorority house" owned by one of eight original DOS slaves, Mexican media heiress Rosa Laura Junco. The dungeon would hold a cave for "a type of surrendering. . . . You were [going to be] in there until whoever was going to let you out."

Salzman read from a DOS rulebook describing master-slave relationships: "Your sole highest desire must be to further your Master from whom all good things come and are related. . . . The best slave derives the highest pleasure from being her Master's ultimate tool. . . . It doesn't matter what the command is, it matters that you obey. It doesn't matter that you understand the command, it matters that you obey."

A master's goal was to have 100 slaves in his or her stable and eventually select one to run for public office, taking the cult out into American society. In light of some of Raniere's beliefs, it would be important for NXIVM to have people in power in the future. Testimony revealed that he thought the government had spied on him—because of his exceptional intelligence—and that some under his sway, who called him "Grandmaster," were convinced that he had the power to change weather patterns. Another story floating around NXIVM was that President Bill Clinton had worked to ruin Consumers Buyline.

As Raniere's trial unfolded, the FBI continued investigating NXIVM and running down leads from some of those who had escaped the group and were in recovery. Sarah Edmonson began writing a book about her experience with Raniere and his followers and about getting branded. It was published in 2019 under the title *Scarred: The True Story of How I Escaped NXIVM, the Cult That Bound My Life*. On June 19, 2019, the trial concluded with the jury convicting Raniere of several federal crimes, including sex trafficking, conspiracy, and conspiracy to commit forced labor, with all the charges connected to the inner workings of DOS. As of this writing, he faces a mandatory minimum prison term of fifteen years and a possible life sentence.

2

SAUL NEWTON AND THE SULLIVANIANS

People often think of cults as preying on the downtrodden and disadvantaged, but they can flourish anywhere—among the uneducated and the highly learned, in rural or urban settings, with the rich and the poor, among the vulnerable and those who appear strong. Usually they arise from what their founders see as the very best intentions. This one began with a single goal: "We were going to create better people." Over recent decades, cults have depended on either mostly physical violence or mostly psychological violence, but a common thread in almost all of them is an attempt to control sexual behavior.

In the 1930s, a number of young Americans, especially those living in major cities, were radicalized by the political climate of those times. The world was suffering through an economic depression, the Nazis were on the rise in Europe, and the global success of the Communist Revolution in Russia still hung in the air. From the Little Red School House in Greenwich Village to socialist meetings on the Upper West Side of Manhattan, leftist ideas and ideals were rampant, and some people acted them out boldly. One who answered the call was Saul Newton, born in 1906 and a native of New Brunswick, Canada. Educated at the University of Wisconsin, he became a member of antifascist circles at the University of Chicago. He fought in the American Lincoln Brigade on the Republican side in the Spanish Civil War and then in the U.S. Army in World War II. For the rest of his life, he espoused left-wing politics combined with unconventional social ideas.

In 1957 in New York City, he and his wife, Dr. Jane Pearce, founded the Sullivan Institute for Research in Psychoanalysis, although neither of them had formal psychiatric training. Both had been members of the U.S. Communist Party and had worked at the William Alanson White Institute but had quit after the 1949 death of Harry Stack Sullivan, one of the institute's founders. Some in the psychiatric community regarded Sullivan as having provided "America's greatest contribution" to that field after he was given credit for taking schizophrenia off the list of incurable disorders. Newton and Pearce named their institute after Sullivan, and the cult they built became known informally as the "Sullivanians," a group of highly educated people living in one of the more intellectually sophisticated neighborhoods in New York City.

Like Newton, Pearce was a Marxist, and their political beliefs gradually shifted into the realm of family dynamics. They wrote about that subject in their 1963 book *The Conditions of Human Growth* and began attracting a local audience made up of largely middle- to upper-class New York intellectuals. As they developed a following, they laid down rules and guidelines that would become stricter over time. The couple supported a nonmonogamous lifestyle, instructing others not to have exclusive relationships and stating that conventional family ties were the root cause of social anxiety and mental illness. Like many Marxists around the world in the twentieth century, once they'd come to power, they had difficulty not letting their rule turn into a dictatorship.

Adults in the group were encouraged to sever all relationships with outsiders, including family members—that is, unless they needed money. People were told which jobs to get to support the group financially and which to avoid. Their therapeutic patients were ordered to end their current marriages and have new ones that might legitimize children and secure more health insurance benefits (to pay for more therapy with

Sullivanians). Children raised under the institute's umbrella weren't raised at home but had caretakers or were sent to boarding schools. They were allowed to interact with their parents for perhaps one hour one night per week so that deeper emotional bonds and dependencies wouldn't develop as strongly as they did in traditional nuclear families. Children were rotated from adult to adult on "dates"; one of the parents later claimed that in seven days his son had had "dates" with twenty-three different people.

Community members were required to undergo three weekly therapy sessions, and the leaders of the group recommended which hobbies to embrace or shun. Men and women weren't supposed to turn down any offer of sex from anyone in the community and to have intercourse with someone different every night of the week or at least five nights out of seven even if one was married. Both therapists and patients went on those dates. Gay and lesbian members were asked to have heterosexual sex with the others and vice versa. (The American Psychological Association's statement of ethical principles says, "Sexual intimacies with clients are unethical.")

By the 1970s, liberation movements were happening everywhere, and they were fully in bloom among the Sullivanians, who hoped to rise above the decadence of bourgeois conformity and achieve a higher and freer state of being while boosting their own sense of moral and psychological superiority. To accomplish this, they believed, one had to cleanse one's personality and values, along with holding all the right political views. On Manhattan's Upper West Side, where the institute was situated, these things had deep significance. Twenty years after the Red Scare of Senator Joseph McCarthy in the 1950s, one could still hear heated arguments about which "comrade" had hung on to his or her convictions and integrity and which had sold out. Those who identified as Sullvanians knew where they stood: they wanted to remake American politics with a leftist bent and rebuild the family structure.

One way to attract followers to their way of thinking and acting was to throw elaborate sexually open Saturday-night parties at a summer house in Amagansett, Long Island.

Newton and Sullivan believed that those with the greatest ability to change and conform to their visions and therapeutic treatment would be creative types. They sought out noted artists such as the painter Jackson Pollock, the writers Richard Ellmann and Richard Price, and the singer Judy Collins, who later wrote about her Sullivanian leaders commanding her to send her son to boarding school. The group also included the art critic Clement Greenberg, the cartoonist Jules Feiffer, and several well-known choreographers. As the membership grew, some of the followers (there were about 200) began moving into three buildings on the Upper West Side and living in sex-segregated apartments.

In 1978 the leadership paid around $200,000 for an upstate retreat, and five years later it spent $1.4 million for a building on Broadway. By then Newton had divorced Pearce. His second wife, the actress Joan Harvey, aggressively attempted to sign a lease on property occupied by a West Side theater group. When the troupe refused to vacate the premises, scores of Sullivanians charged into the space and unleashed chaos, destroying the sets. Three people were arrested. Harvey eventually commandeered the building and launched the Fourth Wall Repertory Theater. From 1978 to 1985, she wrote all the plays produced by that group, most of them about the troubles within the nuclear family.

As Harvey asserted her power, Newton became more volatile and erratic. After the partial meltdown of a nuclear reactor at Pennsylvania's Three Mile Island in March 1979, he ordered the Sullivanians to leave New York to avoid the radioactive fallout and go to Orlando, Florida. On their return to New York, Newton exhibited uncontrolled paranoia, demanding that one room in their building have steel-plated walls to keep out interference from the CIA. He wanted to take over the breeding habits of his flock, deciding who could have children and with which partner. When one man attempted to flee the cult, a pair of Sullivanians (including Newton's son) caught the offender in a subway station and held him over the tracks, threatening instant death if he didn't return to the fold.

In the early '80s, the Sullivanians, now paranoid about the spread of HIV, adopted "AIDS rules," insisting that shoes be removed when one entered an apartment and that dogs' paws be washed after each walk. For minor violations, the leaders inflicted financial penalties and revoked social privileges. A group of high-minded progressives that had begun with the notion of expanding freedom was tilting in the direction of many similar groups—run by those whose deepest needs seemed to be not freedom and personal responsibility but rather telling their followers how to live. And if telling wasn't enough, it was necessary to force one's will on them.

Cults usually appeal less to the intelligence of their members and more to their emotions, which is both a strength and a weakness. Although this can help pull people into the cult because it offers absolute answers to life's challenges and mysteries, keeping them in can be another matter. If it was naive for the Sullivanians to think they could rebuild human nature with a handful of Newton and Pearce's directives, it was more naive to believe they could control others once children became part of the mix. Biology, some say, is destiny. The bonds between parents and children are different from those between adults or even those between cult leaders and followers. Those bonds eventually moved the Sullivanians away from their imagined paradise and into familial conflict, legal challenges, and heated courtroom battles.

Trying to get out of this particular cult—as with others—was not a simple thing. When attempting to exit the group, one ex-member, Michael Cohen, recorded a phone conversation he had had with Newton. On the tape, which was played in court at a 1986 trial, an elderly man says: "You cannot do this to me. Nobody can do this to me. Not you in your arrogance, not [New York City] Mayor Koch, not Hitler. . . . If I have to go to the work of mobilizing 200 people to find you, believe me I will find you."

After Cohen refused to meet with him, Newton said, "All right, you declare war. We'll get you."

Then he hung up.

The Sullivanian community was falling further into isolation, rejecting the changes occurring in the outside world around them. The culture was evolving, moving away from the idealism of the 1960s and '70s and into the materialism of the money-driven decades ahead. The AIDS crisis had made the Sullivanians reluctant to recruit new followers. Members who questioned the direction in which Newton was taking them could be thrown out of their apartments and sent packing by their therapists. As Newton gave in to outbursts of violence, other leaders in the group began to fall away. Some remained proud of what they'd tried to achieve, but others were embarrassed by their association with a "psychotherapy cult." Under attack from many sides, the community received a crucial blow from what might have seemed an unlikely source: the nation's first successful alternative newspaper, known for its liberal point of view.

On April 22, 1986, the *Village Voice* published the article "Escape from Utopia," triggered by a former Sullivanian who was now locked in a child custody battle. The escapee had hired private investigators and then violated the deepest of taboos within the group: going public with a damning story about the institute by contacting the media. The floodgates opened, and the cult's secrets and scams tumbled out: allegations of therapeutic misconduct, corrupt financial dealings, sexual coercion, and a long list of other charges. Ex-members banded together to create PACT (Parents Against Cult Therapy) to publicize their opposition to Newton and his dwindling membership.

Then the lawsuits began.

Screenwriter Mike Bray, an ex-Sullivanian, filed a suit seeking custody of his twin daughters. Another former Newton follower, computer analyst Paul Sprecher, sought custody of his five-year-old son, David. He went to the state supreme court in Manhattan to do battle with the boy's mother, Julia Agee (the daughter of the renowned writer James Agee). Sprecher's lawyer, Sanford Katz, told the judge that his client had been "robbed of his autonomy, robbed of his self-respect, robbed of adulthood and, finally, robbed of his funds."

The Sullivanians, Katz continued, were an "'insidious and dangerous cult whose goal is not to help, but to control and enforce total obedience of its members . . . a sick, insane, revolting group that indulges in bizarre practices and maintains a manic bunker mentality."

At one legal hearing, PACT advocates showed up in court, led by mothers claiming that they'd lost all contact with their adult children who were still under Newton's sway. One said that her grandchildren, whom she'd never met, were being kept from her. Newton struck back, calling

his accusers liars and saying that he and his group had continued fighting the good fight for progressive political ideas such as stopping nuclear war. Anyone who wanted to leave their community, he contended, was free to go.

A few years later, institute therapist Helen Fogarty had her license revoked for recommending that her patients sleep with her husband, Saul

MICHAEL BRAY AND PAUL SPRECHER.

Newton. In 1997, the New York State Board of Psychology's hearing panel found Fogarty guilty of "practicing the profession fraudulently, with gross negligence, with gross incompetence, with negligence on more than one occasion and with incompetence on more than one occasion." One accusation maintained that Fogarty had told her live-in babysitter/patient to engage in sex with her husband, a charge she denied. The board alleged that Fogarty had informed a patient that his mother loathed him, was as "murderously violent as a concentration camp person," and that she'd billed insurance companies for nonexistent therapy visits.

As Fogarty struggled to regain her standing in psychiatric circles, she defended herself by saying that she was young when she met Newton and had been his patient before becoming his lover. She eventually had four children with him. While she provided explanations, or rationalizations, for her behavior with the Sullivanians, other members came forward to push back. Author and sociologist Amy B. Siskind came of age at the institute, where she claimed she was sexually assaulted as a child.

Ex-member Jon Mack of Newfane, Vermont, had a different perspective, feeling that cult members had to take responsibility for their actions, although he was talking about the adult Sullivanians.

"Very few of us from that time, therapists and patients alike," he said in a statement about his experience with Newton, "have a legitimate claim to naiveté. We were—with the exception of the children of patients—consenting adults who knowingly, if not necessarily sensibly, reaped the benefits and paid the price of an unconventional life-style and practice of psychotherapy. Some clearly suffered more enduring harm than others, but the time has come long ago for people to go on with their lives—not forgetting the past, but learning from it and going ahead as best we can."

In 2014, after years of effort on her part, Helen Fogarty's license was reinstated, but she was placed on two years' probation.

In the 1950s and '60s, while writing for the *New Yorker*, press critic A. J. Liebling reported, with his tongue mostly lodged in his cheek, that as his criticism of the media became more acute and penetrating, the press itself had somehow "dis-improved." His words are a warning to cults like the Sullivanians that form with the hope of making "better human beings." When that happens, sometimes people get worse.

3

MAGDALENA SOLÍS, THE HIGH PRIESTESS OF BLOOD

In 1962 the Hernandez brothers, Santos and Cayetano, wandered into the tiny village of Yerba Buena in Mexico. Tucked away in a northeastern corner of that country, it was hot and remote, dusty, and cut off from the world, the sort of place people rarely visit. The modern world had left it alone—it still lacked electricity and telephones. Only about fifty people lived in the impoverished town, most of them poor, illiterate farmers. The Hernandez brothers were chiselers, small-time con men looking for a quick score, and Yerba Buena appeared to be an easy mark. They had their story ready as soon as they arrived in the unsuspecting community.

They explained to the locals that they weren't just ordinary Mexicans but prophets of the exiled ancient Inca gods. The brothers were messengers come to tell the people that the gods would be returning soon to reclaim their authority over Yerba Buena and punish the infidels who refused to believe in their divinity. If the townspeople simply would agree to worship the gods and pay tribute to the brothers, they'd soon gain access to the gold and other treasures buried in caves outside of town. The citizens of Yerba Buena were so desperate for hope and financial help—and so uneducated about their native mythologies—that they accepted the story without question and began handing over food and money to the brothers, pledging to do whatever Santos and Cayetano demanded of them in return for their rewards.

For a while the ploy was effective. While the brothers banged on drums and chanted gibberish made up on the spot, the locals followed their orders. The brothers were able to control their victims through the use of psychoactive drugs and orgies held in the caves. But gradually, a few people in Yerba Buena began to wonder when they'd receive their riches, since none of the promised wealth had shown up. When a couple of men confronted the brothers, Santos and Cayetano didn't have a ready answer. Sensing a rebellion brewing, they knew they had to find a solution quickly or face an all-out mutiny. They wondered if they should expand on their original idea and bring in new people as part of the farce.

The brothers left Yerba Buena and drove to Monterrey, the capital and the largest city in the Mexican state of Nuevo León. They cased the nighttime streets and back roads, looking for someone to take back to the village. Then they saw her: a prostitute named Magdalena Solís and her pimp brother, Eleazar.

Magdalena appeared to be nothing more than a dark-haired, dark-eyed pretty woman (although her work was taking a toll on her attractive features). To the brothers she was just another downtrodden female in a city full of them, one who had begun selling her body at age twelve.

Born into poverty in the 1930s, she'd had few ways to earn a living and, having slipped into the sex trade, had been there ever since. Wouldn't she jump at the chance to get away from prostitution and do something different, something that might even be fun? What Santos and Cayetano didn't know was that life as a streetwalker had exposed Magdalena to all manner of darkness and hardened her in ways that her appearance didn't reveal. Little did the con men realize that they had picked up not just anybody but a woman with a taste for things far beyond their imagining.

The brothers, along with Magdalena and Eleazar, drove back to Yerba Buena, where they introduced her to the community not as a former prostitute but as the reincarnation of the Aztec goddess Coatlicue, mother of the gods and goddesses of the sun, moon, and stars. Eleazar joined the brothers as the third high priest of the cult.

To reinforce the illusion of Magdalena's mystery and superpowers, Santos and Cayetano created a literal smoke screen in front of the villagers, and Magdalena walked through it and into a crowd of worshippers as if being conjured from death or another dimension. The locals were so stunned by the display of magic and by Magdalena's presence that they eagerly accepted the notion of having a goddess in their midst. The brothers' trickery had worked to perfection, but they hadn't counted on one thing: Magdalena had a hidden streak of deep religiosity, what some have called "religious psychosis," and it now surfaced. Like other cult leaders before and after her, she began to believe that she was far above the common run of humankind and did indeed have special powers. The law didn't apply to her—nothing did—and she was willing to try anything she could get away with.

According to Aztec mythology, blood was the only decent food for the gods; by drinking it, they preserved their immortality. To stay young forever, a goddess had to have a steady and fresh supply of the precious liquid. Before long, Magdalena began acting as though she were indeed a goddess living outside all normal human boundaries, preparing to refer to herself as the High Priestess of Blood.

Magdalena began to force the townspeople into sexual slavery, and orgies were held in the caves. Anyone who resisted was subject to severe beatings. If that wasn't enough to make the locals give in to her whims and desires, she set them on fire. Then she turned to bloodletting, cutting them open and pouring their blood into a chalice, where it was mixed with peyote and the blood of a chicken. In front of the horrified onlookers, she gulped the concoction down, claiming that it would give her eternal life. After having her fill, she passed the chalice to the Hernandez brothers and her sibling, assuring everyone that all four of them now had extraordinary powers.

For a while this ritual was captivating, but then Magdalena grew bored and began indulging in more bizarre and dangerous behaviors. Embittered by her early sexual exploitation, the streetwalker from Monterrey was transforming into a paragon of violence whose acts went far beyond the petty scams and crimes of the Hernandez brothers, whom she had brushed aside. Taking over Yerba Buena, Magdalena ran the cult of the Aztec goddess exactly as she envisioned her role in it. When a few villagers challenged her rule, she called them before the high priests and had them hanged to death. She continued to force the living into incest, fetishism, sadism, and pedophilia, her carnal appetites matching her so-called religious fervor.

Yet even this wasn't enough to sate Magdalena's bloodlust. After identifying another renegade, she and her henchmen took him into a cave for a session of lethal bloodletting. For six weeks in early 1963, she oversaw the butchering of at least four people chosen for sacrifice in the caves. During the ritualistic killings, she would remove the victims' hearts while they were still alive and drink from her chalice the special mixture of their blood and hallucinatory substances, standing over their mangled bodies and writhing. By that point everyone, including the Hernandez brothers, had become wary of opposing her reign of terror, which looked as if it might go on for as long as there were townspeople to dispose of. The death toll had reached a minimum of six (although later the authorities speculated that the number could have been considerably higher). But then, almost as if the gods had decided Magdalena had gone too far, fate intervened.

One day that May, she and her followers went out to the caves for another round of bloodletting. They were in the middle of one of their rituals when a local boy, fourteen-year-old Sebastian Guerrero, was taking a walk past the scene of their sacrifices. From inside a cave, he detected lights and heard screams. The sounds were so disturbing that he felt compelled to move closer to the noise. Poking his head inside, he watched in disbelief, transfixed as Magdalena and her cult bent over a new victim, cutting out his heart while engaging in a sex orgy. Horrified, Sebastian was momentarily frozen, but then he whirled and ran as fast as he could, not stopping for fifteen miles until reaching the town of Villagrán, Tamaulipas, the site of the closest police department. Trembling and in a hysterical tone of voice, he told the officers about seeing "*vampiros*" and "a group of murderers who prey on ecstasy and who were gluttonously drinking human blood."

The police stared at him and laughed; his story was too outlandish for anyone to find credible. He repeated it, more passionately this time, and then again, but they continued dismissing him. Regardless of what the teenager actually had seen, he was so clearly shaken that one of the cops, Luis Martinez, offered to accompany him home. Along the way, Sebastian insisted on showing him the location of the scene he'd witnessed. Martinez was curious enough to lead the two of them into the cave for a better look. The boy and the officer were never seen alive again.

A day or two passed, and the Villagrán police realized that Luis Martinez wasn't coming back. They knew where the pair had been going and surmised that Sebastian might have taken him into the suspect caves. A small group of officers, accompanied by Mexican soldiers and Inspector Abelardo Gomez, formed a search party. When they reached the caves, they stumbled upon six dismembered corpses, all presumably former cult members. Now they knew that Sebastian had told them truth, although it was too late to help the missing duo. Following the thread of Sebastian's story, they went into Yerba Buena, where they found the Hernandez brothers and were soon in the middle of an armed standoff. The villagers barricaded themselves inside their mud houses, but the attacking police force blasted away at the facades until the mud crumbled and they'd killed numerous town members. Santos Hernandez died in the gunfire, and his brother Cayetano most likely was shot to death by another cultist, Jesus Rubio, who'd once tried but failed to join the high priests. By murdering Cayetano, he thought that he too could enter the priesthood.

The police arrested Magdalena and Eleazar—both in possession of a sizable marijuana stash—and about two dozen others who had survived the gun battle. As they continued searching, they found the carved-up bodies of Sebastian Guerrero and Luis Martinez, with the latter's heart removed, near a farm where the Solís siblings had been taken into custody. All the suspects except Magdalena and her brother were offered a deal. If they would tell the officers everything they knew about the Hernandez brothers and the Solíses, the authorities not only would show them leniency but be able to charge Magdalena and Eleazar with all eight murders. The offer was refused as the men and women of Yerba Buena were too frightened and traumatized to speak out against their former slave master and her brother. As a result, the locals were accused of six murders. They would maintain their silence about the cult leaders for many years to come. Magdalena and Eleazar were charged with only the murders of Sebastian Guerrero and Luis Martinez.

Those who failed to testify received thirty-year sentences for gang murder or lynching, and Magdalena and Eleazar got fifty years each in

Beautiful Teenager Held in Cult Orgies

United Press International
CIUDAD VICTORIA, Mexico, June 5. — Federal police held a beautiful teenaged priestess and about 40 other persons today in an effort to find out exactly how many farmers were lured into a weird cult that ripped the hearts out of human sacrifices.

The exposure of the cult has already cost the lives of six persons in the farming community of Yerba Buena, in addition to the lives of persons offered as sacrifices in a cave temple.

POLICE INSPECTOR Abelardo G. Gomez, who brought the priestess and members to Ciudad Victoria, capital of Tamaulipas, for questioning, thought at least 12 persons may have been sacrificed.

Farmers around Yerba Buena could not or would not account for 12 missing persons. Federal troops from Tampico checked cemeteries at Yerba Buena to find out whether the remains of the missing persons were buried after they were sacrificed.

THE PRIESTESS questioned in Ciudad Victoria was Magdalena Solis, 18 or 19. Eleazor Solis, said to be no relation to her but a power behind the cult and perhaps its founder, also was questioned. The other cult members questioned were farmers and their wives.

With the temple broke up and all but a few of known members in jail, Gomez thought he had the situation under control. The temple near Yerba Buena, called "La Mina," was broken up Tuesday.

TROOPS looked for another temple in the nearby farming community of Delgado. Other troops hunted through the hills for cult members who fled.

Yerba Buena is about 175 miles below Laredo on the Mexico-U.S. border.

STORY IN THE *EL PASO HERALD-POST*, JUNE 5, 1963.

prison. Magdalena's scheduled release date was 2013, but her whereabouts are unknown. She goes down in the history of cults as one of the very few established cases of a female leader with a sexual motivation. Her extreme sexual desires fall under the psychological diagnosis of paraphilia, a condition that sometimes afflicts serial killers.

Some think that Magdalena died while incarcerated or had additional years tacked on to her sentence for bad behavior and is still locked up somewhere in the Mexican prison system—or perhaps she was released some years ago and slipped into obscurity. Others speculate that when set free, she went deeper into the countryside and resumed her life as an imaginary goddess, performing blood sacrifices.

4

BHAGWAN SHREE RAJNEESH AND THE RAJNEESHEES

Bhagwan Shree Rajneesh was born Chandra Mohan Jain on December 11, 1931, in Kuchwada, India. In later years he would dazzle his followers with tales of his boyhood adventures on late-night hikes, teetering along a cliff's edge far above a rushing river where one false move meant death. He liked to test himself and his young friends, nudging them into risky situations so that they could confront their limitations or their fears—a pattern he would carry into adult life. As a high school student, he was tormented by spiritual questions, fighting off severe headaches and forcing himself to eat. To cope with stress, according to his own accounts, he ran five to eight miles a day until he achieved an "explosion" of enlightenment at age twenty-one in March 1953. Some of his critics felt that his enlightenment story was borrowed from that of Gautama Buddha, who had experienced an awakening sitting under a Bodhi tree in India in the sixth century B.C. Buddha had come from wealth but renounced it on his path to becoming a guru. Bhagwan (which means "God") Shree Rajneesh would go in the opposite direction.

After graduating from high school, he attended Hitkarini College in Jabalpur but soon came into conflict with a professor and transferred to D. N. Jain College, where he earned a bachelor's and then a master's degree in philosophy. After finding enlightenment, he liked to tell his devotees, he discovered "dynamic meditation" and gradually attracted an audience for his teachings. He took a job at Raipur Sanskrit College but departed after getting in trouble with the administration. The theme of his life had been set. Despite being a man who preached peace and spiritual grace, he unleashed controversy everywhere he went, much of it driven by his evolving belief system. He found a new position at the University of Jabalpur and began traveling across India, instructing his followers that sex was the first step toward achieving "superconsciousness."

"The primal energy of sex has the reflection of God in it," he wrote in *From Sex to Superconsciousness*. "It is the energy that creates new life. And that is the greatest, most mysterious force of all."

His reputation quickly spread across India, and he began lecturing to audiences as large as 15,000 people. His ideas on sexuality appealed to some of those in his native land as much as they would to certain Americans in the future.

"Rajneesh," said John Ephland, an ex-disciple of the guru who eventually wrote for the Spiritual Counterfeits Project in Berkeley, California, "gives you the opportunity to sin like you've never sinned before. Only he doesn't call it sin. The path to desireless is desire."

Women would come to occupy a special place in Rajneesh's life and work, especially after he moved to the United States. He had firm notions about their gender, describing females as infinitely patient beings who operated not from the head but from the heart and dismissing the notion that they could be logical or scientific. "Because of the womb being a central phenomenon in the feminine body," he said, "the whole psychology of woman differs: she is non-aggressive, non-inquiring, non-questioning, non-doubting, because all of those things are part of aggression. She will not take the initiative. She simply waits—and she can wait infinitely."

However, what the women he gathered around him most closely did for his sect once they had resettled in America undermined nearly everything he claimed to believe about their innate qualities and capacities.

In the mid-1960s, Rajneesh ran camps in India, recruited believers, and introduced dynamic meditation to his flock so that others could do as he had done and experience divinity. As word of his powers spread, Westerners trekked to India and joined the sect at his six-acre ashram in Pune. Donning orange and red clothing, as he insisted they do, they experimented in group sessions involving sexual promiscuity. Like many cult leaders before and after him, Rajneesh used the twin lures of sex and the promise of material comfort to draw in new members.

Early on, Rajneesh had sought out wealthy Indians around Bombay, offering them the kinds of sensual opportunities generally shunned in their nation's long and rich spiritual traditions. Rajneesh, said an Indian reporter who'd covered him when speaking with the newspaper *The Oregonian*, "knew what the rich people want. They want to justify their guilty consciences, to justify their guilty acts."

As he became more successful, Rajneesh expanded his contacts internationally—with Prince Welf of Hanover, Germany (killed in 1981 in an accident in a Rajneesh karate group in India); the Marquis of Bath; and American heirs and heiresses to the Baskin Robbins,

Learjet, and *San Francisco Chronicle* fortunes. As his organization grew, he awarded the sect's top leadership positions to wealthy women: first to the well-connected Ma Yoga Laxmi and then to the notorious Ma Anand Sheela, the daughter of a prosperous Indian landowner.

From the beginning, Rajneesh's strategy was clear.

"Money [is] easier to get from those who have it," read the notes from a coordinators' meeting of the Rajneeshees. "If anyone knows any people with some connection with Bhagwan who have money, give the name to Mrudula to call them."

By the end of the 1970s, the Pune ashram was overflowing with followers and Rajneesh hoped to relocate his burgeoning sect and escape the growing conflict around himself and his practices. His movement owed around $4 million in income, sales, export, and property taxes in India. Then, in 1980, a Hindu fundamentalist tried to assassinate him. Rajneesh survived and made plans to go west with 2,000 disciples in tow. Many of his followers were from Western countries—Europe, the United States, and West Germany in particular. They tended to be in their thirties, college-educated white professionals from middle-class to affluent backgrounds.

In 1981, Rajneesh's advance guard came to the United States and bought a 64,000-acre tract in far northern Oregon known as Big Muddy Ranch, where they began building a commune called Rancho Rajneesh. They worked fervidly, installing culverts, bulldozing roads, and launching the construction of numerous buildings. Rajneesh then followed his followers. His pretext for getting into the United States was that he needed America's advanced health care; his followers claimed that his back problems required a laminectomy, the surgical removal of a compressed disc in his spine (although a London specialist had expressed doubt that his situation was that serious). Strings were pulled, and in the summer of 1981 the guru began his trek to the United States. By October, when it had become clear that he had no need for a back operation, Rajneesh asked the Portland immigration office for a visa extension so that he could stay in the country a few more months.

The Rajneeshees arrived en masse in the American West with money, ambition, plenty of devotees, and big plans, but they lacked—or were eager to ignore—one thing: the rule of law and due process as it was practiced in the United States. The great expanse of landscape around them might have looked wild and open and free, but it was bounded by customs, rules and regulations, and other strictures. Within a few years, Ma Sheela would be referring to Oregon officials as "bloated pigs" and the sect would be plotting a series of crimes in reaction to what most Americans would consider normal compliance with government bureaucracy: the ins and outs of land-use law.

Serving as Rajneesh's chief of staff, thirty-one-year-old Ma Sheela led the relocation to the juniper-laden hills and imposing canyon lands surrounding ranch headquarters. When Rajneesh first saw Big Muddy on August 29, 1981, he was sharply disappointed, having hoped for a wetter and lusher environment like the one he'd left behind in India. He had expected more trees on the property, the first inkling that he had little concept of what awaited him out west. Still, he and Sheela decided to incorporate a new city, Rajneeshpuram, on the rugged terrain.

One hundred fifty laborers working with hammers, shovels, and heavy machinery began constructing a school, an office, a health center, a canteen, a warehouse, a garage, a gourmet restaurant (Zorba the Buddha), a private airstrip, and fifty homes. At sunset, after a hard day's work, the staff cooled off and relaxed with a keg of beer. The first wave of Rajneesh disciples settled quietly in rural Oregon, but before long they were wandering into The Dalles, a nearby town of around 13,000 residents, and the much smaller Antelope, whose population was under 100. The spirit of live and let live still pervaded much of the West, with its assortment of tax resisters, survivalists, drug dealers, nudist hot springs, meth labs, UFO enthusiasts, and countless spiritual retreats. Wasn't this just one more oddball sect, the locals probably thought.

The Rajneeshees' mandatory reddish clothing and malas—bead necklaces holding a photo of their guru—stood out and, at least in Antelope, put residents in mind of an invasion. A number of bewildered locals, like many in small towns across the nation, initially tried to be friendly and accommodating to the visitors. After all, the stated purpose of their presence in the region seemed harmless enough.

According to an October 1983 affidavit from sect president Yoga Vidya, the main activity was for sannyasins (the guru's followers) to grow spiritually by "working/worshiping in the commune in the presence of Bhagwan Shree Rajneesh. . . . Members of the commune have come from all over to participate. They have invested their personal assets, their labor, their expertise and their love to build a home here for themselves and their families."

In Volume 2 of his book *Sufis: The People of the Path,* Rajneesh had described his religion this way: "When you join me as a sannyasin, you are dropping yourself, disappearing. When you join the commune then you have to utterly efface yourself. If a little bit is hanging there then you will be a trouble to yourself and to the commune too. And you will not be benefited by me."

Rajneesh, however, would benefit quite well. The sect had at a minimum twenty-eight bank accounts in five countries, including a dozen in Switzerland. On the ranch, Rajneesh wore a jewel-encrusted watch, spangled robes, and designer eyeglasses and was always in the market for another Rolls-Royce (he reportedly had a fleet of them worth $7 million). While he indulged his materialistic impulses, he kept his flock in fear and under control by declaring that 1984 would ring in fifteen straight years of global disaster: nuclear detonations, volcanic explosions, earthquakes, and floods. The faithful were to hunker down at Big Muddy to await the apocalypse.

In the beginning, Ma Sheela charmed Oregon ranchers and politicians, inviting them to a dance in Madras, a town of 6,000 residents in Jefferson County, where the cowboys partied till the sun crept over the horizon. She attempted to impress the locals by purchasing fifty head of cattle even though the commune was vegetarian, all the while continuing with the construction of housing compounds, warehouses, and other support structures. As Rancho Rajneesh grew, her guru applied for permanent residency in the United States.

Lawyers in Portland told Sheela that to proceed successfully and peacefully with all of her building projects she needed to befriend the environmental group and land-use watchdog 1000 Friends of Oregon. Befriending people, as the state was about to learn, just wasn't her style. She met with two attorneys from 1000 Friends and told them that she intended to construct an incorporated city for the thousands of Rajneesh followers continuing to move onto Big Muddy. The environmental lawyers challenged her, raising the issue of a sect controlling a city, which appeared to violate constitutional provisions ensuring the separation of church and state. She asked whether a substantial contribution to 1000 Friends of Oregon would change their point of view. Offended, they resisted the bribe, and Sheela quickly turned nasty, commenting on the run-down appearance of their work space. The environmental group retaliated with an aggressive effort to stop the city, using Sheela's picture on its literature to raise money for its cause.

The building of Rajneeshpuram went forward, and the city rose from the landscape with more homes and places of worship. To satisfy the guru's desires, they built him a $200,000 swimming pool and meticulously cared for his garden. Never one to take an insult without giving a harsher one in return, Sheela made a point of naming Big Muddy's sewage lagoon after the 1000 Friends' executive director. She'd made her first major local enemy but hardly her last.

Some in the sect who watched how Ma Sheela operated wanted her to tone down her hostility, but Rajneesh gave her his full support. In his philosophy, women might have lacked initiative or aggression, but that belief couldn't contain Ma Sheela or her female cohorts. Concerned with his immigration status in America, Rajneesh usually stayed in the background, collecting more Rolls-Royces while trying to avoid being deported because of issues with his visa. He put Sheela on the front lines of the sect's controversies, where she seemed most at home, but not everyone appreciated her combative style.

One day Ma Yoga Vidya, a mathematician also known as Ann McCarthy, the commune's president, called Sheela's conduct toward the Oregon authorities "outrageous" and detrimental to their cause. The next day, in front of the guru, Sheela exploded at Vidya as Rajneesh instructed the mathematician never to challenge Sheela because she spoke directly for him.

By 1983, in an effort to lure entertainment celebrities to the movement, Sheela was expanding her outreach to a Beverly Hills mansion that had been given to the Rajneesh Foundation by the trust funder Dhyan John. The Rajneeshees did this by conducting Tantric sex orgies orchestrated by a member known as Kaveesha, the "Tantra Queen." They also hoped that the Los Angeles crowd would chip in the funds for a few more Rolls-Royces in Rajneesh's stable. One of those Sheela attracted was Ma Prem Hasya, alias Françoise Ruddy, the former wife of Albert Ruddy, who had produced *The Godfather*. She helped purchase Big Muddy and served as personal secretary to the guru.

While courting Hollywood, Sheela oversaw the creation of police departments for two cities—Rajneeshpuram and Rajneesh, as they had renamed Antelope—while employing a private security force and stocking a substantial arsenal with shotguns, revolvers, and military-style, semiautomatic weapons. They also made efforts to purchase submachine guns and fully automatic weapons even though Rajneeshpuram heralded itself as free of both vice and violence. Proclamations aside, they were plotting a series of major crimes in reaction to what most Americans would consider predictable government regulations.

After bringing a contingent from Hollywood onto the land at Big Muddy, Sheela began making a list of those people and others whom she considered a threat both to the commune and to Rajneesh. She hid microphones around the ranch to monitor what was being said and who was saying it and placed a bug on a table leg next to the guru's favorite chair. She put together undercover squads to spy on her enemies, but when that wasn't effective enough, she turned to poisoning, enlisting Ma Anand Puja, a nurse previously known as Diane Onang, the supervisor of the ranch's medical department. The more resistance Sheela met over land-use laws, the more paranoid she became and the more she availed herself of Puja's services. While the nurse medicated Sheela daily for stress and exhaustion, she carried out her orders regarding suspect Rajneeshees or those from Hollywood. If they were deemed dangerous, the nurse forced them to live in isolation, based on trumped-up diagnoses. Puja also kept a secret lab in a ranch cabin, where she experimented with viruses and bacteria.

In the summer of 1984, Sheela was ready to use what the nurse had been cooking up in the cabin. Puja began distributing unlabeled vials filled with brownish liquid to

MA ANAND SHEELA.

Sheela's minions. The vials were transported to The Dalles, the seat of government and the largest city in Wasco County. The brownish liquid, which was believed to contain diarrhea-inducing salmonella, was strategically placed in the men's restroom at the county courthouse, aimed at public officials and regular citizens alike. Rajneeshees also smeared the poison around at a local political rally and a nursing home. Then they hit a grocery store, where Sheela and a small band of followers targeted the produce section with a vial she'd stashed up her sleeve.

When this strategy failed to cause widespread illness in the community, Sheela resorted to less subtle tactics. She invited three Wasco County commissioners, including wheat farmer Bill Hulse, to Big Muddy to tour the commune. The trio thought they were there to generate trust and goodwill after they'd taken measures to restrict growth at Rajneeshpuram. When they returned to Hulse's car after the tour, it had a flat tire. While the commissioners stood in the blazing August sunlight and waited for it to be fixed, Puja came outside and offered each of them a glass of water. They quickly drank the liquid, which put Hulse in the hospital for the next four days. If he hadn't been treated as quickly as he was, his doctor told him, he probably would have died.

When Hulse stated publicly that the Rajneeshees had poisoned him, they disputed his account. Giving him water, a Rajneeshee PR person wrote to the commissioner, was "a simple act of human kindness on that sweltering day. Now you are making a hysterical accusation that you were poisoned." Only later, when things had begun to change at the commune, did the sect acknowledge that Hulse's accusation had been right.

After attacking the commissioners, Sheela upped the stakes with plans to undermine the Wasco County political system. The commune selected a Rajneeshee who appeared to have cut off all ties with the ranch to move to The Dalles and run for office. To ensure the candidate's victory, Sheela ordered commune residents to register to vote, but she also had a backup plan: lowering the election turnout by poisoning Wasco County voters. She diligently studied land maps and conducted surveillance on the local reservoirs and water systems, but in the end it proved too difficult to find a means to poison enough people to alter the vote count to favor her candidate. Once again she relied on Puja, who donned a wig and regular clothing when she went into cafés and poured a substance onto the salad bar, waiting for mass illness to descend. Again the plan wasn't as successful as Sheela had hoped, but commune members were wearing down the locals in other ways.

In The Dalles and Antelope, sect members lounged in the streets and had sex on people's lawns, living out the principle of superconsciousness in a way that the small-town residents never could have imagined. Many were horrified. Under Sheela's leadership, the Rajneeshees were increasingly in no mood to make peace with the locals, and vice versa. The townspeople had no concept of what was coming next.

Rajneesh was living in luxury on the ranch and also in silence. Testifying in a written deposition in Multnomah County circuit court in 1984, he claimed that he wanted the world to know that he'd stopped talking and was "finished with doing. . . . I am going to be contradictory to myself many times for the simple reason that I am trying to bring all the religions to a higher synthesis. . . . Different approaches have to be joined together. I am creating an orchestra."

Surrounded by conflict and plagued by sleeplessness and ever-growing tension, Sheela relied on more medications and laid more grandiose plans. To get her people in power in county government, she needed a new strategy and turned toward the reckless and bizarre. From one coast to another, she scouted out cities and then chartered buses, packing them full of the homeless—mostly men—to bring to the commune. The Rajneeshees spun this as a massive humanitarian effort to help the downtrodden with a new spiritual home in the beautiful countryside, along with food and other possessions and a healthy supply of beer. Many of the homeless were only too willing to get on the buses.

The real reason for their pilgrimage to the commune, they discovered in time, was for them to establish residency in Big Muddy, register to vote, and support Ma Sheela's candidate for county commissioner. What she hadn't factored into her equation, however, was that a significant number of the incoming were suffering from a variety of illnesses, especially mental illnesses. Most couldn't work, and so they stayed around the ranch drinking too much or self-medicating in other ways. They quarreled among themselves, flew out of control, and got into verbal scrapes and fistfights. As they slid into chaos, Sheela came up with a solution: shoot the tranquilizer Haldol into their beer kegs. When that wasn't enough to tame them, the Rajneeshes put them in buses, drove them into the surrounding small towns, and dropped them off drunk on street corners, letting the unfortunates fend for themselves with no money or other resources. The shock to the communities generated so much anger and fear that the Oregon State Police and the National Guard made contingency plans to mobilize 10,000 soldiers.

Lawsuits against the sect were piling up; one administrative case alone sought $1.4 million in penalties for electrical code violations. Criminal cases were being brought against Rajneeshees who registered to vote under different names in both Rajneeshpuram and The Dalles. When Oregon Governor Vic Atiyeh's staff met with Sheela to defuse the crisis, she went on the attack, demanding that the governor solve Rajneesh's ongoing deportation issues and that the state cease trying to get rid of Rajneeshpuram. She wanted the officials to remove the land-use obstacles so that the commune could expand. As a bargaining chip, she contended that if the state would do this for her, she'd help get the homeless out of the small towns. When the state rejected the deal, Sheela hurled obscenities at the governor's staff and ended the meeting.

With no assistance from Big Muddy, Oregon had to pay $100,000 to send the homeless back to their states of origin.

Dan Durow, the Wasco County planner, began taking steps to shut down construction at the ranch because of various code violations. Commune leaders sent two of their soldiers at midnight into The Dalles, where they broke into Durow's office and lit eight candles to start a fire that would burn official documents. A motorist passing by noticed the flames and called in firefighters, who quickly doused them before much paperwork was lost.

Sheela had underestimated the toughness of rural Oregonians. Local governments were fighting back, and none of her strategies was paying off. Troubles were mounting on every side, and some Rajneeshees wanted her out. The guru had become more detached from the day-to-day running of the ranch, as though he couldn't be bothered with the ramifications of his decision to flee India for the American West. He was still concerned about his Rolls-Royce collection—rumored, at ninety-three, to be the world's largest—and with having Sheela obtain for him a million-dollar watch. It didn't matter where or how she got the money as long as he got his timepiece.

Tensions were growing between the two as well. Sheela was too busy fighting the surrounding power structure and scrambling for new tactics to pay as much attention to her guru as she had before. At a state hearing in Salem held to expose improper construction practices at the ranch, a Rajneeshee poisoned the drinking water with enough Haldol to cause overdoses, leaving the state's chief electrical inspector and assistant attorney general severely ill (the latter's jaw froze up during questioning). The hearing resulted in a $1 million fine against the commune, and a federal jury awarded $1.7 million to an aging ex-sannyasin who hadn't been repaid a loan. Sheela tried to poison that woman, too, but her efforts failed.

Nothing was working, and at that point some cult leaders might have pulled back and reassessed their plan of perpetual conflict and harm—but not Ma Sheela. In May 1985, she held a meeting of commune leaders in her bedroom and declared that change was in order, but not the kind of change that some of them had been anticipating. It was time, she declared, to shift from poisoning and arson to more serious tactics—such as murder. She was working on putting together a hit list of their enemies and needed assassins to carry out her vision.

This provoked an immediate reaction among some who hadn't joined the cult to engage in mayhem but to act out the ideals their guru had once talked or written about. Others were on the fence about Sheela's next move.

"I can't kill anybody," one woman said in response to the notion of the hit list, "but I support you if you do it."

In a rare moment of reflection Sheela went to Rajneesh for his input. Maybe her critics were right and murder was going too far. He indicated that if 10,000 people had to perish to save a single enlightened master, that was the way it had to be. She continued working on her list.

A primary target was Charles Turner, the U.S. attorney for Oregon, who was running an investigation into immigration fraud at Big Muddy. If the case went forward, it was possible that Rajneesh might be indicted along with Sheela. This was unthinkable. Sheela's crew purchased some untraceable pistols and created a safe house in Portland where the would-be killers could keep watch on Turner's residence. They monitored his comings and goings, when he was with others and when he was alone. While they surveilled him, another Rajneeshee posed as a Bible salesman to scout out Dave Frohnmayer, the state's attorney general, who also had been marked for death. Yet another squad was plotting to kill former Wasco County commissioner James Comini, who'd relentlessly hounded the sect and was now laid up in Portland's St. Vincent Hospital after ear surgery.

The hit list wasn't limited to those outside the ranch. It also included Rajneesh's physician, Dr. Swami Devaraj, who was British and was also known as George Meredith, along with caretaker Ma Yoga Vivek. Sheela saw the two as a threat after she'd made a clandestine recording of the doctor consenting to obtain the necessary drugs if the guru decided to commit suicide. She picked Ma Anand Ava and Ma Anand Su to kill Vivek with a combination of potassium and adrenaline, but late at night when they went to fulfill the mission, they took the wrong key and couldn't unlock the door to her bedroom.

In July 1985, the commune held its annual world festival, and that July morning the dance hall was filled with swirling bodies and pounding music. A woman named Ma Shanti Bhadra (aka Jane Elsea) approached Devaraj and stuck him in the buttock with a miniature syringe filled with adrenaline. He looked at her in shock, as if suddenly knowing, before the adrenaline kicked in, that he'd become an assassination target. A quick flight to a hospital in Bend was credited with saving his life.

By now, the commune's rank and file was openly rejecting Sheela's murder plots and starting to defect. Between the lawsuits, the rising rebellion against her, and the money woes the ranch was wallowing in, she was preparing to flee. Then Rajneesh turned on her publicly, outlining her crimes and those of her associates. After state and federal investigators came onto Big Muddy to collect evidence against the cult, two of Sheela's staunchest allies—Rajneeshpuram mayor Krishna Deva and dirty trickster Ma Anand Ava—cut deals with the prosecutors. The mayor's allegations against Sheela took up ninety-six pages, with sect members accusing her of arson, assault, wiretapping, and attempted murder. The cult had carried out the largest biological terrorism attack in American history, with at least 700 victims. It had overseen the biggest illegal wiretapping operation ever uncovered in the United States, along with a massive case of immigration fraud to harbor foreigners. It had toyed with the idea of crashing a bomb-carrying airplane into the county courthouse in The Dalles but ultimately couldn't bring it off.

In September 1985, Sheela fled to Europe, taking along commune notes, taped conversations regarding the guru, and miniature hypodermic needles. Many of her allies quit along with her. Ma Prem Hasya (aka Françoise Ruddy) succeeded Sheela as the Big Muddy experiment began to collapse. Nurse Ma Anand Puja and church treasurer Shanti Bhadra made deals that sent them to federal prison. Sheela would plead guilty in the salad bar poisoning case but employed the "Alford plea," in which a person doesn't actually admit guilt but concedes that the state's evidence could have convicted him or her. She accepted the deal, she said later, because she lacked the $2 million her lawyers told her was necessary to fight the charges in court. She claimed victory in this negotiation, with the prosecutors giving her only a two-year sentence when they had been after twenty.

While his followers were confessing to his and Sheela's crimes, Rajneesh took a chartered jet across the country, hoping to escape from America. Grounded in North Carolina, he returned to Portland in handcuffs and was booked into jail. His lawyers managed to have him quickly deported, but as a convicted felon. He changed his name to Osho and went back to India, where he died of heart failure in 1990. His original ashram—renamed the OSHO International Meditation Resort—remains a functioning enterprise, with the faithful in red robes running his meditation centers around the globe. Other former disciples, disillusioned with Rajneesh and what had happened at Big Muddy, turned away from the cult and were labeled as traitors. Some were afraid to speak out about their experience with the guru for fear of reprisals.

After Sheela served prison time in America, she relocated to Europe, where she ran restaurants in Germany and then Portugal. In 1990, facing new charges in the United States, she sought sanctuary in Switzerland, where she could not be extradited back to the States. Still angry and unrepentant about her years in the Northwest, she was always eager to blame Oregon officials for the collapse of Rancho Rajneesh. In Switzerland, she initially found work walking a retired man's dog and then assisted three elderly women, eventually launching a home-care business.

Rajneeshpuram is now called Washington Family Ranch, a summer camp for the Christian teen organization Young Life.

5

JOSEPH DI MAMBRO, LUC JOURET, AND THE ORDER OF THE SOLAR TEMPLE

Some people believe that the universe in its infinite complexity never creates precisely the same thing twice. Conditions change and people change with them, so it's not possible to redo what happened long ago. Such thoughts might stand as a warning to those who hope to bring into the present what vanished hundreds of years earlier—especially when it didn't end well back then. In A.D. 1120, nine knights met in Palestine and formed a Catholic military order to protect Christian pilgrims on their way to the Holy Land. They took as their prototype the Temple of Solomon and held their order together for nearly two centuries until the Pope banned the Knights Templar in 1312. Two years later their last grand master, Jacques de Molay, was burned at the stake as a heretic. Another 680 years passed before a new set of Templars arose in their shadow, with similarly grandiose ambitions.

Born in 1924 in southern France, Joseph Di Mambro became a clockmaker and jeweler while developing a great interest in the occult. In 1956, he joined the Ancient and Mystical Order Rosae Crucis (AMORC), an American Rosicrucian group that became popular in France after World War II. By 1960, he was head of the AMORC lodge in Nimes, and he remained active in AMORC for the next decade. In 1973, he founded the Center for the Preparation of the New Age in Annemasse, France. Then he started a communal group, La Pyramide, in Geneva, Switzerland, before opening the Golden Way Foundation. He promoted himself as a representative of the Great White Brotherhood, a collection of highly evolved persons who would steer the forward progress of the human race. He was, he also told people, an incarnation of the biblical Moses and the Egyptian Pharaoh Akhenaton.

In 1984 Di Mambro came into contact with a New Age holistic health teacher, Luc Jouret, who was connected to a revived occult group, the Renewed Order of the Solar Temple, who claimed to be the successors to the Knights Templars. Jouret was born to Belgian parents in 1947 in the Belgian Congo—now Zaire—and grew up handsome, charming, and articulate, with a gift for public speaking. In 1974, he graduated as a physician from the Free University of Brussels and associated with Belgium's Walloon Communist Youth. After a stint as a surgeon, he turned to homeopathy and other forms of alternative medicine, including psychic healing.

Jouret made a strong positive impression on Di Mambro and began lecturing at the Golden Way. He was exactly what Di Mambro had been seeking—a charismatic figure who could reach the public and present it with the foundation's philosophy and plans for the future. Combining their ideas about the occult and the coming New Age, they founded a new organization in 1984: the Order of the Solar Temple. As Jouret went out into the world to recruit new members, Di Mambro established the esoteric rituals for the men and women coming to him, some of them living in his home. Di Mambro worked hard to convince the members that the end of the world was at hand and would require alterations to their bodies and spirits; thus they trained themselves for passage into the next phase of the human experience. If they lived according to the order's dictates, they would be whisked off the earth at the appropriate time and reborn on a planet revolving around the Dog Star, Sirius. Jouret, hinting at things to come, once said, "Liberation is not where human beings think it is. Death can represent an essential stage of life."

Di Mambro had fathered a daughter, Emmanuelle, whom he touted as a cosmic being who would usher in the New Age. Like other cult leaders, he gained more power over his followers by deciding who would marry whom to produce the special children who would assist Emmanuelle in creating global change while he was making plans for the supreme changes just ahead. In 1984, the Golden Way Foundation sent Di Mambro and his spouse to live in Canada, where he continued working behind the scenes. Jouret had become the public spokesman for the group in Canada, France, and Switzerland, making radio appearances to spread its message and help others prepare for the coming transition.

Although the two men promoted the imminent arrival of the New Age and a radical shift in the human experience, their ideas, as with many similar groups, were based largely on looking backward to biblical times. The days to come would be apocalyptic, they believed; the end of the world was near, and it would leave reality unrecognizable. Because of this, a messiahlike figure (or figures) was required to lead humanity away from the approaching disasters and into a safer and better place. Di Mambro convinced the group that through his mystical powers he received and transmitted divine messages coming to him from the masters during cryptic ceremonies. He commanded order members to live humbly and make sacrifices now so that they could receive much greater rewards later on. In giving up a normal life, they would become part of an elite sect at the forefront of humanity that would ascend to a higher plane. To symbolize their elitism, they occasionally wore plastic bags over their heads to show their alienation from lesser people and from nature itself. During rituals, they placed a painting of a Christ-like figure above their heads and burned incense in a golden chalice. Members wore red, white, or black capes, with the different colors signifying people's ranks within the organization.

As the Order of the Solar Temple focused on lofty concepts and talk of departing the earth, it didn't pay much attention to the day-to-day efforts needed to cope with life in the present. It taught adherents little about dealing with conflict within themselves or between people or how best to get along with one's spouse, children, and others close to a person. Not much time was spent on managing stress, anger, or fear—issues far too mundane for those who saw themselves as planetary saviors. Besides, as both Di Mambro and Jouret had learned over years of cult building, it was hard to create and hold a following without using the threat of impending doom and the belief that one was part of an extremely select group. Picking up on these clues and this language, members of the order began describing themselves as noble travelers in possession of secret knowledge and hidden truths.

A message from an order leader reveals the group's mindset: "I personally believe in a cosmic law. I believe that messages were received 2,000 years ago, and I am striving to live by them. I believe in a life ethic that my parents taught me and that I am working hard to apply. I believe in a consciousness that I am capable of finding. If I follow this path, I can't go wrong. And these claims, whether true or false, will not derail me from what I must do. I will continue to work in the Order and for the mission for as long as you need me and I am able to do so."

Jouret had become known for choosing a woman to have sex with before making a proclamation or speech, saying that this gave him "strength." In October 1987, he codified the Order's beliefs in this way:

> Re-establish the correct notions of authority and power in the world;
>
> Affirm the primacy of the spiritual over the temporal;
>
> Give back to man the consciousness of his dignity;
>
> Help humanity through its transition;
>
> Participate in the assumption of the earth in its three planes: body, soul and spirit;
>
> Work toward the union of the Churches and to work toward the convergence of Christianity and Islam;
>
> Prepare for the return of Christ in solar glory.

As it evolved, the Order of the Solar Temple divided itself into three different structures. The Amanta Club disseminated the group's philosophy and focused on bringing the members into a higher state of consciousness. Its leaders spoke throughout North America, including the United States and Canada, as well as in parts of Europe and the Caribbean. The Archedia Club offered followers advanced knowledge to prepare for the looming earth changes. The most elite club of all, the International Knighthood Organization, held esoteric initiations for the most elevated within the order. In 1989, through the combined efforts of all three branches, the order reached its greatest popularity, with 442 members, many of whom were contributing financially to its growth. Things were going well, and Di Mambro's vision was to keep expanding the group and using its resources to construct health centers around the world.

One of his most notable successes was infiltrating Hydro Quebec, the province's electrical utility. Jean-Pierre Vinet was a sect member and the company's projects manager, and in 1988 and '89 Jouret gave a series of paid lectures to its executives on subjects such as "Self-Realization and Management" and "The Meaning of Life." Some of those who heard him speak were impressed enough to become linked to the sect.

Until 1991, the order grew without much trouble. Then one member claimed it was a cult and filed a lawsuit. The Canadian police suspected Jouret of criminal activity and, when he came to Quebec, began gathering information on him from the Swiss police. The Swiss authorities believed that he was behind a paramilitary group known as Q-37, which had threatened to kill Quebec's public security minister, Claude Ryan. The order also was investigated for possible links to bombings of two Hydro Quebec transmission towers. Jouret was arrested for trying to buy illegal weapons, placing the order under more scrutiny.

But the sect's deeper problems were closer to home. As Di Mambro told others, through his prophecy and revelations about the impending apocalypse, his battles were becoming more personal and intimate. His health began to fail: he developed kidney problems and then cancer. As he deteriorated, Emmanuelle rebelled against the role her father had assigned her—that of a cosmic being sent to earth to bring about the New Age. Then others began questioning Di Mambro's authority. His son, Elie, also challenged his visions after discovering that the "messages" Di Mambro said he was receiving during order events were staged using holograms and special effects. When Elie spoke out about this, fifteen members quit the sect.

More grumblings came from the ranks about Di Mambro's lifestyle in Canada. While preaching to others about the need to live sparsely, he had surrounded himself with wealth and luxury. He also developed a haughty attitude. He had long since disdained taking part in the group's daily chores, he traveled first class, and he owned several spacious homes. In the past he had tolerated some differences of opinion and been somewhat open to those questioning his views, but he now demanded complete subservience. If members dissented from his leadership, he pitted them against one another to increase his control, producing even more resistance. Conflict was mounting. Di Mambro might have had a strategy for the next life, but this one was descending into division and chaos. Membership in the order began declining, as did donations, with revenues dropping by nearly four-fifths between 1991 and 1993.

In 1994, Di Mambro's followers wrote a letter castigating him; many doubted they were still on the path to higher consciousness and a divine purpose. After a few members from Martinique decided to go to Canada to investigate the order, they began spreading word about the dangers of its mission and its possible connections to money laundering and paramilitary activity. Di Mambro and Jouret were now confronted with the most basic questions: Could they utilize their teachings and alleged special powers to help themselves and the order in a time of crisis? Would they turn to fight or flight, or try to find another way to deal with the rebellion brewing around them?

Di Mambro had the answer. He introduced his followers to the notion of "transit"—voluntary departure to a different planet, where they would unite with "the Father" and create a new world. Transit could be effected in two ways: using mirrors or spaceships. Di Mambro sent out letters to public figures explaining the transit concept but then destroyed all the documentation in an effort to generate more mystery around the order's looming departure to Sirius. All members, he commanded, had to be on twenty-four-hour alert for when the transit came—and some could only hope that would be soon.

On April 19, 1993, when the federal raid on David Koresh's Branch Davidian compound in Waco, Texas, left scores dead (see Chapter 14), Di Mambro and Jouret worried that that tragedy would overshadow their transit event. Tension between the two men had been growing over money, leadership, and who represented the true beliefs of the order, not to mention who should make the final decision about the transit and when that should come. The police recorded the men talking about what had happened in Texas:

Di Mambro: People have beaten us to the punch, you know.

Jouret: Well, yeah. Waco beat us to the punch.

Di Mambro: In my opinion, we should have gone six months before them . . . what we'll do will be even more spectacular.

On October 4, 1994, Di Mambro distributed 300 letters to his followers for mailing out three days later. One went to the French minister of the interior and was intended to explain what would happen during the transit. Di Mambro held the French government responsible for several deaths of the order's members, and wrote to the minister: "We accuse you of having attempted to deliberately destroy our Order for reasons of state. Mr. Pasqua, we accuse you of premeditated group murder. As a result, we have decided to leave the terrestrial plane ahead of time because we are aware of your desire to destroy the Work we have accomplished."

Several Quebec organizations, including the investigatory group Info-Cult, received a letter from those inside the sect outlining their worries about the order's mind-control techniques. Another police investigation that included wiretapping was opened because of reports that order members were trying to buy guns with silencers and were plotting terrorist attacks. This turned out not to be true, but the investigation led to Luc Jouret and two others in the order being sentenced to a year's probation and a $1,000 fine for possessing illegally purchased firearms. This only heightened the sense

"T.S." INSIGNIA OF THE ORDER OF THE SOLAR TEMPLE.

of victimization within the order and Di Mambro's sense that they were being punished for their beliefs.

The investigation widened into allegations that Di Mambro and his spouse were engaged in illegal currency dealings and further questions about her efforts to obtain a passport. The French were looking into fraud by Di Mambro, who, in early 1994, convinced that the group was under international surveillance, issued a statement to his dwindling band of believers: "We are rejected by the whole world. First by the people, the people can no longer withstand us. And our Earth, fortunately she rejects us. How would we leave [otherwise]? We also reject this planet. We wait for the day we can leave . . . life for me is intolerable, intolerable, I can't go on. So think about the dynamic that will get us to go elsewhere. . . .

"We don't know when they might close the trap on us—a few days? A few weeks? We are being followed and spied upon in our every move. All the cars are equipped with tracing and listening devices. All of their most sophisticated techniques are being used on us. While in the house, beware of surveillance cameras, lasers, and infra-red. Our file is the hottest on the planet, the most important of the last ten years, if not of the century. However that may be, as it turns out, the concentration of hate against us will give us enough energy to leave."

On October 2, 1994, Di Mambro and his closest advisers held a feast. Two days later, the police in Morin Heights, Quebec, answered a call about a cottage fire. Arriving at the scene, they found the charred bodies of Colette Rochat and Jerry Genoud. Two days after that two more adults and their infant son were found dead in the same vicinity inside a closet. The bodies had medallions around their necks engraved with "T. S.," probably meaning "Temple Solaire," or "Solar Temple" in English. Autopsies confirmed that the three victims—Tony Dutoit; his wife, Suzanne Robinson; and their young son, Christopher Emmanuel Dutoit—had been murdered on September 30, 1994. Before the killings, Di Mambro had identified Christopher as the Antichrist. Police determined that the killers had fled to Switzerland.

Near midnight on October 4, locals returning home from a celebration at a restaurant saw a fire raging at a hillside stone farmhouse known as La Rochette in the Swiss village of Cheiry. Volunteer firemen drove to the scene and were able to preserve much of the house. Within the structure, they found the body of seventy-three-year-old Alberto Giacobino, who had bought the twenty-acre farm five years earlier. Around 5 a.m., when the firefighters descended below the barn's main floor, they found twenty-two other bodies. Most wore white, red, or black capes, and a few of the women were draped in long golden ceremonial robes. The room with the majority of the dead had a photo of Jouret and led into a small space with mirrored walls and an altar holding a chalice, a rose, and a cross. Of the twenty-three victims, ten were men, a dozen were women, and one was a ten-year-old boy. The ages of the adults ranged from eighteen to seventy-two. Seven were Swiss, five were French, four were Canadian, and the rest European.

The Cheiry victims had been called to a meeting at the farmhouse on October 2 and probably died that day. Most of them had taken a sedative, and sixty-five bullets were recovered from their bodies. Five had been stabbed. They lay in a circle with their heads pointing outward, positioned near what appeared to be a small chapel. The lack of fingerprints at the scene and the disappearance of evidence led the authorities and the victims' relatives to believe that this was not a collective suicide but a well-planned massacre.

Another fire soon broke out in three cottages in Granges-sur-Salvan, forty-five miles east of Cheiry. The police found twenty-five more bodies there, all dead from poisoning. Overall, in Switzerland and Quebec, fifty-three order members had been killed, fulfilling Di Mambro's ideas regarding the first transit.

Fourteen months later, on December 15 and 16, 1995, the second transit occurred when thirteen adults and three children were burned to death on a plateau in the Vercors massif in France. Fourteen of them had taken sedatives before being shot twice. Two cult members had been assigned to do the killing and then had shot themselves in the head. The message Di Mambro and Jouret delivered after the mass death was that the victims had sacrificed their lives to save the world and open the way for more transits.

According to Gilbert Lavoué, the legal expert running the investigation into the Vercors deaths, the victims would not have burned as they did during a firewood ritual. Instead, they had been doused with phosphorus before the blaze was ignited. Violent marks on their bodies showed that they had not died willingly. Two victims were members of the general information office, which Jouret had suspected of infiltrating the sect to "destroy the Order of the Solar Temple." Two days after the bodies were found, the Swiss police issued arrest warrants for Jouret and Di Mambro. The Quebec police also suspected murder. Yet according to Alain Vuarnet, the parent of two of the victims, the investigation into the order was muddied from the beginning. He alleged that the sect functioned essentially to "white wash money," as several million francs ($186 million) was found in Australian accounts on behalf of Di Mambro and other individuals, some of them prominent individuals outside of the order. The police quickly denied this, but Vuarnet was adamant: the authorities wanted the public and the media to believe that all the deaths were part of a mass suicide, thereby stopping the probe from reaching beyond the sect. He further alleged that the police asked the victims' families to withdraw their complaints about the investigation. In a sense, it was all moot as Jouret and Di Mambro were later identified as victims of the Quebec fire.

But the transit wasn't over. Its third and final segment came on March 22, 1997, in Saint-Casimir, Quebec, when five people, including

ORDER OF THE SOLAR TEMPLE SUICIDE, 1997.

four order members and the parent of one of them, committed suicide. They left behind a letter explaining that they had done this to open a path to the new world. Three teenagers, the children of a couple who died in the fire, were found in a shed behind the house. They were alive but had been heavily drugged.

In 2001, one person was tried for contributing to the seventy-four deaths of the order's members. Michel Tabachnik, a former conductor with the Canadian Opera Company, was in court for nine days in Grenoble, France, after being indicted for "participation in a criminal organization" and murder. Prosecutors attempted to link him with Di Mambro through the Golden Way Foundation. Tabachnik's name was on a list of order members found in a Quebec chalet, but the prosecution failed to connect him to the cult. He was acquitted of all charges, and the legal issues and mysteries around who had shot the victims ended there.

The speculation over the exact times of death for the sect's creators was that Jouret had perished in the fire in Quebec with the others on October 4 or 5, 1994. Di Mambro had died at approximately the same time. Both men had met the same fate as the last grand master of the Knights Templar, Jacques de Molay, who was burned at the stake in 1314. Thus, they did in fact re-create a piece of the distant past but surely not the one they had had in mind when founding the Order of Solar Temple.

6

JIM JONES AND THE PEOPLES TEMPLE

I represent divine principle, total equality, a society where people own all things in common, where there's no rich or poor, where there are no races. Wherever there are people struggling for justice and righteousness, there I am.

—Jim Jones, founder, Peoples Temple

The road to hell is paved with good intentions.

—Henry G. Bohn

As a young man, Jim Jones bounced from one thing to another before finding his direction and calling. He passionately wanted to be a minister and in 1952 was hired as a student pastor at the Somerset Southside Methodist Church in a poor white neighborhood in Indianapolis. He understood being both poor and white, since he had grown up that way, and he had strong convictions about helping the downtrodden. A natural-born preacher, he was soon building a congregation, but with a twist for that time and place. He didn't want to deliver standard sermons only to white people like himself; he also wanted to talk about social justice to black people and anyone else who wanted to hear his message. Somerset Southside Methodist might have promoted harmony, acceptance, and loving one's fellow man or woman from the pulpit, but it didn't want to bring those whom such virtues might invite into its own backyard.

Jones left the church and in 1955 started his own place of worship, the Wings of Deliverance, which he soon would rename the Peoples Temple. He didn't just air his sermons from the sanctuary but scraped together enough funds to buy airtime and broadcast them over a local AM radio station. His congregation was growing at the same time that he was getting more concerned about the future. Restless and fearful of calamities such as nuclear war—he said it would come on July 15, 1967—he took his followers to Brazil in 1962, but that venture was short-lived and he relocated in 1965 to northern California with a few hundred of the devoted. They resettled in the small towns of Redwood Valley and Ukiah in the beautiful and relatively isolated forest country, but Jones soon itched to branch out again and opened a church in San Francisco in the early '70s.

Jones was finding his purpose and mission while trying to escape the difficult circumstances of his life, which had begun in Crete, Indiana, in May 1931. His father, James Thurman Jones, who had served in World War I and been a victim of mustard gas, drank and lived on disability checks. Fighting off his depressions and bad memories, he showed little interest in his young son. His mother, Lynetta, was outspoken and known to alienate others with her independent spirit and freewheeling tongue. When someone in the neighborhood told her that her behavior was going to send her to hell, she didn't argue with that person; she laughed. But Jim's upbringing wasn't particularly funny. With a damaged father who held racial views that his son could not abide and a mother usually absent from home and working, the boy felt alone, if not abandoned. To occupy himself, he conducted deadly experiments on animals—a hallmark of a seriously troubled youth.

"I didn't have any love given to me," he once told his congregation. "I didn't know what the hell love was."

As a youngster, he was often by himself on the streets, hanging with society's underdogs. He took on bullies who bothered smaller kids, rescued stray cats and dogs, and made a point of being kind to the less fortunate. He once described himself as "the trash of the neighborhood," a young man looking for a way out of his circumstances and a path to salvation. With a neighbor, he went to churches in Lynn, Indiana, where he had moved in 1934, and became friends with a Pentecostal preacher, thinking he'd like to follow in the man's footsteps. Weaving together pieces of different branches of Christianity, he began ministering to the local children. His hope was to join a religious group, but after studying a few—the Methodists, the Quakers, the Church of Christ, the Nazarenes, and several other denominations—he found something lacking in their beliefs. He felt he had to strike out on his own.

Jim knew how to draw attention to himself. Once he came up with a clever scheme for a pep rally before a high school basketball game: staging a funeral for the other team. He conducted the memorial and delivered a sermon over the dead opponents. His fellow students loved it. Another part of his appeal was physical: he had thick black hair, penetrating eyes, and a handsome stare that could make those he looked on feel special. He came across almost as a rebellious hipster, which was the thing to be in some circles in the 1950s (think James Dean and Marlon Brando).

Dressing all in black, he made an impressive appearance, and not just with his looks. From the pulpit, he brought fire and brimstone, hope, and the promise of something better, not only moving people spiritually but getting them to contribute financially to his church and dreams. Jones had it all—for what he eventually had in mind.

Jim's parents split up when he was still young, and he and his mother moved to Richmond, Indiana. He found work as a hospital orderly and met Marceline Baldwin, a nursing student a little older than himself. He graduated early from high school and enrolled at Indiana University in January 1949. He dropped out after his first semester and married Marceline that year.

Jim continued preaching on the side and attracted some followers. Although he discouraged dancing, romantic relationships, and sex for his flock, he indulged in adulterous affairs and fathered at least one child. Building his skills as a pastor, he took an unconventional model for one with his background. George Baker, aka "Father Divine," was a black preacher who in the 1920s had founded the International Peace Mission movement. He led a multiracial congregation, and some of his sermons focused on avoiding the sexual act (a message Jim borrowed from him). He didn't just try to save souls but called for empowering his followers through political and financial action. This entailed pooling their resources so that more of them had a chance at a better life. Father Divine was inspirational in igniting Jones's racial consciousness, which few white ministers had at that time, spurring him to try to end segregation in Christian churches. Father Divine and his wife, Mother, lived on a Pennsylvania estate. When Divine died in 1965, Jones made a play for the Peace Mission organization, telling Divine's followers that he was the reincarnation of the great minister who'd just passed. Mother Divine responded to Jim's claim by expelling him from the movement.

His predatory behavior notwithstanding, Jones was sincere in his racial convictions, at least in the beginning, and used religion to promote integration and equality. He and Marceline adopted three Korean children and a youngster who was part Native American, and they were the first white couple in Indiana to adopt a black child, to whom they gave their own last name. Jones referred to his growing clan as his "rainbow family," a moniker he later applied to his religious followers.

As the head of the Indianapolis Human Rights Commission, to which he was appointed in 1960, Jones worked to desegregate restaurants, hospitals, and the city's police department and telephone company. The Peoples Temple provided free food and housing for the elderly and mentally ill, along with drug counseling for addicts. In Indiana, this unleashed a backlash against his family, who became the victims of threats and letters from people who prayed for Jones to die. He found more openness in California, especially in San Francisco in the 1970s, where his congregation reached into the thousands.

Jones fit in well with the Bay Area's rebellious character. He offered not just sermons and material goods but a heated combination of antiwar, antipoverty, anti-imperialist, and anticapitalist messages. People were listening and responding. If they came for the preaching, they stayed for the "faith healings," a longtime staple of religious revivals in which the minister seemed to perform miracles in healing the sick. Jones was just charismatic enough—with his slicked-back hair and the trademark dark sunglasses he now wore nearly all the time—to pull it off.

In 1975, Jones's followers campaigned door to door to get Democrat George Moscone elected mayor of San Francisco. Moscone then praised Jones for bringing peace and harmony to poor and frustrated people, and in 1976 he appointed Jones to the San Francisco Housing Authority Commission. Jones was politically engaged at the same time as Harvey Milk, the first openly gay person to be elected, in November 1977, to the city's board of supervisors. Milk and Moscone went to Jones's church services, and Governor Jerry Brown praised his work. Milk and Jones advocated for "radical equality," and the former spoke at Peoples Temple events and once wrote to a friend after a church rally: "Rev Jim, It may take me many a day to come back down from the high that I reach today. I found something dear today. I found a sense of being that makes up for all the hours and energy placed in a fight. I found what you wanted me to find. I shall be back. For I can never leave."

In November 1978, Milk was gunned down a year after his election, his death only nine days separated from Jones's.

Jones had reached the height of respectability in San Francisco, where renowned columnist Herb Caen wrote about him in his society column, describing the sect leader as "soft-spoken, modest, publicity shy" (this despite Jones having been arrested in December 1973 for lewd conduct at a movie theater in Los Angeles). As the Peoples Temple leader became more popular in San Francisco, his style began to change and his demons, which he'd mostly been able to suppress until then, grew stronger. He became dependent on prescription drugs, and his sexual views were turning stranger. He was obsessed with homosexuality, calling out men he thought were gay while bragging about his own heterosexual prowess. Some of his followers wondered if all this was to mask his being gay himself and incapable of facing the truth or publicly coming out.

As time passed, Jones's tendencies became more flagrant. There were accounts of him using a rubber hose to beat the genitals of a man, suspected of pedophilia, in front of a group until the man bled. "Jim said that all of us were homosexuals," ex-Temple member Joyce Houston claimed in the documentary *Jonestown*. "Everyone except [him]. He was the only heterosexual on the planet, and that the women were all lesbians; the guys were all gay. And so anyone who showed an interest in sex was just compensating."

In classic cult fashion, Jones accumulated more power over others by separating families or trying to end marriages. At least one couple, Tim and Grace Stoen, signed an affidavit saying that Jones was the father of their son, John Victor Stoen. Grace fled the sect but, fearing for the lives of everyone in her family, left the child with the church. Tim, a lawyer, also departed and tried to reclaim John through the legal system. After much wrangling, the boy stayed with the sect. Not all of the Jones's conflicts involved court battles. Stories of violence against the disobedient were mounting. Jones told people that he could read their minds, and some believed him. He ordered them to sell their homes or other assets and give him their sources of income. His followers tried to rationalize all this, reminding themselves of what he was accomplishing in San Francisco and how many people he'd brought into the church.

As Jones's eccentricities increased, he grew more restless. He was thinking of making another major move, this time far to the south. In mid-1977, *New West* interviewed some of those who'd left the church, who described a sometimes violent, sometimes phony prophet sliding out of control. When Jones was unable to kill the story before publication, he packed up his belongings and led his sect to the English-speaking South American country Guyana, leasing 3,800 isolated acres of jungle from that nation's government. There he could fulfill his long-held concept of creating his own community and calling it Jonestown, away from the clutches of society, other religions, the media, and the law. A thousand followers were ready to leave their lives in San Francisco and go where he led them.

In Guyana, Jones's followers were quickly organized into various teams that would be in charge of future operations: education, medical, day care, and agricultural. They raised chickens and pigs and planted crops. Jonestown was intended to be a utopia, far from the American scene and those who wanted to attack the sect and its leader. But the move to Guyana did nothing to lessen Jones's ravings and punishments for those who questioned his vision or goals or mental abilities. Jones thought that the CIA was trying to undermine the community's efforts by poisoning its rice supply. Armed guards were put in place to stop anyone from attempting to escape from the compound. If they managed to get outside, they had no money or passports. If they somehow made it back to San Francisco, Jones's thugs would find them and retaliate. Failed escapees were taken to the "Extra Care Unit" and routinely drugged into submission. Loudspeakers around the compound often played through the night, using the mind-control techniques of sleep deprivation.

"True believers accepted that whatever [Jones] did was right," Jeff Guinn wrote in *The Road to Jonestown*. "Those increasingly disaffected with Jones but still loyal to the Temple's professed socialist cause shrugged the experience off as one more example of Jones's increasingly bizarre behavior. Many, sleep-deprived and emotionally exhausted, were just glad to get back to their beds."

The one creature to whom Jones showed kindness was Mr. Muggs, a chimpanzee that Jones claimed to have saved from a grim scientific experiment but that more likely came from a pet store. In 1973, the church's periodical, the *Temple Reporter*, said of Mr. Muggs: "Only 18 months old, he has the intelligence of a four year old child. . . . It may sound anthropomorphic, but Muggs will follow every command of Pastor Jones, and will defend him when anyone comes up casually to pet the chimpanzee."

As the Peoples Temple mascot, the chimp got better treatment than the humans in the compound. Jones preached over loudspeakers, driving home his sermons and visions and demanding that temple members conduct suicide drills during which they were awakened in the middle of the night, given a cup of a red liquid supposedly containing poison, and made to drink the concoction. Later, they would be informed that this had been nothing more than a test of their loyalty and that they had passed.

The Good Samaritan from Indiana was morphing into a monster whom no one inside the sect could challenge or speak to honestly for fear of retribution or being forced to live in worse conditions than they already did. Food was sparse. Jonestown members were forced to work a dozen or more hours at a stretch in the heat, and at night they were expected to learn the Russian language, as their leader believed that the Soviet Union— "paradise" according to Jones—supported what they were doing in the forests of Guyana. Cheese was used as a reward and a punishment: if you were good, you got more; if you were bad, less.

Jones repeatedly showed his followers, especially his black sect members, *Night and Fog*, a movie about the Jewish concentration camps, to convince them of what the United States planned to do to minorities. That was why, he said, it was absolutely essential for them to carry out his every order and build their home elsewhere. He was now taking Valium and synthetic morphine. He drank too much and when drunk spewed venom against his enemies, real and imagined. He practiced more "fake suicides" with his followers and talked about the nobility of "dying for the cause."

In early 1978, after announcing that an armed force was coming to kill everyone, Jones demanded that all the compound members drink from a vat of poison, announcing that they would die in less than an hour. They did as they were told, but it was just another loyalty test and all survived.

Some tried to call attention to Jones's decline, but that was dangerous. Others tried to escape. He meted out punishment to the disloyal and raged against anyone attempting to defect. He sent cheery videos of Jonestown to his former followers in San Francisco, showing how happy his people were in Guyana, living freely in their new cabins. But stories of the actual reality there were leaking out and growing more troubling.

After considerable effort, Peoples Temple member Yulanda Williams persuaded Jones to let her and her family leave Guyana with the promise that they would return. In San Francisco, she was contacted by Representative Leo Ryan, a California Democrat, who had begun investigating Jones and his followers. An unconventional politician, he was sympathetic to their plight. Earlier, Ryan had served a short stint at California's Folsom State Prison to see how the prisoners fared behind bars and whether their situation could be improved. He also had traveled to Canada to investigate the slaughter of baby seals. When he began receiving complaints about the Peoples Temple from the relatives of those in the sect, who thought that their kin were being held against their will, he felt he had to act. Ryan fired off a letter to Jones and, similarly to what he'd done at Folsom, asked to come there and take a look. That was the last thing Jones, whose kingdom was up and running in the jungle, wanted to hear, but turning down the congressman might produce a worse outcome. He let Ryan visit.

Ryan put together a delegation that landed in Guyana on November 17 with a pack of reporters, his staff, and others representing "Concerned Relatives"—made up of Americans who'd fled the Peoples Temple and family members of those still living in Jonestown. As they toured the compound with a television crew in tow, Ryan invited anyone who wanted to quit the sect to leave with him. For some, it took no persuasion. Sixteen people met with the congressman and begged to go back to the United States. He was the answer to their hopes and prayers, having seen enough to understand their fears and take them home.

They packed up for the flight, but six miles from Jonestown, right by the airstrip at Port Kaituma, they were ambushed by a man inside their group who was working undercover for Jones. Larry Layton opened fire with a handgun, and other armed loyalists showed up on a truck holding more weapons. They shot Representative Ryan at least twenty times and killed the Jonestown escapee Patricia Parks. When the shooting stopped, Ryan and four others lay murdered on the airstrip. They included NBC correspondent Don Harris, NBC cameraman Bob Brown, and *San Francisco Examiner* photographer Greg Robinson. One of the wounded was Ryan's aide, Jackie Speier, twenty-eight years old at the time and now a U.S. congresswoman. For years afterward she spoke of Ryan's good heart and sincere convictions in trying to help Peoples Temple members. For his courage and compassion, Ryan received a Congressional Gold Medal in 1983; in 2009, a post office in his San Mateo, California, district was named for him.

In the wake of the attack, a teacher at the temple, Richard Tropp, apparently penned a note about what was coming and explained why temple members now needed to take their place among the dead. Although there are some who believe that he was not the author of the note, he claimed that Jones had not ordered the murder of Congressman Ryan and the others, concluding, "If nobody understands, it matters not. I am ready to die now. Darkness settles over Jonestown on its last day on earth."

On November 18, the forty-seven-year-old Jones brought his followers together in the pavilion area one last time. Surrounding the leader were armed guards with pistols, shotguns, semiautomatics, and crossbows. Vats had been prepared with cyanide-laced drinks for distribution. His words would be captured on audiotape and recovered by investigators.

"How very much I loved you," Jones told them while holding a microphone. "How very much I tried to give you a good life."

In the background was the sound of babies crying.

Jones attacked those who had defected from the Peoples Temple and "committed the betrayal of the century." The recent visit by government officials from California, he said, was just a hint of what the government was about to do to the sect: "They won't leave us alone. They are now going back to tell more lies, which means more congressmen. There's no way, no way we can survive. . . .

"My opinion is that we be kind to children and be kind to seniors and take the potion like they used to take in Ancient Greece, and step over quietly."

"What about going to Russia?" an aging woman asked.

"It's too late for that," said Jones.

"But," she pushed back, "I look at all the babies and I think they deserve to live."

"I agree," he answered. "But what's more, they deserve peace."

There was no time to wait, he went on. The defense forces of the Guyana government were on their way to the compound, and when they arrived, they would torture and shoot all of them.

"Please get us the medication," he said. "It's simple. There's no convulsions with it. Don't be afraid to die."

His mistress, Maria Katsaris, agreed. "There's nothing to worry about," she told them. "Everybody keep calm . . . and the oldest children can help love the little children and reassure them. They're not crying from pain. It's just a little bitter tasting, but they're not crying out of any pain."

As the people began drinking the cyanide concoction, the air was filled with the sounds of vomiting. Mothers gave the drink to their children and then swallowed it themselves. The older ones observing this began to weep as the children slumped over to their deaths.

One follower grabbed the microphone and said, "The way the children are laying dead now, I'd rather see them lay like that than to see them have to die like the Jews did, which was pitiful. And the ones they take captive, they're gonna just let them grow up and be dummies like they want them to be, and not socialist like the one and only Jim Jones. . . . Thank you, Dad."

Others applauded.

Jones took the microphone and said, "Die with respect, die with a degree of dignity. Stop this hysterics. . . . This is not the way for people who are socialistic communists to die. We must die with some dignity."

"That's right," someone said.

"Some people," Jones said, "assure these children of . . . stepping over to the next plane. . . . We didn't commit suicide. We committed an act of revolutionary suicide protesting the conditions of an inhumane world."

His words hung in the air, accompanied by an organ playing "We Shall Overcome," the hymn of the civil rights movement of the 1960s, when Jones was carrying out his mission of preaching racial and social justice. At the close of his life, he returned to his roots, as though this song somehow could bring back the glory and promise of those days. When the music stopped, the audiotape held only the sounds of silence, followed by faint static.

Within twenty-four hours, 918 members of Jones's cult were dead. Sometime later, the FBI would recover the tape in Jonestown on which the Peoples Temple leader instructed his flock to drink poison. His minions had mixed Valium and cyanide into a grape-flavored powdered drink and handed it out to sect members. Children died first, but some of the adults resisted Jones's command. Armed guards forced them to follow orders and imbibe—but not Jim Jones, for whom death came more swiftly. Members of his inner circle shot him, or perhaps he shot himself, in the head. Next to him were his wife, Marceline; his nurse, Annie Moore; and several other top officials of the Peoples Temple.

Mr. Muggs, the cult's favorite chimpanzee, was killed by a gunshot that day. John Victor Stoen, who'd come with the sect to Guyana after his parents had failed to win their custody battle with Jones, was among the roughly 300 people under age seventeen who perished in Jonestown. Photos revealed hundreds of bodies lying facedown on the grass in the largest mass death by suicide in American history. It gave us the phrase "drinking the Kool-Aid" as a reference to any person or group that unquestioningly accepts what someone else is saying or doing—taking something on faith without doing any critical thinking. (The people at Jonestown didn't actually drink Kool-Aid but a similar brand called Flavor Aid.)

Around a hundred of Jones's followers escaped or survived the mass suicide on November 18. Two of them were Jones's sons—Jim Jones, Jr., eighteen, and Stephan Jones, nineteen—who were attending a basketball game in Guyana's capital city of Georgetown. One mother told her three-year-old son they were going on a picnic and walked thirty-five miles to escape the mass suicide. Three other Temple members—Mike Prokes, along with the brothers Tim and Mike Carter—were sent out that day to deliver a suitcase holding $550,000 in cash to the Soviet embassy in Georgetown. They also carried letters to the embassy that left all the Peoples Temple's assets, totaling around $7 million, to the Soviet Union's Communist Party.

An elderly black woman, Hyacinth Thrash, had slept in her cabin on the compound as all those around her were committing suicide. The next morning, she got out of bed and walked to the senior citizens' center, seeing rows of corpses covered with sheets. One body belonged to her sister, Zipporah Edwards. "There were all of those dead being put in bags," she wrote in her 1995 memoir, *The Onliest One Alive*. "People I'd known and loved. . . . God knows I never wanted to be there in the first place. I never wanted to go to Guyana to die. . . . I didn't think Jim would do a thing like that. He let us down."

As reporters made their way in helicopters to the site of the tragedy, the stench of death below hit them at 300 feet above the earth. From that perspective, one journalist said, the bodies looked like a bunch of discarded rag dolls, as they were dressed in bright shades of blue, green, and red. Once the choppers had landed, the newspeople wrapped handkerchiefs around their mouths and noses to ward off the smell. The jaunty colors of the clothing made the scene seem even more surreal and macabre.

DEAD BODIES LIE NEAR THE COMPOUND OF THE PEOPLES TEMPLE ON NOVEMBER 18, 1978, IN JONESTOWN AFTER OVER 900 COMMITTED MASS SUICIDE.

Long after November 18, 1978, the casualties connected to the Peoples Temple would continue to mount. In 1979, Mike Prokes, the cult's media-relations person who had escaped the carnage in Jonestown, held a press conference at a California motel to defend the temple's actions under Jones's leadership. When the presser was over, he went into the bathroom and killed himself with a gunshot to the head. In 1980, Al and Jeannie Mills, two of the sect's defectors, were murdered at their Berkeley, California, home. No one was arrested for the double homicide. Three years later, ex-Temple follower Paula Adams and her child were murdered by Laurence Mann, her ex-boyfriend and a former Guyanese ambassador to the United States. Mann then took his own life. In 1984, Tyrone Mitchell, whose mother, father, and siblings had all died at Jonestown, killed one person in a Los Angeles schoolyard and wounded more than ten others before committing suicide. Chad Rhodes's mother, Juanita Bogue, was pregnant with him in Jonestown, but they survived. Near the thirtieth anniversary of the mass death in Guyana, Chad was charged with murdering an Oakland police officer.

Forty years after being shot in Guyana, Jackie Speier spoke with an ABC affiliate about the trauma, then and now. After the attack on Congressman Ryan's entourage, she was flown to the United States and underwent ten surgeries. Cheryl Jennings was the interviewer.

"Every time I go back to that moment," Speier said, "I thank God that I'm still alive, because there's no reason why I am alive."

Their dialogue about the assault and being hit five times with bullets, including once in the back, continued:

> *Speier*: And then Ryan started to run, so I ran under the plane. And as I was running, he was hit once. And then he was hit again. And fell. And I just ran to one of the wheels and tried to hide there, pretending I was dead.
>
> *Jennings*: Do you remember the physicalness of being hit?

Speier: The first thing I felt was the impact and then I looked onto my right side and my right arm was blown up and there was bone sticking out. My right thigh was totally destroyed, but the femoral artery was still intact. If that had been severed, I would have bled to death.

Jennings: You were basically left for dead.

Speier: We were on that airstrip for twenty-two hours without medical attention.

Jennings: Do you still have shrapnel in your body?

Speier: I do. I have two bullets still and then shrapnel as well. . . . I always get my hackles up when people say it was suicide. Those people were murdered.

More than four decades after the bodies were recovered from Jonestown and the Peoples Temple had been long since abandoned, jungle growth overtook the landscape, leaving it as it had been before the Americans arrived with their loudspeakers and watchtowers, their fears and their Flavor Aid. Plant life flourished everywhere. A few years ago, a survivor of the mass death went back to the site and searched around, but it was empty except for the big vat that once had held the poison that killed more than 900 people.

7

JAMES ARTHUR RAY

On Thursday morning, October 8, 2009, James Arthur Ray posted a question on his Twitter account: "For anything new to live something first must die. What needs to die in you so that new life can emerge?" Several hours later at the Angel Valley Retreat Center outside Sedona, Arizona, Ray led sixty-three people into a twenty-foot-square tent made of tarps and blankets that was pitch black inside; the tent was just over four feet tall in the center and two and a half feet high at the edges. Every fifteen minutes Ray's assistants raised a flap on the tent, brought in more volcanic rocks the size of cantaloupes, and doused them with hot water, raising the enclosure's temperature to 122 degrees. Ray was attempting to simulate a Native American sweat lodge purification ceremony designed to cleanse the body and spirit. Unlike those who took part in the ancient Indian rituals, the Angel Valley participants had paid Ray $9,695 for this experience, the culmination of a five-day "Spiritual Warrior" retreat in the desert outside Sedona, having fasted for the last thirty-six hours before eating breakfast that morning. In his 2008 *New York Times* best-selling book, *Harmonic Wealth*, Ray contended that one could become a multimillionaire, like him, by focusing one's intention on becoming rich and practicing the kind of discipline needed to endure the rigors of the sweat lodge.

This retreat, he promised, would "absolutely change your life."

"911," the Yavapai County, Arizona, police dispatcher said, responding to an incoming call at 5 p.m. that afternoon. "Where's your emergency?"

"Angel Valley," a female voice answered, explaining that a man and woman on the property had lost consciousness. "Two people not breathing. There's no pulse."

"Is this the result of a shooting or something?"

"No, it's a sweat lodge."

The dispatcher sent emergency personnel to the retreat as Ray's staff frantically dismantled the thrown-together tent structure. By nightfall, Angel Valley was crowded with EMS vehicles, fire crews, police officers, ambulances, and helicopters. The unconscious man and woman were forty-year-old James Shore of Milwaukee and thirty-eight-year-old Kirby Brown of Westtown, not far north of New York City. They were rushed to Verde Valley Medical Center, where both were pronounced dead. Nineteen others were hospitalized for dehydration, respiratory arrest, kidney failure, elevated body temperature, and other ailments. All but four soon were released, but forty-nine-year-old Liz Neuman of Minnesota remained in a coma caused by multiple organ damage. With the casualties mounting around him, Ray left for Los Angeles and a speaking engagement at the Ritz-Carlton Hotel.

"We attempted to interview Mr. Ray at the scene," Yavapai County Sheriff Steve Waugh told the media. "He refused to talk to us."

In the years leading up to the sweat-lodge incident, Ray had found great success in the self-help business, appearing on *Larry King Live* and landing a role in the hit film *The Secret*, touted on television by Ellen DeGeneres and Oprah Winfrey. The movie was based on the book *The Secret*, which contended that by employing positive thinking and the "Law of Attraction," one could bring about improved health, personal happiness, and wealth. Author Rhonda Byrne wrote that Asking, Believing, and Receiving were the three most important aspects of this "Universal Law," which had been known about for centuries but kept secret by some of the world's most famous people. Within months of the release of the book and a companion DVD, nearly 2 million copies of the book were in print and 1.5 million DVDs had been sold. After Ray's appearance in the film, his $1-million-a-year company, James Ray International, began doing $10 million in business annually.

Although Ray didn't immediately comment on the deaths outside Sedona or offer condolences to the victims' families, others were not so reticent. Native Americans came forward and talked about how easily white people can abuse and exploit their age-old ceremonies, which had been created not to make money for tribal leaders but to restore inner balance and change people's attitudes and self-image. Some Indians referred to people like James Ray as "plastic shamans." Traditional sweat lodges held only ten to twelve participants, who were given breaks during the ritual cleansing to make certain they didn't become dehydrated or overheated.

"The sweat lodge needs to be respected," said Joseph Bruchac, author of *The Native American Sweat Lodge: History and Legends*. "When you imitate someone's tradition and you don't know what you are doing, there's a danger of doing something very wrong. If you put people in a restrictive, airtight structure, you are going to use up all the oxygen."

The day after James Shore and Kirby Brown died, Yavapai County sheriff's deputies served search warrants at Angel Valley while autopsies were conducted and blood samples were checked for poisons. The county's building-safety manager, Jack Judd, said that there was no record of an application or permit for a sweat lodge on the property and that on October 8 the structure hadn't been inspected for problems before it was quickly torn down. Four years earlier, another Angel Valley sweat lodge participant had lost consciousness before being revived.

Sheriff Waugh then stunned Ray by announcing that the two fatalities were not accidental and were being investigated as homicides. Ray made a countermove, putting together his own investigative team to uncover the real truth behind the deaths in the desert. The police were unimpressed, and they were not alone.

On network and cable television, Tom McFeeley had emerged as the family spokesman for Kirby Brown's survivors, recalling her life as an avid hiker and surfer and "the least selfish, kindest person I knew." McFeeley said that Ray's message regarding the sweat lodge experience— that people should push themselves beyond their boundaries—"could be flat dangerous. Something clearly went wrong. Something wasn't done correctly."

Ray's public relations spokesman, Howard Bragman, called Sheriff Waugh's characterization of the fatalities as "homicides" irresponsible; the local police, he said, were tarring his client to promote their own political futures. "I find it very interesting the police are trying to escalate the case in the media," Bragman said, "and frankly, I think the escalation should be in getting the facts. We have one goal and that is to find out what happened so that it never happens again."

A week after the deaths, Ray still hadn't talked with Arizona authorities, but he did speak to his supporters at the Los Angeles Ritz-Carlton, where he broke down and declared that he was "being tested" by those events. It wasn't his first test.

In May 2005, a New Jersey woman shattered her hand after Ray allegedly bullied her into performing a board-breaking exercise to overcome self-esteem issues. Diane Konopka filed a negligence lawsuit, charging Ray with recklessness; the case was settled for an undisclosed sum. In July 2009, Ray held a three-day seminar in San Diego that cost attendees $12,000. He ordered the participants to wander through the downtown area in shabby clothes and without an ID, money, or cell phones so that they could learn what it feels like to be homeless. During the event, Colleen Conaway, a forty-six-year-old Minnesota woman, jumped three floors to her death from the balcony of a mall. Drugs and alcohol were not involved. For seven hours she lay in a morgue without any identification before someone from Ray's business stepped forward to claim the body. In recent years, James Ray International had made people paying for these events sign waivers exonerating the company from any responsibility in case they got hurt.

On October 17, 2009, Liz Neuman, the sweat-lodge victim who had been in a coma for nine days, passed away.

With three people dead, a few survivors of the Angel Valley retreat began talking publicly about what had happened that afternoon and evening. Texas orthodontist Beverley Bunn told the Associated Press that in the days leading up to the ceremony, the group had undergone grueling physical and mental games. In one, Ray had assigned himself the role of God, donning white robes and encouraging people to commit mock suicide, but everything that week had culminated with the sweat-lodge challenge. Within an hour of entering the tent, Bunn told the AP, people began vomiting, gasping for air, and collapsing, yet Ray urged them to stay inside.

"I can't get her to move," Bunn heard someone say in the darkness. "I can't get her to wake up."

"Leave her alone," Ray responded, according to Bunn. "She'll be dealt with in the next round."

When somebody lifted up a back flap on the tent, letting in sunlight and fresh air, Ray demanded to know who was doing it and said the person was committing a "sacrilegious act."

Melinda Martin, a James Ray International employee who quit after the retreat, had tried in vain to save Kirby Brown.

"After giving her mouth to mouth," Martin recalled, "I would breathe into her mouth, her stomach would go up, and when it would go back down again, she'd vomit into my mouth. And this happened four times. And I really thought I was going to bring her back. I really thought that she was going to survive."

While Martin attempted to rescue Brown, Ray stood off to one side of the tent, being cooled down with a hose by his aides. In the aftermath of the tragedy, he continued traveling the country to hold seminars until he was tracked down and hounded so severely by CNN's Anderson Cooper and Gary Tuchman that he eventually canceled the rest of his 2009 schedule. He went into retreat at his Carlsbad, California, headquarters or inside his $4.5 million Beverly Hills home to await the next round of legal developments (facing mounting attorney fees, he put the house up for sale). His lawyers made available two extensive "White Papers" that tried to refute what Bunn and Martin were saying and to clear Ray's name with the press and public. PR man Howard Bragman continued releasing statements, but Ray stayed mum.

As a boy growing up in Tulsa, Oklahoma, Ray had watched his father try to make ends meet as a preacher, leaving the youngster with a permanent sense of shame. The Ray family often had no place to live but his father's Church of God office. "The hardest part of my childhood," Ray wrote in *Harmonic Wealth*, "was reconciling how Dad poured his heart into his work, how he helped so many people and yet he couldn't afford to pay for haircuts for me and my brother. How could a loving God keep me from Cub Scouts on account of not being able to afford a uniform?"

In time Ray became a top producer and trainer at AT&T, with a natural flair for salesmanship and business. The more success he had, the more determined he was to use his spiritual ideas to make money and be a player at the highest levels of the self-help industry. He eventually got the fast cars and the Los Angeles mansion, living the life of a media star surrounded by celebrities. In his book, he nakedly laid out his beliefs about the ties between spirituality and getting rich:

"It takes a bigger person to make $100,000 per year," he wrote in *Harmonic Wealth*, "than to make $10,000."

"Growth leads to what? Money."

"To take control of your destiny, you must begin to take full responsibility and accountability for everything in your life."

"I can spend fifteen minutes with you and tell what you've been up to for the past five years."

"Money is nothing more than a measuring stick of your growth."

With his speaking and writing, Ray attracted numerous followers who had turned away from traditional religions and were looking not just for wealth but for a new relationship with their own spirituality. Many were educated, sincere, and successful people, and some remained convinced that Ray had helped them. Even after the sweat-lodge deaths, Ray's approach appealed to the desires of tens of millions of other Americans and other seekers engaged in similar activities.

After the tragedy, Native American leaders denounced Ray, and the Lakota Sioux Tribe sued him and his company, demanding that he be prosecuted under the 1868 Treaty of Fort Laramie for appropriating an Indian ritual. The lawsuit employed the original language of the treaty: "If bad men among the whites, or among other people subject to the authority of the United States, shall commit any wrong upon the person or property of the Indians, the United States will, upon proof made to the agent, and forwarded to the Commissioner of Indian Affairs at

Washington city, proceed at once to cause the offender to be arrested and punished according to the laws of the United States, and also reimburse the injured person for the loss sustained."

Ray, the Sioux leaders believed, was a bad man among the whites, and several families of the dead or injured at Angel Valley agreed and filed civil cases against him. The authorities in Yavapai County interviewed the sweat-lodge survivors and put together 700 pages of information and evidence to present to a grand jury. In *Harmonic Wealth,* Ray claimed that he knew the laws of the universe, but he was about to come face to face with American due process.

On one occasion, when talking at a seminar about encountering the unexpected and the painful in life, he had said, "I fully know, for me, that there is no blame. Every single thing is your responsibility . . . and nothing is your fault. Because every single thing that comes to you is a gift . . . a lesson."

On February 3, 2010, Ray was indicted, arrested, and charged with three counts of manslaughter. He was taken into custody in Prescott, Arizona, and jailed at the Camp Verde Detention Center, which stood by itself on a windswept, sandy, desolate patch of desert far removed from the money and metaphysical gift shops of Sedona. Because of his financial resources, Ray was considered a flight risk, and his bond was set at $5 million. His lawyer, Luis Li, said that both the charges and the bond were unjust, promising that his client would refuse to take a plea bargain in the case but go to trial and win an acquittal.

"This was a terrible accident," Li said, "but it was an accident, not a criminal act. James Ray cooperated at every step of the way, providing information and witnesses to the authorities, showing that no one could have foreseen this accident."

Three weeks after the arrest, Judge Warren Darrow lowered Ray's bond to $525,000 but ordered him to surrender his passport and not to organize, supervise, or conduct any sweat-lodge ceremonies or other activities that might be harmful to people. If convicted, Ray faced three to twelve years in jail on each count.

After the deaths at Angel Valley, Ray's former high-profile supporters, including Deepak Chopra and Oprah Winfrey, did not step forward to defend him in public. In a *Daily Beast* article, anticult therapist Steven Hassan said, "Oprah has mainstreamed a lot of very questionable characters, in my opinion. I would like to believe that this incident could be something that would cause people like Oprah to do more responsible research and to question whether or not they are serving their viewers, as opposed to just promoting people and ideas that are fundamentally flawed."

In 2011, Ray was convicted of three counts of negligent homicide. He served two years in an Arizona state prison and was released under supervision in July 2013. Upon his release, he attempted to relaunch his career as a motivational speaker.

8

SHOKO ASAHARA AND AUM SHINRIKYO

Shoko Asahara began life with severely limited vision in his left eye and lesser problems in his right. Born on March 2, 1955, as Chizuo Matsumoto, he grew up in a Japanese village on the southern island of Kyushu, the sixth of seven children in an impoverished family crowded into a tiny living space. His father struggled as a tatami-mat maker, and one of his older brothers, who was almost completely blind, went to a school for his special needs that offered financial aid. Asahara could see, and so could a younger brother, but their parents sent both of them to the older brother's school, where they all received a government subsidy and free meals.

His eyesight problems notwithstanding, Asahara was physically gifted and soon earned a black belt in judo. He developed an early fascination with accumulating power and money, and he was in a good place to exercise those desires. Because of his partial sight, he had an advantage over many of his fellow students and was positioned for leadership. Years later, classmates would recall him using his clout at school to bully others, a hint of things to come.

To get them to follow him, Asahara took his classmates to restaurants off campus, and in return they bought his food. The ploy was only partly effective. He ran unsuccessfully for student body president in elementary, junior high, and senior high school. The memory of losing three times stayed with him and would echo through his developing ambitions and actions. Although he failed to attain office at the school, he had a knack for making money and getting others to contribute to his vision of the future; some estimates have him saving up $30,000 by the time he left high school. He did not pass his college entrance exams and soon found work as an acupuncturist in a Tokyo suburb. In 1978, he met Tomoko Ishii; they married and had four daughters and two sons.

In the early 1980s, Asahara opened a store selling Chinese medicine and did well hawking tangerine peels steeped in alcohol. Two years later, he was arrested and fined for peddling fake drugs. He went into seclusion and claimed to have traveled to India and Nepal to study Hinduism and Buddhism and returned home with photos of himself with the Dalai Lama. In the Himalayas, Asahara said, he had achieved enlightenment and discovered that he was the reincarnation of Shiva, the Hindu god of destruction. Back in Japan, he became a yoga teacher and taught a group of followers his own combination of Eastern religions and prophecies of an impending apocalypse. He started a company called Aum Shinrikyo, whose name derived in part from "*Aum*," which in Hinduism represents the cosmic power behind all creation—the vibration by which God brings all things into manifestation. He also managed a yoga school and sold health drinks, working as a senior executive at Aum and transferring the same bold and charismatic qualities he'd used in school into the world of commerce. Over time, he built a business stretching across national boundaries that was worth tens of millions of dollars. He liked assuming the role of overlord and commanding his employees while riding around in a Rolls-Royce.

Aum attracted members of elite families, scientists, and young university graduates. It was recruiting followers at the right moment, as many young students in Japan were rebelling against a culture that forced them to spend 240 days in the classroom every year, one-third more than their American counterparts. Cramming for exams began in kindergarten, and nights were devoted to homework. Japan churned out highly educated young people who often were lacking in social skills and ignorant of the world beyond school. Some were looking for something to believe in, a cause to take up—a leader they could follow without question. Others wanted to escape the urban landscape of Tokyo, with its maze of new roads, new power lines, and new steel and concrete structures rising everywhere. Some wanted to get away from all the people and the difficulty of trying to feel special in a megalopolis: Japan was the same size as California, with four times more people. Aum was there to offer inner peace, along with teachings that declared that because the outside world probably would end soon, it was extremely important to have a balanced inner life. For harried students looking for an escape from their rigid lives, Aum seemed to have the answers.

By the close of the 1980s, Asahara had drawn to him some of the best young doctors, computer programmers, biologists, and chemists in Japan who were seeking something more than their scientific learning. Scores of Aum followers were working in the country's top ministries and in the legal system, construction, engineering, journalism, education, the military, and telecommunications. They worked for IBM Japan, Toshiba, Hitachi, and other major companies. Some gave thousands to the organization, some gave more than that, and some went to work for Aum full time. Forty active-duty members of the Self-Defense Forces joined Asahara's army, along with some veterans. A few passed classified data to Asahara. All those followers assisted him in launching the communes of his religious sect, which he'd designed to mimic the culture of his old school for the blind.

The father of six children, polite, and soft-spoken, Asahara was known for his intelligence and friendly appearance, with his partial blindness adding to his aura of benevolence. Sporting a long beard, a big smile, and a manner that could be friendly when needed, and often clad in pink robes, he looked kind—but that provided cover for the plans he was laying.

"As we move toward the year 2000," reads one of Aum's booklets, "there will be a series of events of inexpressible ferocity and terror. The lands of Japan will be transformed into a nuclear wasteland. Between 1996 and January 1998, America and its allies will attack Japan, and only 10 percent of the population of the major cities will survive."

Asahara harbored a deep hatred of the American government, believing that U.S. military planes had dropped the nerve gas sarin on Aum's communes even though there was no evidence to support that theory. He was also angry about Japan's government, and by 1997 he hoped to create a new and independent nation within Japan that would be set up with his own "Ministry of Education," "Ministry of Finance," and "Ministry of Construction." He began stockpiling sarin, first created by the Nazis, which was a very challenging thing to do because he wasn't connected to the government and its supplies of the chemical. If he could get his hands on enough of the gas, he imagined, he could kill between 4 million and 10 million people.

His followers were increasingly instructed to engage in bizarre rituals, such as drinking his bathwater and wearing electrical caps to synchronize their brain waves with his. Despite the demands or perhaps because of them, his yoga school was highly successful and he officially changed his name to Asahara. Aum focused on Tibetan Buddhism, meditation, yoga, and controlled breathing, yet one of the best-known aspects of Tibetan Buddhism—compassion—wasn't emphasized. The sect did, however, promote belief in miracles and the notion that it could help members develop supernatural powers; it claimed that Asahara, who dressed in Chinese-style pajama tunics and told people that he had extrasensory powers, was capable of telepathy and of levitating for hours on end. They put out photographs depicting Asahara and his followers levitating in yoga positions, several inches off the ground (an effect that can be achieved by aggressively bouncing on the floor and having somebody snap pictures when one is in midbounce).

Asahara was at the top of the organization with many directors below him. His head spokesman, the lawyer Yoshinobu Aoyama, was a brilliant man and the youngest ever to pass the national exam for attorneys. He graduated from Kyoto University and began his association with Asahara by taking yoga classes at Aum. Then he renounced his wife and daughter and became a monk in the sect.

In building his combined order and business, Asahara blended aspects of Hinduism, Christianity, Buddhism, and certain prophecies. He borrowed from Nostradamus, Saint John's revelations in the New Testament, other sources, and what he claimed were his own divine revelations. Shiva, the Hindu god, appealed to him because of that deity's association with destruction in order to allow new creation. In the sect's belief system, salvation came only when the last battle, Armageddon, was over and its members had achieved a higher state of consciousness and being through the teachings of their "Supreme Master"—Asahara. Even if one died during the coming bloodshed, one could be saved if he or she had followed those teachings to completion and was prepared to reincarnate in an enlightened state. In 1989, Asahara published his book *The Destruction of the World*, which prophesied war between the United

States and Japan around 1997. He intended for Aum to be prepared for that great event.

That August, the Tokyo Metropolitan Government made Aum one of Japan's 185,000 religions, with corporation status. This gave the sect massive tax breaks and immunity from oversight and prosecution, allowing it to edge forward with what would turn into criminal activities. That immunity covered nearly everything the sect did, including making money, because the Japanese government was loath to investigate organized religions. Asahara and his followers had achieved this status for Aum through a concerted lobbying campaign, by pressuring politicians, and by aggressively protesting at the agency that could grant it official status.

With that status, Aum's net worth leaped to around $4.3 million and then $1 billion six years later. Membership expanded from a handful of followers in 1984 to 10,000 in 1992 and 50,000 in 1995, spread throughout a half dozen nations, with branch offices in Osaka, Sapporo, Nagoya, Fukuoka, New York, and Russia. As it extended its global reach, Aum became more suspect and many labeled it a dangerous cult.

In November 1989, the lawyer Tsutsumi Sakamoto, who had been working on a class-action case against Aum, was found murdered, along with his wife and child; the homicides were later linked to the cult. According to prosecutors, Aum members had entered the Sakamotos' home during the night, injected them with lethal doses of potassium chloride as they slept, and strangled them. Far away, on a western Australian sheep farm, Asahara's scientists began carrying out one of his long-range goals by testing sarin. They also made a botched attempt to manufacture automatic rifles.

In 1990, Asahara and twenty-four aides, in an apparent final effort to work within Japan's political system, ran for seats in the upper house of the Japanese parliament, but all lost, which became a turning point in the development of the sect's future. Resigned to not being able to gain power by conventional means, Asahara became more insulated and more fanatical in his beliefs and leaned more toward violent solutions. He demanded that Aum members live in communes and end relationships with their families. He wanted total obedience, access to their financial resources, and no resistance from any quarter. People soon accused the sect of attacking, kidnapping, and murdering its opponents.

Women who joined Aum alleged sexual harassment. One woman who left the sect remembered being summoned to the room of the "Venerated Teacher" around midnight one evening. "There were just the two of us in the room," she wrote in a pamphlet for some lawyers, "and he asked me if I had had any experience with men. And he asked me how many men I knew, and then he asked me to take off my clothes. I didn't think he could do anything wrong, and I was nervous and didn't want to resist, so I did as he said." Asahara made her promise not to tell anyone about the encounter.

Besides sexual manipulation, Aum subjected followers to sleep and food deprivation along with sensory deprivation and hallucinogens to induce visions and exert mind control. People sometimes were allowed to leave the sect, but only after they had agreed to turn over their property to Aum. Some who refused disappeared or died. Asahara regularly denied any connection to sect killings and was not yet under much scrutiny. Reporters trying to write honestly about

SHOKO ASAHARA ANNOUNCING A PLAN IN TOKYO TO RUN IN THE LOWER HOUSE ELECTION. STANDING ON THE RIGHT IS FUMIHIRO JOYU, A ONE-TIME SPOKESMAN FOR ASAHARA'S AUM SHINRIKYO CULT.

Aum were harassed or had their phones tapped, and before long most of them moved on to other stories.

A man who claimed to have been kidnapped by the sect told the press that for nearly 100 days he had been injected with an unknown medication. He also was ordered to drink two and a half gallons of hot water a day and then throw it up to clean out his system. This was accompanied by a weekly bowel-cleansing technique. He was able to leave Aum only after promising to become a sect member and hand over his money to Asahara.

The police eventually did conduct a raid on the Aum training compound in the village of Kamiku Isshiki, where they found fifty people in advanced states of dehydration and malnutrition and on the verge of unconsciousness. This led to the arrests of four doctors on the premises, but the rescued Aum followers refused the police's efforts and medical attention. They still believed in Asahara and resisted any negative media coverage of the sect.

At its height, Asahara's "Supreme Truth" cult, as it was now called, had, in addition to its Japanese followers, as many as 30,000 followers in Russia. All were told that to survive the coming nuclear attack by the United States they had to adhere strictly to their leader's dictates. "World War III will certainly occur," he said during a 1993 lecture. "I will stake my religious life on that."

As the group grew, it attracted more and more bad press. In 1993, Tokyo residents were angered over an Aum office giving off the smell of "burning flesh." After hundreds of demonstrators gathered outside the office, Asahara arrived in a Mercedes-Benz limousine. He tried to dispel the crowd by telling it that the odor came from a combination of "soybean oil and Chanel No. 5." The protesters were not mollified.

Asahara had begun saying in public that he might have liver cancer. True or not—and in the coming years it appeared to be a false report—his health was failing in other ways, and that seemed to radicalize him more. In a videotape recorded around that time, he said, "My body is considerably damaged now," words that soon were broadcast on Japanese television. He said he was infected with Q fever, which he believed had resulted from the authorities spraying chemicals on his compound from airplanes. His illness, serious or not, was pushing him toward a catastrophic view of the future. Only someone like him, he was more and more convinced, could save the world. He continued to compare himself to Shiva, a deity of both creation and destruction who must end life so that it could be reborn.

In 1993, Asahara intensified his proclamations about the coming Armageddon. In his book *Shivering Predictions,* he stated, "From now until the year 2000, a series of violent phenomena filled with fear that are too difficult to describe will occur. Japan will turn into waste land as a result of a nuclear weapons' attack. This will occur from 1996 through January 1998. An alliance centering on the United States will attack Japan. In large cities in Japan, only one-tenth of the population will be able to survive. Nine out of ten people will die."

Later that year his next book, *Second Set of Predictions*, offered more revelations. A third world war was about to explode across the planet, he wrote, and "I am certain that in 1997, Armageddon will break out. By 'break out' I mean that war will erupt and that it will not end soon. Violent battles will continue for a couple of years. During that time, the world population will shrink markedly."

In 1994, Asahara said somewhat mysteriously, "It has become clear now that my first death will be caused by something like a poison gas such as sarin." In fact, in a vast compound in Kamikuishiki at the foot of Mount Fuji, Aum had built and was running a chemical plant that mass-produced sarin and another plant that assembled illegal automatic rifles. In June 1994 they took a quantity of sarin to Matsumoto, a city in central Japan, and, driving slowly around an apartment complex in the middle of the night, released the gas, killing 8 people and injuring 100.

Despite Asahara's recent public talks about sarin, his cult was not at first linked to the attack and continued making more chemical weapons for another, far larger assault on the public.

Asahara, born after World War II, hadn't lived through the horrors of August 1945, when nuclear bombs were dropped on Nagasaki and Hiroshima, killing hundreds of thousands, injuring countless more, and exposing people to deadly radiation that killed well into the future. He wasn't part of the immediate aftermath of the war or the ongoing residual trauma that became part of Japanese life in the decades ahead. He had come of age in a country that had been disarmed and had been relatively peaceful for the last fifty years. For someone his age, mass destruction was something seen in old films or current horror movies, a couple of steps removed from reality.

Then, on January 17, 1995, a major earthquake hit Kobe in central Japan, knocking over apartment buildings, crumbling freeways, and killing 5,500 people. It was Japan's single biggest instance of mass destruction and death since World War II. Aum's chief scientist, Hideo Murai, offered his opinion of what had caused the disaster: "There is a strong possibility that the Kobe earthquake was activated by electromagnetic power or some other device that exerts energy into the ground," he told an assembly of international journalists. The device, he said, was perhaps controlled by the U.S. military, an idea the reporters dismissed. Asahara, however, took the earthquake as proof of the looming apocalypse, and it became the catalyst for his next act of violence.

It began right before 8 a.m. on Monday, March 20, 1995, calculated to hit Tokyo's subways during the height of the morning rush hour. Five cult members went underground and into the transit system and, using umbrellas with sharpened tips to poke holes in plastic bags containing liquid sarin, released the poison at three different locations. Trains were scheduled to arrive at the central Kasumigaseki station four minutes apart, exposing the greatest possible number of passengers to the gas.

The cult intended not just to kill all those on the trains but to deliver sarin to main subway interchanges used by thousands of passengers.

After the assailants distributed the gas and fled, it spread into the packed subway cars. Commuters knelt down on the train floors and struggled for breath, coughing up blood and foaming at the mouth. Some were able to make it upstairs to street level before collapsing onto the pavement, with the residue of what smelled like paint thinner still filling their nostrils.

"Liquid was spread on the floor in the middle of the carriage," Sakae Ito would tell Agence France-Presse in the aftermath of the attack. She had been in the subway when the sarin was released. "People were convulsing in their seats. One man was leaning against a pole, his shirt open, bodily fluids leaking out."

As the survivors struggled to get out of the subway, members of Tokyo's self-defense forces dressed in face masks and hazmat suits ran down flights of stairs to get to victims trapped below Tokyo. No one in authority realized that they were confronting a lesser version of the recent earthquake's casualties: Japan's worst-ever terrorist attack killed thirteen and injured more than 6,000. If the five Aum assailants had been more competent and able to fulfill their goals with the sarin, according to the Federation of American Scientists, "tens of thousands could have easily been killed."

The attacks affected Japan more profoundly than could be understood through the number of victims alone. When the fuller story of Aum began to emerge, many in Japan were shocked to learn that the mastermind behind the crime was one of their own. Asahara hadn't recruited among the uneducated and the poor but inside the elite circles of Japanese society: doctors, lawyers, and corporate executives, the ones with significant resources who had given their money to Aum's cause. Over the years, Aum members had been prominent enough to be featured on live television, touting their leaders and publicly supporting the sect. They had helped normalize Asahara's ideas. Something in his teachings had drawn in a disillusioned portion of that culture who were tired of the regimentation and constant striving for worldly success, but it led them into activities that brought massive harm to their country. In the aftermath of the sarin attack in Tokyo, some recalled the bombs dropped half a century earlier and how Asahara's assault had punctured the sense of calm and security many had felt in postwar Japan. Asahara himself did not offer any answers.

Before the disaster, Asahara had gone underground and while in hiding had issued statements denying any involvement in the event. He was immediately a suspect, but he was able to elude the police for the next two months before they found him in a tiny space at the cult's compound, concealed behind a wall and surrounded by piles of cash and a sleeping bag. After his arrest, he was indicted on seventeen counts, including drug charges, illegal production of weapons, and murder.

Besides Asahara, 191 other sect members were indicted for murder, attempted murder, abductions, producing nerve gases, and buying illegal

SUBWAY PASSENGERS LIE DOWN ON A STREET AT HATCHŌBORI STATION IN TOKYO FOLLOWING A SARIN GAS ATTACK ON MARCH 20, 1995.

automatic rifles. The Japanese government banned Aum, but it would come back to life in 2000 as Aleph, with its members making a point of decrying Asahara and agreeing to pay compensation to the gas attack victims. Based on information from Japan's public security intelligence agency, Aleph and two splinter groups gradually would rebuild a corps of about 1,650 Japanese followers and about 460 followers in Russia while holding more than 1 billion yen (US$9 million) in assets.

Asahara continued to deny any connection to the subway attacks, but some in the cult had joined the sect for other reasons and were appalled at the incident. Former Aum spokesman Fumihiro Joyu was overcome with guilt and acknowledged having a "heavy shared responsibility" for the group's crimes. "I would like to apologize to the victims," he said at a press conference. "I would like to work on compensation and to make sure such crimes never happen again."

Near the end of 1996, Asahara finally took responsibility for the attacks, adding that he wasn't personally involved but had been "instructed by God" to accept the blame. Having offered a partial apology, he made a threat: the lawyers who were questioning other Aum Shinrikyo members would die if they didn't shut down their inquiries and leave his followers alone.

The prosecution of Asahara began with the state seeking the death penalty against not just the sect's leader but a handful of the members. During the exhaustive legal proceedings to come, Asahara delivered long spontaneous chaotic monologues in both English and Japanese but gradually fell into complete silence as the trial dragged on for eight years. He went deeper into isolation, turning aside all requests for visits, including those from his own relatives. When he spoke to his lawyers, what usually came out was streams of gibberish that led his attorneys to tell the court that he wasn't mentally competent to stand trial. It was difficult to say whether he was feigning insanity to obtain a legal advantage or had gone mad. He had shaved his head and no longer dressed in pink, looking very different from the man who once had commanded Aum. In his cell at the

Tokyo Detention Center, he sometimes burst into what sounded like extended sermons, but now he was preaching only to himself.

The *Nishiyama Report*, which described his activities while incarcerated, wrote, "In April 2005, just before the accused's lawyer entered a visiting room, the accused exposed his penis and began masturbating, continuing until he had finished while the lawyer stood before him the entire time. He has repeated this act of masturbation in the visiting room, as well as in his solitary confinement cell since being placed under observation in May. He also performed the act in front of his daughters when they came to visit him in August of the same year."

The *Report* maintained that Asahara was not mentally impaired and should be in court for his trial. Others in the mental health community disagreed with that conclusion, but the authorities were unbending. "Based on the diagnosis by a psychiatrist, he [Asahara] maintains body functions and at least has no explicit psychiatric disorders," read a document submitted in court in May 2015.

After his conviction, Asahara was sentenced to hang and placed on death row; a dozen more Aum members were given the same sentence for the 1995 attack and related crimes. From his prison cell, Asahara had a small following and wielded as much influence as he could, including on some of those who had joined Aleph. They still used his writings and recordings for conducting their meditations. Several dozen had moved into Aleph's headquarters on three blocks of apartments in suburban Tokyo, and the police kept them under constant surveillance. At the Tokyo Detention House where Asahara was being held, he was able to stand up without help only when he had to bathe every few days. Now his strength and health were truly failing him.

Asahara was convicted of not only the Tokyo crimes but the murders of lawyer Tsutsumi Sakamoto, his wife, and their one-year-old son, along with the sarin gas attack in Matsumoto, Nagano Prefecture, in June 1994. In 2006, the Japanese Supreme Court rejected his appeals and finalized his death sentence; he was declared legally sane and held responsible for his actions.

When he received the news of his conviction and then his death sentence at the detention center, he cried out, "Why? Damn it! Why! Damn it!"

In its final analysis of Asahara's state of mind, the high court was fully aware of his aberrant behavior since his arrest but not persuaded that that should affect the justices' rulings. "It was obvious that he was aware of the death sentence," the Tokyo court concluded. "It cannot be recognized that he developed mental illness as a result of being detained."

Asahara was executed on July 6, 2018. Japan's chief cabinet secretary, Yoshihide Suga, reported that six other senior cult members were hanged the same day: Tomomasa Nakagawa, fifty-five; Kiyohide Hayakawa, sixty-eight; Yoshihiro Inoue, forty-eight; Masami Tsuchiya, fifty-three; Seiichi Endo, fifty-eight; and Tomomitsu Niimi, fifty-four. Six more were scheduled to join them on the gallows. Executions in Japan were carried out in secret, without advance warnings to the prisoners, their families, or their legal representatives. Only hours before they died did inmates realize what was going to happen that day.

After Asahara's death, some of the survivors celebrated and found peace in this resolution, but others spoke of their regrets that those who had survived the subway attacks were not able to witness the executions of Asahara and his followers. Still others thought that Asahara's remaining followers might seek revenge for his hanging.

Organizations around the world that opposed the death penalty were quick to criticize the hangings. "The attacks carried out by Aum were despicable," said Hiroka Shoji, East Asia researcher at Amnesty International, "and those responsible deserve to be punished. However, the death penalty is never the answer. . . . Justice demands accountability but also respect for everyone's human rights. The death penalty can never deliver this as it is the ultimate denial of human rights."

Shizue Takahashi, the widow of a Tokyo subway employee killed in the attack, told a group of reporters of her surprise at the sudden hangings. "When I think of those who died because of them," she said, "it was a pity [my husband's] parents and my parents could not hear the news of this execution. I wanted [cult members] to confess more about the incident, so it's a pity that we cannot hear their account anymore."

A few of those who had joined Aum with good intentions claimed to be stunned by the way the sect had devolved into a cult carrying out criminal activities. Some said they had been drawn to Asahara because of their idealism and in the hope of doing something positive and useful in the world. Dr. Tomomasa Nakagawa had come to Aum with those intentions yet had gone on to play an important role in Aum's production of sarin gas. After the Tokyo attacks he seemed filled with remorse and tried to explain, if not exonerate, himself, pleading with the sect's leader to come forward and speak publicly about what he was trying to accomplish through violence. Asahara never gave him or others that satisfaction but continued offering mumbo jumbo to those who asked him to try to justify what they had done in his name to the subway system of Japan's largest city.

In a court hearing in 2016, Dr. Nakagawa broke into tears when telling the court, "I didn't enter the priesthood [of Aum Shinrikyo] to produce sarin or choke someone's neck." He made one more appeal to Asahara: "Please explain your ideas to the people who believed in you."

In 2018, on the same day Asahara died, Nakagawa was hanged for his part in the production of sarin gas and the 1989 murders of the Sakamoto family. He was hardly the first person to realize too late whom he had once sworn allegiance to and given his power to and what that leader actually represented and how he would—without any apparent grief—bring down everyone close to him. It was for others to look back and cry, not for the partially blind boy named Chizuo Matsumoto, who had bullied his way to infamy.

9
THE FALL RIVER CULT

In 1979, Doreen Levesque, a seventeen-year-old runaway from New Bedford, Massachusetts, was found behind the Diman Vocational High School in Fall River, about twelve miles from her home. Her wrists were bound with fishing line, she had been stabbed, and examination of her head wounds revealed multiple skull fractures. Police believed that she had been assaulted by multiple people and that from the evidence on her body she might have been stoned.

A month later, forty-four-year-old Andy Maltias showed up at the Fall River police station and filed a missing-persons report on his girlfriend, Barbara Raposa, a twenty-two-year-old prostitute who conducted her business downtown on Bedford Street. While describing her to the police, he brought up a local "satanic cult" and let it drop that he knew something about the murder of Doreen Levesque. The police were uncertain how to take his ramblings: Maltias was known around town as a mentally disturbed pedophile, a sexual sadist, and a violent rapist. How could anyone trust what he had to say about a homicide?

Maltias told the police that he recently had become a devout Christian. "Jesus Christ is my personal Lord and Savior," he told the detectives while holding a small Bible. "Once I worshiped Satan . . . now I worship Jesus."

All this was strange, the police knew, but lots of strange and troubling things were unfolding in Fall River at that time. When the American economy went into a recession in the late 1970s, the impact was greater on the formerly prosperous textile city in Bristol County than it was in many other places. Buildings were shuttered, factories were closed, and much of the downtown was abandoned. Petty crime and sometimes not-so-petty criminal acts involving drugs and hustling were common, and they all occurred around Bedford Street.

In late 1979 and early 1980, two young prostitutes in the area were tied up—one with fishing line—and then tortured, raped, and beaten to death. A third victim's body was never located except for a skull fragment and some hair in a nearby forest. By then there had been enough unsolved murders around town to produce a growing local scare and talk of a "Satanic Panic." The killings conjured up one of the darker moments in Fall River history and the town's most notorious daughter. In 1892, Lizzie Borden stood trial for having savagely killed her father and stepmother, unleashing sensational headlines and inspiring a memorable poem:

Lizzie Borden took an axe,
And gave her mother forty whacks;
When she saw what she had done,
She gave her father forty-one.

Almost ninety years later, Fall River residents wondered if the Devil had decided to pay them another visit.

Andy Maltias confessed to the police that both he and Barbara Raposa had been practicing satanists when she had disappeared. Before her murder, he said, Doreen Levesque was also in their group; he was pretty certain that a cult of satanists was responsible for her death. The police were skeptical but didn't have any other good leads and were willing to listen. Within a few days, Maltias had brought them two of the alleged cult members: Karen Marsden and Robin Murphy. Marsden, a twenty-year-old single mother, was a runaway, a drug addict, and a prostitute. Murphy, seventeen, was a prostitute and an aspiring pimp. The two women were roommates and lovers.

Marsden was more open with the police than Murphy, who later would claim that Maltias had been molesting her since she was eleven. In the middle of her police interview, she broke down and blurted out, "Carl Drew killed Doreen Levesque."

Drew, a twenty-six-year-old pimp with a bad reputation, conducted his business from the Bedford Street district. He already had a substantial felony record, with convictions for armed robbery, assault, and weapons possession. A New Hampshire native, he later would say that his painful upbringing had helped make him a criminal. When he was a boy, his alcoholic father had cinched a rope around the youngster's ankles and dropped him into a well to remove dead rats. The experience had never stopped haunting him. At fourteen, after running away from his father and the farm he had been raised on, he hooked up with the Fall River underground and drifted into managing his own prostitution ring. One woman in his stable was Doreen Levesque, but none of the physical evidence in her murder could be connected to him.

When speaking to the police, Marsden tried to distance herself from Drew and his loose band of followers, which she described as a cult. "I'm a good person," she said. "I believe in God." According to her, Drew organized his prostitution outfit like a satanic coven with him as the absolute ruler. He liked to use Devil references when threatening the women who worked for him with punishment or death. "Satan will take his toll" was how Marsden claimed he talked to them.

Marsden brought in Carol Fletcher, another young prostitute with cult connections, and they led the police to Freetown–Fall River State Forest, a known site for aberrant behavior and violent crime. Locals said that the 5,000-acre reservation was cursed, with its abandoned shack holding an altar—a big flat stone slab where candle-lit rituals were performed over naked prostitutes and animals were sacrificed to honor Satan. The forest was perfect for the cult to carry out its black-robed midnight events: orgies that involved the killing of stray cats and goats, whose blood was utilized for mock baptisms and poured over the attendees' heads. Sometimes those present allegedly spoke in tongues or passed out—or Satan began to chant his orders directly through them.

Drew, Marsden claimed, had demanded from her a vow of silence about what went on in the woods: if she ever went to the police with what she knew, he would put her body in an algae-covered pond after "injecting battery acid into her veins" and then "offering her soul to Satan."

A prostitute named Cookie (Mildred Jukes) offered corroborating evidence of Drew's violence: if a woman he pimped for ever got arrested, "he was going to kill her for it . . . tie her to a tree to be sacrificed and pour warm blood from a live goat all over her face."

Cookie added more about the cult's activities: "They kill every thirty days or so—on the full moon. It's always a ritual that they offer up the victim as a sacrifice to Satan."

It wasn't long before another body turned up: Barbara Raposa's bloodied, frozen corpse was found lying in the woods behind an empty factory, her wrists bound with fishing line. Her skull had been crushed, and she had been sexually assaulted. The police called in Andy Maltias, but he said adamantly that he had no knowledge of the crime. Within a week, he had reached out to the police to report that he had picked up details of Barbara's death in "a psychic dream."

Detectives took Maltias to the crime scene, where he laid out what he had witnessed while sleeping. Some of it was astonishingly accurate; he knew precisely where the body had been located and its positioning, he knew the method of murder and the time of death, and he gave the police a few other correct details not yet known to the public. The police arrested him and charged him with the murder.

When she learned of this, Robin Murphy called local law enforcement, wanting to testify against Maltias. She was with Maltias when he killed Raposa, she told the detectives, and she was also a witness to the murder of Doreen Levesque. The prosecutor's office found her credible enough to give her a deal: in return for her recollections in court, she would be granted immunity for both homicides and placed in protective custody.

Under oath, Murphy testified to being with Maltias and Raposa on the night of the crime and said that Maltias had killed his girlfriend after finding out she had been unfaithful. While all three of them had been partying that night, an argument erupted and Maltias then raped his lover before beating her with a rock. He and Murphy drove away, leaving Raposa to die. Murphy failed to report this, she said, because Maltias threatened to kill her if she talked. Now that he was locked up and unable to harm her, she could tell the whole story. But was that the truth, the whole truth, and nothing but the truth?

Murphy went on to say that the Raposa homicide and the Levesque murder were two entirely different crimes; the only connection was that she happened to have been present at both events. "The killing of Doreen Levesque," she told the police, "was an offering of the soul [to] Satan."

Drew, Murphy contended, had murdered Doreen over a business matter: she had tried to drop him as a pimp and take charge of her own work as a prostitute. He had stalked her on Bedford Street, Murphy said, and forced her to take a ride with Murphy herself, Karen Marsden, and another passenger named Willie Smith who associated with the Fall River underground. Murphy identified Smith as yet another satanist. As the three sat silently, Drew began hitting Doreen in the face. While the two women stayed in the car—again based on Murphy's retelling of that night—the men went to an empty high school field and killed her under the bleachers. Murphy and Marsden claimed to have heard nothing of the brutal crime, yet it had included torture, sexual assault, and an extremely violent death. Only later did Murphy flip her story about the homicide to the police when she provided them with some horrific details and allusions to satanism.

Marsden had her own story, which was very different from Murphy's. She implicated Murphy in the satanic cult and the killings, saying that Murphy had ordered everyone at the crime scenes, as part of one of their rituals, to mutilate Raposa's and Levesque's bodies.

But then again, was Marsden, who didn't want to testify under oath as Murphy had done, credible?

On February 9, 1980, Marsden went missing. A couple of months later, not far away in the town of Westport, a man was out walking and came upon the top half of a human skull. Investigators searching the area found sheep bones, three dead cats, and human hair, along with a high-heeled shoe, fragments of a woman's sweater, and jewelry. The skull belonged to Karen Marsden. A woman named Maureen "Sonny" Sparda told the police that Robin Murphy had killed Marsden. Sparda was an ex-hooker living in a Fall River apartment where she held satanic gatherings with runaways, drug addicts, and young prostitutes. Was she to be believed or was she protecting something or some-

one? Sparda and Murphy once had been intimate, and Sparda now claimed that Murphy had let slip that she had murdered Marsden.

Carol Fletcher, the prostitute with connections to the cult, came forward with contradictory information: Murphy and Drew had *both* executed Marsden, and Carl Davis, a Fall

ROBIN MURPHY OF FALL RIVER, MASSACHUSETTS, WHO WAS EIGHTEEN WHEN SHE PLEADED GUILTY TO SECOND-DEGREE MURDER IN THE STABBING DEATH OF KAREN MARSDEN.

River pimp, had been there during the murder. Fletcher said she knew this because she had driven all of them out into the woods for a satanic sacrifice.

The police arrested Murphy, along with Drew and Davis.

"I worship Satan," Drew told the police during his interrogation. "I worship him like you worship God."

Under hard questioning from detectives, Murphy cracked and confessed that because Marsden had watched the murder of Doreen Levesque and gone to the police with information about it, Drew commanded her to die. According to Murphy, she had to participate in the killing to show her loyalty to the cult, and so she was the one who had pulled out the victim's hair. Then they all stoned her and Drew sliced off one of her fingers and broke her neck. Claiming to have been in a trance, Murphy told the police that she cut Levesque's throat and that the men pulled off her head and kicked it around. Drew carved an "X" into her torso and, Murphy said, gave her soul to the "Dark Lord." Using Marsden's blood, he marked Murphy's forehead with an "X" and forced her to have oral sex with the corpse. At the end of the ritual killing, they poured gasoline on Marsden and set her on fire.

This was a stunning set of revelations about the inner workings of the cult, but was all of it, some of it, or very little of it real? The police were fully aware that no one who had confessed to any of these crimes was a truly credible witness, and so they kept investigating and trying to learn more about satanism.

A pair of detectives from Fall River's major crimes division went to Sparda's apartment and watched a black mass, with Murphy and Drew also on hand. A large painting of the Devil hung on a living room wall, and the assembled cultists made a circle and chanted, "Hail. Satan. Hail. Satan."

As word of the murders and the ongoing law enforcement probe reached the public, the Satanic Panic set in around Fall River, driven by religious quackery, armchair psychiatry, and the tabloid press, which couldn't get enough of the fantastic tale. Speculation ran rampant, and every imaginable projection of evil was made. Was there indeed a satanic organization operating not just in Fall River but all across America, carrying out these and other Devil-ridden crimes? Wasn't the public seeing a spike in the number of reports of human sacrifice and cannibalism? No, not actually—but the rumors continued to spread.

The first trial was for Andy Maltias in January 1981, and Robin Murphy was the main witness against him. After his conviction for the first-degree murder of Barbara Raposa, he was given life with no possibility of parole. (He died of cancer in 1998.) Because of all the publicity around the killings, the next three scheduled trials—for Davis, Drew, and Murphy—were moved to Fitchburg, Massachusetts. Murphy's planned defense was that she had been controlled by a local satanic cult, but then she was allowed to plead guilty to second-degree murder in exchange for testifying against the other defendants. As part of the deal, she could not be charged in the Levesque or Raposa killing; she got life, but with the possibility of parole. The evidence against Davis for his part in the abduction and ritual slaughter of Karen Marsden did not hold up, and he never went to trial. A year later he was back in jail for attacking Sparda with a deadly weapon. After a seven-year stint behind bars, he was set free.

At Drew's trial, two witnesses depicted him as the main force behind the cult and its sadistic crimes. Murphy portrayed him as the leader, and her testimony was backed up by his former girlfriend, Leah Johnson. Drew had admitted to her, she told the court, that when he was drugged up, he had murdered "a girl" with the help of Murphy, Davis, and a third, unidentified woman. The jury convicted him of the first-degree murder of Karen Marsden; he got life without parole at the Massachusetts Correctional Institution in Shirley.

The charges against Drew and Willie Smith for the murder of Doreen Levesque were dismissed, but the legal wrangling over the cases would go on for decades, with Murphy regularly asking for and being denied parole. In 1984, hoping for a new trial, she changed her account of the criminal activities of Maltias and Drew while trying to rationalize her own actions. "I believe Carl Drew was guilty of killing Karen and many, many other women in the area," she told the parole board. "I believed he belonged in jail, but also knew justice was not taking place. So I made the story up."

Murphy had also made up, she now said, her testimony about not being present during the Raposa murder and lied about it to convict Maltias because he had sexually abused her. Witnesses besides Murphy also changed their recollections, claiming that the police had coerced them into confessions or they had been high during interviews or their memories had been faulty until now. Carol Fletcher said that it was Murphy, not Drew, who had killed Marsden and that the murder hadn't taken place in the Westport woods but at Fall River's Harbor Terrace housing project. Others said other confusing things.

It was impossible to sort out who was telling the truth or lying, who was in love with and having sex with whom, who wanted revenge on whom, and whose interest was best served by having his or her version of the murders altered in this direction or that. Whatever the ultimate reality behind the murders, there was clearly no honor among those thieves, killers, and cultists when it came to covering up their secrets, rituals, and crimes. Within the police department, there was no common agreement about who

DEFENDANT CARL DREW, TWENTY-FIVE, TALKS WITH COURT SECURITY OFFICER DURING HIS TRIAL.

led the cult, called for the killings, and carried them out. Some were certain that Drew was the mastermind, but others were convinced that Murphy was the main person behind the death of Karen Marsden.

In an autobiographical account for the press and public, Carl Drew insisted that he was never part of a satanic cult. In fact, he was all but innocent: "I was [thrown] into the middle of a mass nightmare that involved macabre accusations of devil worship and human sacrifice. Totally off the wall accusations that was right out of some thriller novel. None true as far as I was involved and nothing like what was being said."

Were all of them lying, and had they committed more crimes than anyone had imagined? In autumn 1978, fifteen-year-old Mary-Lou Arruda was abducted from Raynham, Massachusetts, and found dead in the Freetown–Fall River State Forest, tied to an oak tree by the throat with her hands knotted behind her. A cross was close to her body, which was near where evidence of the other Fall River murders had been located. A man named James Kater was arrested and convicted of the crime, but questions remained. Within the next decade, nine prostitutes were killed by strangulation and discovered along Bristol County highways. A cross was left by the first victim, and those cases were never solved.

In 2004, after spending nearly two and a half decades behind bars, Robin Murphy was set free, but then she was arrested again for violating her parole. She was returned to the maximum-security prison in Framingham, Massachusetts.

In 1988, years after the Satanic Panic had faded and stories about the cult were passing into local lore, a hunter in the Freetown–Fall River State Forest uncovered a camouflaged bunker near an isolated hiking trail. He checked it out and found animal bones, a small wooden chair, children's clothing, a rusty butcher knife, and dolls with their eyes gouged out. The same year a dozen mutilated calves were found in the Freetown–Fall River State Forest. Someone had exhumed the corpse of Elizabeth Gregory, which had been buried in the woods in 1868, pulling her from her plot and leaving her remains exposed to the elements. The cult or an offshoot of it was thought to be involved.

10

CHARLES MANSON AND THE FAMILY

You know, a long time ago being crazy meant something.
Nowadays everybody's crazy.

—Charles Manson

From childhood on, Charles Manson had a knack for spinning stories about himself—whether they were true or made up on the spot. Some were so good that in time he persuaded people that he was the Messiah, the Second Coming of Christ.

Born in Cincinnati to sixteen-year-old Kathleen Maddox, Manson later would tell listeners that his mother was an alcoholic prostitute who had left home for a life on the streets a year before his birth. (She wasn't, in fact, a hooker, just an unwed mother.)

"Mom," according to his recollection of his childhood, "was in a cafe one afternoon with me on her lap. The waitress, a would-be mother without a child of her own, jokingly told my Mom she'd buy me from her. Mom replied, 'A pitcher of beer and he's yours.' The waitress set up the beer, Mom stuck around long enough to finish it off and left the place without me. Several days later my uncle had to search the town for the waitress and take me home."

When Charles was eight, his mother was arrested for grand larceny. Facing jail time, she began shuffling him from one relative to the next, but none was suited for parenting the boy. An uncle he stayed with for a while chastised him for having feminine traits, his grandmother pounded her religion into him, and another uncle killed himself while caring for the child. In 1947, at age thirteen, Manson was picked up by the police for stealing and sent to a Catholic-run school for boys in Indiana. After his release, he was desperate to reunite with his mother, but she rejected him, leaving him to fend for himself.

According to one of his later disciples, Charles "Tex" Watson, Manson developed "a special hatred for women as mothers. . . . This probably had something to do with his feelings about his own mother, though he never talked about her. . . . The closest he came to breaking his silence was in some of his song lyrics: 'I am a mechanical boy, I am my mother's boy.'"

Back on the street from the boys school, he was soon arrested again. He already had learned a useful strategy to keep older, larger inmates from hurting or raping him in jail: act really crazy and they might leave you alone. When that tactic failed, he mastered the art of escape, skipping out of penal institutions nearly twenty times in three years, building a criminal record that was long but involved only relatively minor crimes.

After stealing a car, he was arrested in Utah and eventually wound up at Virginia's Natural Bridge Honor Camp, where he raped a boy at razor point. In 1954 he was paroled and wed a seventeen-year-old waitress, Rosalie Willis. He then stole another car. Rosalie became pregnant, which allowed him, as an expectant father, to get probation instead of more prison time. In March 1956, Rosalie gave birth to Charles Manson, Jr., but Manson senior had his probation revoked and was sentenced to three years in Terminal Island prison in San Pedro, California. Rosalie bolted with the child and divorced Manson in 1957. He married a prostitute named Leona "Candy" Stevens and fathered a second son, Charles Luther Manson, but Candy divorced him a few years later. By June 1960, Manson had been arrested again and received a seven-year sentence at McNeil Island Penitentiary in Puget Sound. One of his sentencing judges said, "If there ever was a man who demonstrated himself completely unfit for probation, he is it."

Behind bars, Manson dabbled in Scientology while learning to play guitar and attempting to turn his natural storytelling ability into songwriting, penning dozens of tunes about his life experiences and romantic fantasies. In the mid-'60s, as he tried to hone those skills, he watched the British Invasion that sent the Beatles, the Rolling Stones, the Dave Clark Five, and numerous other bands to America, where they topped the charts. Why couldn't he, Manson wondered, write some catchy tunes and get a toehold in the music business? Couldn't that be his ticket to fame and fortune? Or maybe he should give up those dreams and live out his life in prison, away from all the temptations on the outside.

In 1967 he was scheduled to be released but had reservations about it. By that point he was so completely "institutionalized" and so dependent on the penal system to contain and control him that he didn't want to leave his cell. "Oh, no, I can't go outside there," he told the officials who had decided to turn him loose. "I knew that I couldn't adjust to that world, not after all my life has been spent locked up and where my mind was free."

They let him go, and he immediately headed for San Francisco, arriving at one of the most creative and tumultuous times in the city's history. He was obviously—at the very least—eccentric, and being eccentric in 1967 in the Bay Area, especially in the Haight-Ashbury neighborhood where he landed, was an asset. From all over America, people who had felt like outsiders or nonconformists were streaming into the Haight for the "Summer of Love." The new norm was to shed one's past and give oneself over to total personal freedom and experimentation. The area's most popular up-and-coming band, the Grateful Dead, was indeed grateful to have died to the culture they had been born into and determined to build something new. In San Francisco, a guru selling liberation was standing on every corner. Some were peddling peace and harmony, while others . . .

Manson began attracting mostly young women in their late teens and early twenties, repeating to them the mantra sweeping the country in the late '60s: "turn on, tune in, and drop out." His primary recruiter for bringing in women was nineteen-year-old Paul Watkins. Once Watkins and Manson had drawn in the females, Manson used them to attract men who could offer him financial or other forms of support. He was always on the lookout for celebrities. Two females in his group were picked up hitchhiking by Beach Boys drummer Dennis Wilson, and they took Manson to his home. Wasn't this the break he had been looking for? Couldn't Wilson help him get his music produced and launch his career? Then he met the music teacher Gary Hinman, another asset on the path to stardom.

At first Manson charmed Dennis Wilson, moving into his home with several women and playing music, dropping acid, and having sex until some in the group contracted gonorrhea, leading to a $21,000 medical bill. Wilson had had enough by that time; he showed Manson the door, but others would welcome him in.

Manson had a verbal intensity and poetic magnetism that people responded to. He would sit in coffeehouses with his guitar, singing Spanish love songs and pulling in more followers. In addition, he had been an outlaw and could talk prison talk at a time when that kind of character was coming into fashion in movies such as *Bonnie and Clyde* and *Cool Hand Luke*. Those who encountered Manson couldn't be sure if he was a mystic in the middle of a run of very bad luck or an outright sociopath with the gift of gab who could get people to do things they would never otherwise consider doing. The more he talked and the more drugs they all took, the more power he wielded over others and the more he replaced their values with his. He was evolving from a thief and a con man into something far more sinister. Clever in the way of many criminals, he knew how to take bits and pieces of popular culture—some white people, for example, resented the rise of the black power movement—and weave them into an increasingly paranoid fantasy about the American future. At a scrawny five feet six inches, Manson was hardly a commanding figure, but his words made him appear larger and seemed to contain nuggets of truth—especially about the dark side of being human.

Manson once compared himself to a coyote on the hunt: "Have you ever seen the coyote in the desert? Watching, tuned in, completely aware. . . . The coyote is beautiful. He moves through the desert delicately, aware of everything, looking around. He hears every sound, smells every smell, sees everything that moves. He's in a state of total paranoia, and total paranoia is total awareness."

He had a talent for zeroing in on people's needs, especially young women who had had difficult relationships with their fathers. He told them they were beautiful and smart and strong, his pitch always tailored to the person in front of him. Like a pimp with a stable of females, he knew what each one wanted in order to keep her under his control and keep meeting his increasingly outlandish demands. One of the first to take up with him was Mary Brunner, a University of California–Berkeley librarian who invited him to live with her. She quit her job and recruited another young woman, Lynette Fromme, eventually known as "Squeaky." Then others joined them.

Manson wasn't known for reading many books, but in prison he had perused the Bible and diligently studied Dale Carnegie's self-help title *How to Win Friends and Influence People,* which has sold more than 15 million copies worldwide since its publication in 1936. A core Carnegie principle is to use words and emotion to convince others that *your* ideas or plans for doing something are actually *theirs.* With his quick mind and sharp tongue, Manson utilized that concept with those he was forming into his own cult.

Under the guise of teacher/preacher/salesman, Manson gathered a small band of troops for the work ahead. They moved south toward Los Angeles, ending up at the Spahn Ranch, a former film and television set in the western San Fernando Valley owned by the milk entrepreneur George Spahn. There Manson took control of his followers with a strict set of rules: no eyeglasses and no money on your person if you left the ranch. He arranged LSD sessions and orgies and decided who got to participate in the sex and who did not. He encouraged them to think of themselves as a new kind of family unit, and soon they were calling themselves "the Family."

Through all of this, Manson was still trying to forge ahead in the music business. Dennis Wilson had introduced him to the record producer Terry Melcher, the son of the actress Doris Day and boyfriend of the actress Candice Bergen. The daughter of another actress, Angela Lansbury, was also briefly on the edges of the group. Through his growing entertainment contacts in the Los Angeles area, Manson believed he could build a future in music. He invited Melcher to the ranch to hear him perform, but the producer wasn't interested and dumped him. Melcher and Bergen had been living at a house on 10050 Cielo Drive that they would soon vacate.

At night on the ranch, his anger and frustration growing, Manson delivered long lectures to his group, much as he once had held court in prison, teaching them the fine points of dropping acid and his views on the human race. He believed that the song "Helter Skelter" from the Beatles *White Album*, along with the assassination of Dr. Martin Luther King, Jr., had signaled an imminent American race war that would leave thousands or more dead. He and his followers would escape to the desert to wait out the apocalypse. Once it ended, they would emerge from hiding and take over the world. And if that war didn't come fast enough, they might just have to start it themselves, because violence was always an option. (One early cult member, Squeaky Fromme, would act out this notion in 1975 when she tried to assassinate President Gerald Ford, but her gun jammed and the Secret Service quickly subdued her.)

In July 1969, as the tumultuous decade of the 1960s was coming to a close, Manson's grudges were ready to explode. The main one was focused on his failure to get anything going in music and the people he felt had held him back. The Family's first attack came on July 1, when they shot Bernard Crowe, a drug dealer whom Manson mistakenly believed was a Black Panther. (Crowe would survive and testify against Manson.) On July 31, Manson sent out Bobby Beausoleil, Mary Brunner, and Susan Atkins to the home of music teacher Gary Hinman, one of those who hadn't helped him succeed in the recording business. The trio repeatedly stabbed Hinman to death and wrote "Political Piggy" in his blood on the walls of his house. They drew a paw with Hinman's blood to indicate that the Black Panthers had committed the murder to ignite the race war Manson was promoting. Two days after Hinman's body was found, Manson doubled down on his plans by telling his followers, "Now is the time for Helter Skelter," and the troops were ready to go. The cult leader would not carry out any violence directly. He didn't need to because his criminal personality had been transferred to his followers. If there's one solid definition of a sociopath, it's the inability to feel what you've done to another. The whole group had become as deadened as their leader.

On August 8, Manson ordered several of his most committed soldiers to the Cielo Drive address in Benedict Canyon, not far from Hollywood. Manson believed that Terry Melcher still lived there, but Melcher had moved out and the rental property was now occupied by the film director Roman Polanski and his wife, the actress Sharon Tate, who was eight months pregnant with their child. Polanski had directed the 1968 film *Rosemary's Baby* about a cult that fools a woman into birthing the Devil's spawn. The year before, Tate had appeared in *Valley of the Dolls*. The couple had met on the set of a movie that he was directing in Italy, and in the first ten days of August 1969, while Polanski was out of town on business, his wife had stayed home on Cielo Drive.

A decade later, author and California native Joan Didion would write in her book of essays, *The White Album*: "Many people I know in Los Angeles believe that the Sixties ended abruptly on August 9, 1969." The night before, Watson broke into the Cielo address by snipping the screen of a window and crawling into the residence, letting Susan Atkins and Patricia Krenwinkel in through the front door. Linda Kasabian had taken up a post at the bottom of the driveway to watch for anyone passing by or coming home. Watson and the others found four people in the house: Tate, writer Wojciech Frykowski, coffee heiress Abigail Folger, and celebrity hair stylist Jay Sebring. Watson tied Sebring and Tate together by their necks, hanging Tate from the rafters while Folger was hustled away to a back room. Sebring was shot and stabbed seven times. Frykowski wriggled free and fought with Atkins until Watson shot and stabbed him numerous times. Folger escaped from her room and was stabbed twenty-eight times by Krenwinkel and Watson. Frykowski made it outside to the lawn, where Watson stabbed him again—he was shot twice and had fifty-one knife wounds. As Tate watched what was happening around her, she begged Atkins for mercy, but she too was attacked and stabbed sixteen times. Her unborn baby did not survive. A fifth (or sixth) victim, Polanski's gardener Steven Parent, also was murdered. Before the killers departed, Atkins wrote "PIG" on the front door in Tate's blood. The murders went unnoticed until the next morning, when housekeeper Winifred Chapman came to work and, seeing the carnage, dialed the LAPD.

When the group reported back to him, Manson wasn't pleased with what had happened as they had expected he would be but upset because the crimes hadn't gotten enough publicity or unleashed enough panic in LA or started a race war. He sent them all back into LA to look for another upscale neighborhood to terrorize, but this time he rode along. In the car were Manson, Watson, Atkins, Kasabian, and Krenwinkel, along with Leslie Van Houten and Steve "Clem" Grogan. They drove for hours, cruising past a home where they once had partied, and then stopped at the house next door, which belonged to the supermarket executive Leno LaBianca and his wife, Rosemary.

Later, Manson would say that he alone approached the house, but others would tell the story with some variations. He claimed that he went back for Watson and the pair then used a lamp cord to bind the LaBiancas, placing pillowcases over their heads. As the two men collected cash from the couple, Manson told them this was only a robbery and nobody would get hurt. They took Rosemary to her bedroom, and

THE FIVE VICTIMS SLAIN AT THE BENEDICT CANYON ESTATE OF ROMAN POLANSKI. FROM LEFT: WOJCIECH FRYKOWSKI, SHARON TATE, STEPHEN PARENT, JAY SEBRING, AND ABIGAIL FOLGER.

when Krenwinkel and Van Houten entered the house, Manson ordered them to kill the terrified LaBiancas. He left and said that Watson was now in charge. As Rosemary listened from her bedroom, the trio stabbed Leno with a bayonet and carved "WAR" into his chest. Then they came for Rosemary, stabbing her forty-one times after she was clearly dead. Before leaving, they wrote in Leno's blood "Death to pigs" and "Rise" on the living room walls. The refrigerator door was smudged with a misspelled "Healter Skelter."

Now Hollywood and all of Los Angeles, if not southern California, were on terror alert. Celebrities started buying handguns, hiring bodyguards, and installing security systems or took refuge inside the Beverly Hills Hotel, where they were certain they would be safe.

The group went back to the ranch, disappearing into the hills and taking more LSD, seemingly out of the reach of law enforcement after committing eight homicides. But Manson had a record and had associated with a lot of sketchy people. Within a week of the LaBianca murders, the LA sheriff's department had interviewed Al Springer, a motorcycle gang member who knew Manson. He told detectives that just days after the Tate killing, the cult leader had confided to him about it, bragging about "knocking off five" pigs.

Police took their investigation north of LA to where the Family had been formed, and by October Manson had been arrested at another rural location, Barker Ranch, in Death Valley. The police told him that he was being held on suspicion of grand theft auto. Then the rest of the Family was rounded up.

On November 6, the incarcerated Susan Atkins was the first to crack, telling inmate Virginia Castro that she had killed Tate and revealing the cult's motive for doing so: "We wanted to do a crime that would shock the world—that the world would have to stand up and take notice."

She also told Castro of their "death list" of celebrities: Richard Burton, Steve McQueen, Tom Jones, Elizabeth Taylor, and Frank Sinatra.

A week later, the police spoke with inmate Ronnie Howard about her own conversation with Atkins concerning the Cielo Drive and LaBianca murders. As Atkins kept talking with snitches, the investigation spread out across California and Deputy District Attorney Vincent Bugliosi was assigned the case. The LAPD hunted down Watson and tried to take him into custody in Texas, but his lawyers launched an extradition battle that lasted nine months. Eventually, he would be incarcerated with the rest of them. In December 1969, Atkins, Watson, Manson, Kasabian, and Krenwinkel were indicted for the murders of Tate and the others at Cielo Drive, and a grand jury charged all five with the LaBianca murders. In mid-June 1970, Manson, Van Houten, Atkins, and Krenwinkel went on trial, with Manson coming to court famously with an "X" carved into his forehead. Still believing that he could outsmart everyone in any room where he found himself, Manson served as his own lawyer, with some assistance from attorney Irving Kanarek. The case against the cult was built on the memories of Linda Kasabian, the lookout on Cielo Drive, who was given immunity to testify against Manson and his followers.

As the trial unfolded, some of the women in the Family who hadn't been arrested left the ranch and gathered outside the courthouse with X-shaped scars on their foreheads—marks that showed their ongoing support of Manson. Inside the

CHARLES "TEX" WATSON, NAMED IN COURT TESTIMONY AS A KILLER IN THE TATE-LABIANCA SLAYINGS, ARRIVES IN COURT FOR ARRAIGNMENT, MARCH 1, 1971, LOS ANGELES, CALIFORNIA.

courtroom, Bugliosi, who had made his name as a prosecutor and who later would write about Manson in his book *Helter Skelter*, didn't hold back in laying out his view of the Family to the jurors: "These are human monsters, they're mutations. There's no reason for them to go on living."

Van Houten's lawyer countered with, "Don't kill them. Study them. Let's learn from them rather than sending them to the death chamber."

The core of the trial unfolded with Kasabian on the stand for an astonishing eighteen days, describing how no Family member had refused a Manson order. She laid out for the jury textbook answers about the inner workings of a cult and people who hand their power over to others out of fear of challenging or defying the leader. The residue of that control and fear colored everything she said. "We always," Kasabian replied to the prosecutor about their relationship with Manson, "wanted to do anything and everything for him." She created a picture of the young women huddling around a hardened criminal who relished his rule over them as they waited for him to reveal the next step of his plans.

Bugliosi asked her about their return to Spahn Ranch after the murders on Cielo Drive.

"Charlie told us to go into the kitchen," she testified, "get a sponge, wipe the blood off [the car], and he also instructed Katie and I to go all through the car and wipe off the blood spots."

"What is the next thing that happened after Mr. Manson told you and Katie to check out the car and remove the blood?"

"He told us to go into the bunk room and wait, which we did."

In regard to the LaBianca murders, she told the court that she didn't want to be a part of it but went to their home "because Charlie asked me and I was afraid to say no."

On August 3, while she continued testifying, Manson unexpectedly rose in front of the jury, holding a copy of the *Los Angeles Times* with a headline that read "MANSON GUILTY, NIXON DECLARES."

With the president of the United States weighing in on the most spectacular recent American crime, the defense took the opportunity to demand a mistrial because Manson's actions in court had prejudiced the jurors against him. After all the members of the jury told the judge under oath that the president's opinion would not influence them, the trial went forward.

Watkins, Manson's main recruiter of young women, gave the jury a firsthand account of the "logic" the leader used with his followers—and the connections between the murders, the Book of Revelations, the song "Helter Skelter," and the racial component of Manson's thinking, which became a central piece of the Family's convictions. Most of the core cult themes, cutting across national boundaries, age groups, and religions, were all there, pieced together by a master manipulator and racist.

How, Bugliosi asked the young man, did the strategy for their own Helter Skelter and starting a race war begin? In answering the question, Watkins took the jurors right into the middle of the drug-laced late-night discussions Manson was having with his followers in the run-up to August 1969:

"There would be some atrocious murders, that some of the spades from Watts would come up into the Bel-Air and Beverly Hills district and just really wipe some people out, just cut bodies up and smear blood and write things on the wall in blood, and cut little boys up and make parents watch. So . . . in other words, all the other white people would be afraid that this would happen to them, so out of their fear they would go into the ghetto and just start shooting black people like crazy. But all they would shoot would be the garbage man and Uncle Toms, and all the ones that were with Whitey in the first place. And underneath it all, the Black Muslims would—he would know that it was coming down."

"Helter Skelter was coming down?"

"Yes. So, after Whitey goes in the ghettoes and shoots all the Uncle Toms, then the Black Muslims come out and appeal to the people by saying, 'Look what you have done to my people.' And this would split Whitey down the middle, between all the hippies and the liberals and all the up-tight piggies. This would split them in the middle and a big civil war would start and really split them up in all these different factions, and they would just kill each other off in the meantime through their war. And after they killed each other off, then there would be a few of them left who supposedly won."

"A few of who left?"

"A few white people left who supposedly won. Then the Black Muslims would come out of hiding and wipe them all out."

"Wipe the white people out?"

"Yes. By sneaking around and slitting their throats."

"Did Charlie say anything about where he and the Family would be during this Helter Skelter?"

"Yes. When we was in the desert the first time, Charlie used to walk around in the desert and say—You see, there are places where water would come up to the top of the ground and then it would go down and there wouldn't be no more water, and then it would come up again and go down again. He would look at that and say, 'There has got to be a hole somewhere, somewhere here, a big old lake.' And it just really got far out, that there was a hole underneath there somewhere where you could drive a speedboat across it, a big underground city. Then we started from the 'Revolution 9' song on the Beatles album, which was interpreted by Charlie to mean the Revelation 9. So—"

"The last book of the New Testament?"

"Just the book of Revelation and . . . it talks of the bottomless pit . . . about there will be a city where there will be no sun and there will be no moon."

"Manson spoke about this?"

"Yes, many times. That there would be a city of gold, but there would be no life, and there would be a tree there that bears twelve different kinds of fruit that changed every month. And this was interpreted to mean—this was the hole down under Death Valley."

"Did he talk about the twelve tribes of Israel?"

"Yes. That was in there, too. It was supposed to get back to the 144,000 people. The Family was to grow to this number."

"The twelve tribes of Israel being 144,000 people?"

"Yes."

"And Manson said that the Family would eventually increase to 144,000 people?"

"Yes."

"Did he say when this would take place?"

"Oh, yes. See, it was all happening simultaneously. In other words, as we are making the music and it is drawing all the young love to the desert, the Family increases in ranks, and at the same time this sets off Helter Skelter. So then the Family finds the hole in the meantime and gets down in the hole and lives there until the whole thing comes down."

"Until Helter Skelter comes down?"

"Yes."

"Did he say who would win this Helter Skelter?"

"The karma would have completely reversed, meaning that the black men would be on top and the white race would be wiped out; there would be none except for the Family. . . ."

"Did he say what the black man would do once he was all by himself?"

"Well, according to Charlie, he would clean up the mess, just like he always has done. He is supposed to be the servant, see. He will clean up the mess that he made, that the white man made, and build the world back up a little bit, build the cities back up, but then he wouldn't know what to do with it, he couldn't handle it. . . ."

"This is when the Family would come out of the hole, and being that he [the black man] would have completed the white man's karma, then he would no longer have this vicious want to kill. . . .

"Blackie then would come to Charlie and say, 'You know, I did my thing, I killed them all and, you know, I am tired of killing now. It is all over.' And Charlie would scratch his fuzzy head and kick him in the butt and tell him to go pick the cotton and go be a good nigger, and he would live happily ever after."

Near the end of the trial, Manson testified and told the courtroom: "I haven't got any guilt about anything because I have never been able to see any wrong. . . . I have always said: Do what your love tells you, and I do what my love tells me. . . . Is it my fault that your children do what you do? What about your children? You say there are just a few? There are many, many more, coming in the same direction. They are running in the streets and they are coming right at you!"

FROM LEFT: SUSAN ATKINS, PATRICIA KRENWINKEL, AND LESLIE VAN HOUTEN AFTER RECEIVING THE DEATH SENTENCE FOR THEIR PART IN THE TATE-LABIANCA MURDERS.

Lasting more than nine months, it was at the time the longest and most expensive criminal trial in American history. In January 1971, all were convicted, and a decade later they would be held responsible for killing stuntman Donald "Shorty" Shea, whose body was not found until that time. Two months later, Atkins, Manson, Van Houten, and Krenwinkel received death sentences; Watson was found guilty of seven murders and got the same punishment. In 1972, California abolished the death penalty, and the sentences were commuted to life imprisonment. Manson now made a career of coming up on parole with no hope of getting out. Just as in the courtroom when testifying, he showed no remorse for his crimes or any capability of feeling for others.

In October 1972 Manson entered Folsom Prison, and in 1976 he was transferred to Vacaville, where he stayed for nine years. In September 1984, another inmate claimed that "God told me to kill Manson" and set the cult leader on fire, leaving him with serious burns. In July 1988, from San Quentin prison, Manson told Geraldo Rivera during a TV interview, "I'm going to chop up more of you m—f—ers. I'm going to kill as many of you as I can. I'm going to pile you up to the sky." On May 23, 2007, he was refused parole for the eleventh time.

Despite all his crimes and ongoing threats, Manson still attracted women and was scheduled to get married in prison in 2015 to one named Star, but the wedding was called off. In November 2017, Manson, eighty-three, died of natural causes.

Tex Watson got married in prison and then divorced, fathering four children through conjugal visits and becoming an ordained minister.

> *From behind the time locks of courtrooms and from the worlds of darkness, I did let loose devils and demons with the power of scorpions to torment.*
>
> —Charles Manson

11

ADOLFO CONSTANZO AND THE MATAMOROS HUMAN SACRIFICE CULT

When Pablo Escobar was the cocaine king of Colombia from the late 1970s to the early '90s, he was believed to have ordered the murder of around 5,000 people. It could be more—a lot more. Under his rule, he created the template for how drug lords deal with conflict and opposition from law enforcement, judges, other coke traffickers, the press, politicians, or anyone else standing in the way of wider distribution for their product, making more money, and avoiding extradition, in this case to the United States. Escobar—known as "El Patron" or "El Padrino"—changed the game by being ruthless in ways never seen before in an entrepreneur running a private business. America, especially Miami, became a key outlet for the Medellín cocaine cartel, and violence followed it there. In 1981, the Miami-Dade morgue had more dead bodies than it could process and was forced to put the extra cadavers on ice in a refrigerated truck. Miami soon became the U.S. murder capital, with drug killings filling the streets. In 1980 there were 573 homicides, and a year later the number was 621. Escobar was the godfather of the trade, and Miami was about to see an American-born godfather who rivaled him in cruelty.

Adolfo Constanzo was born on November 1, 1962, the son of a fifteen-year-old Cuban immigrant, Delia Aurora González del Valle, and a father who died in Adolfo's infancy. Baptized as a Catholic, he went with his mother to Haiti as a small child and began learning voodoo and practicing Santeria, which has a hundred million followers worldwide. Santeria came about when African slaves combined worship of their own gods and ancestors' spirits with elements of Catholicism. Both Constanzo's mother and his grandmother were *santeras* (Santeria priestesses). In 1972, Adolfo's family moved back to Miami, and the ten-year-old served an apprenticeship to a Little Havana priest who practiced Palo Mayombe, a mixture of voodoo and religion based on African gods that originated in the Congo. Some have said that it represents "evil for evil's sake"; its rituals involve killing animals (but neither Santeria nor Palo Mayombe is known for sacrificing human beings). Adolfo's mother took a new husband who engaged in the drug trade and voodoo. Her neighbors claimed that she settled grudges by putting a headless animal—a chicken or a goose—on their doorsteps.

Adolfo's teenage years were spent telling fortunes, cruising gay clubs, and getting busted for stealing. He enrolled in junior college but was expelled or quit, drifting further into petty crime. In 1983, he moved to Mexico City and committed himself to "*Kadiempembe*"—the Devil. He launched a drug-selling cult with followers named Jorge Montes, Omar

Orea Ochoa, and Martin Quintana Rodriguez, having sexual relationships with the last two. They conducted killing rituals with chickens, goats, lions, zebras, and eventually human remains taken from a cemetery, but they hadn't yet sacrificed a living person. Like many other drug bosses, Constanzo wanted to advance in society, and he recruited more members from the police force and the Calzada mob family, who paid him very well to tell their fortunes. He wanted to go into business with them, but when they declined the offer, he had his group torture and kill seven of their family members, removing their toes, fingers, and brains, mimicking atrocities that Escobar had inflicted on his victims in Colombia.

Constanzo found a suitable partner when he met a tall, attractive, personable Mexican woman, Sara Aldrete. She was known by two names within the cult: "La Madrina" ("the Godmother") and "the witch." In her early twenties, the daughter of a retired electrician, she was an honor student at Texas Southmost College in Brownsville, a school with an enrollment of around 6,000 Mexicans, Anglos, and Hispanic-Americans. Aldrete was a model student—she was well liked on campus, bound for success, and nearly a star. By the late 1980s, she had become president of the soccer booster club and an outstanding physical-education student and had received the National Collegiate Health Physical Award. But she also had a fascination with the dark arts and black magic that came to the fore when she took up with Constanzo and secretly devoted herself to his cause. She began living two entirely different lives: one at the school by day and the other engaged in Adolfo's religious practices and variations on Santeria.

Constanzo had risen in the drug business, and he and Aldrete moved to a ranch in the Mexican desert where they could hide their huge stash of narcotics and be far enough away from civilization to carry out their rituals. He had graduated to killing people now—usually coke dealers who were competing with him or whose deals with him had gone bad but sometimes the homeless or prostitutes. His group's activities went unnoticed even though they were selling as much as a ton of marijuana a week and pulling in several hundred thousand dollars.

To find new recruits, Constanzo used a 1987 movie, *The Believers*, which starred Martin Sheen and Jimmy Smits and depicted a New York City cult that conducts human sacrifices to get access to money and power. Constanzo and Aldrete brought in men to watch the film and either turned them into converts or killed them. By participating in the death rituals, he told his followers, they were taking on the spirit of the victims, praying over the deceased and asking for riches and protection for their drug smuggling. Two cult members began wearing necklaces made from human vertebrae, and some believed that their sacrificial practices at the ranch rendered them invisible and unable to be wounded by bullets. They marked themselves with symbols signifying that they were killers.

On March 14, 1989, the cult murdered a Mexican stranger to ensure the secure passage of 800 kilos of marijuana Constanzo was about to sell. Because he didn't believe the victim had suffered enough during the sacrifice, Constanzo decided to pick another target, this time an Anglo: Mark Kilroy, a premed senior at the University of Texas. Kilroy and three of his friends had gone on spring break to South Padre Island, where the tip of the United States meets the Gulf of Mexico. They crossed the Rio Grande by car and ventured into the booming border town of Matamoros, with its stretch of discos and bars and young American women who also had come looking for adventure or romance. Nothing happened on that first excursion. The next night they retraced their steps back to Matamoros on foot. As they headed back to Texas, just 200 feet from the American border, Kilroy drifted away from the group. His friends weren't able to find him and assumed that he had returned to the hotel with someone else, perhaps a young female. In the morning, he wasn't there.

Kilroy's friends reached out to the U.S. consul in Matamoros, Donald Wells, who forwarded a description of Kilroy to local jails and hospitals. Kilroy's parents, James and Helen Kilroy, came to Texas to search for their son, sending out 20,000 leaflets with his picture and offering a $15,000 reward for any information about him. Under pressure from the American authorities, the Mexican government stepped up its efforts to find the killers. When this produced no leads, the United States and Mexico announced a new investigative drug program, using a dozen helicopters, thirty airplanes, and 1,200 shared agents. Three weeks after Kilroy disappeared, twenty-two-year-old Elio Hernandez Rivera of Matamoros, who was in possession of marijuana, ran a police roadblock, believing that he was protected by the cult's ritual activities. He wasn't. Agents followed him to a small ranch, Santa Elena, twenty miles west of Matamoros, and interrogated him. Rivera named a few narcotics dealers, and on April 11, nearly a month after Kilroy had gone missing, the authorities transported him back to the ranch, where Comandante Juan Benitez Ayala of the Mexican Federal Police discovered seventy-five pounds of marijuana.

The *federales* showed a picture of Kilroy to the property's caretaker, who said that he had seen the man on the ranch, over by a corral and a shack about a quarter mile away. Nearing the corral, the police were overwhelmed by the smell of rotting flesh. They began to search and dig and eventually uncovered a handful of shallow graves holding twelve males. Kilroy's tortured corpse was among them. The men had been shot and cut, burned and hanged. Some had had their eyes, ears, and genitals sliced off and their hearts torn out. One had no head. Three more bodies soon were discovered, bringing the total to fifteen. (There was unconfirmed speculation that there were twenty-five bodies in all.) In addition to the adult victims, they found the corpses of two fourteen-year-old boys.

The shack, lit by candles, held an iron kettle with a blackened human brain, a roasted turtle, a hammer, and a blood-encrusted machete inside it. The *federales* also found an oil drum in which some of the sacrificial victims had been boiled to make them unrecognizable to anyone looking for missing persons. Several members of the group now said that Constanzo had specifically ordered the killing of an "Anglo student," which had led to Kilroy's death. He had been hacked on the back of the neck with a machete, his legs severed at the knee, his brain and spine removed. Experts were brought in to analyze objects found in the shack and Aldrete's room; they identified elements of both Santeria and Palo Mayombe, also known as Ogun, the patron god of criminals. In the run-up to a murder, the head priest, or *mayombero*, becomes possessed by spirits, blowing cigar smoke and spitting liquor in the faces of his victims. Constanzo kept Ogun-like implements—a chain, a horseshoe, and railroad spikes—in the shack.

Other cult members were quick to tell the authorities that El Patrino himself had done the killings on the ranch, assisted by a tall Mexican woman. The police issued arrest warrants for the vanished Constanzo and Sara Aldrete.

Once the graves had been found and the story had broken in the news, Aldrete bolted from Texas Southmost. When her fellow students and the general population heard reports that the police had identified a "witch" in a murderous cult, they were stunned and panicked because of rumors that the group's tendrils stretched into the top echelon of Mexican culture. The *Dallas Morning News* reported that Constanzo had drawn in entertainers, along with high-ranking police and government officials, who had paid $8,000 a session for his ritual "cleansings." Texas Southmost was shocked to learn that the female suspect on the run with Constanzo was their classmate, the affable Sara Aldrete. How could this friendly and upwardly mobile young woman be part of something so heinous? What had lured her in? To understand more about her and the cult she allegedly was in, community leaders in the Rio Grande Valley began scheduling seminars and town meetings to inform people more about the dangers of witchcraft and voodoo. They pulled in huge crowds.

Clearly, the Mexican authorities were worried about what Constanzo had left behind. Two weeks after the last bodies were exhumed from Rancho Santa Elena, they performed a kind of exorcism of the evil lingering at the shack. They lit it on fire and reduced it to ashes, covering the ashes with a wooden cross. Accompanying the conflagration was a rite of purification conducted by a *curandero* (healer), who made the sign of the cross and tossed white powder onto the flames.

Within two weeks, the police encircled an apartment complex in Mexico City where Constanzo was hiding with Aldrete and five other suspected cult members. Gunfire was exchanged. Constanzo threw handfuls of cash out the window and opened fire at not just the police but pedestrians. The standoff lasted forty-five minutes and involved 180 police officers. With the agents closing in, Constanzo commanded Alvaro de Leon Valdez to kill him and his longtime companion, Martin Quintana Rodriguez. Valdez resisted at first but then followed orders. In Constanzo's apartment, the police found two swords, black candles, a skull made of white wax, and a blindfolded doll holding another doll, along with the bodies of Constanzo and Quintana, stuffed together inside a closet, their shirts covered with blood.

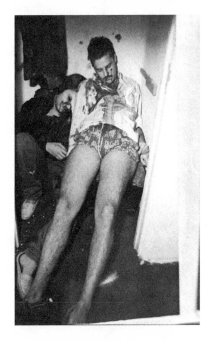

Valdez, Aldrete, and three other cult members were taken into custody on multiple charges. In all, a dozen people were indicted for damage to property, criminal association, wounding a police agent, and homicide. Valdez and several other arrestees were presented to reporters at the office of the Mexico City attorney general. Valdez explained that he

THE BODIES OF ADOLFO CONSTANZO AND MARTIN QUINTANA RODRIGUEZ (LEFT) ARE DISCOVERED INSIDE A CLOSET AT A MEXICO CITY APARTMENT FOLLOWING A SHOOTOUT WITH POLICE, MAY 8, 1969.

SARA ALDRETE, TWENTY-FOUR, SPEAKS WITH REPORTERS AFTER HER ARREST IN MEXICO CITY, MAY 1989.

shot Constanzo and Quintana with a machine gun after Constanzo hit him for failing to do so when he first made the request.

"He went crazy, crazy," when the police came, Valdez said. "He grabbed a bundle of money and threw it and began shooting out the window. He said, 'Everything, everything was lost. No one's going to have this money.'"

Aldrete told the press, "He [Constanzo] was telling him [Valdez], 'Do it, do it. If you don't do it, you're going to pay with circumstances in hell.' He said that he wanted to die with Martin."

Valdez went on to acknowledge his involvement in the killing of Mark Kilroy and others on the ranch, providing more details about what had happened after the student's kidnapping in Matamoros. After wrangling him into the back of a car and driving him to the ranch, they bound and gagged him with tape and held him in the shack. No harm would come to him, they promised when feeding him eggs, bread, and water. Twelve hours later, Constanzo delivered the fatal machete chop to his neck.

Aldrete denied participating in the ritual slayings and said she knew nothing about the killings at Santa Elena until she saw the reports on television. For her, she claimed, the cult was "like hell. They treated me like a prisoner. . . . If I had known it was like this, I wouldn't have been in it."

The police, along with many others, thought she was lying and had herself lured at least one of the victims, Gilberto Sosa, to his death. Her efforts to distance herself from the cult did not succeed.

After the Mexico City shootout, the *New York Times* wrote that Constanzo might not have died in the gunfire but had escaped and was at large, sending yet another shock wave of terror through the border towns. This report was lent some credence when Armando Ramirez, the agent in charge for the U.S. Drug Enforcement Administration in Brownsville, said that the faces of Constanzo and Quintana were so bullet-riddled that they couldn't be positively identified. Only dental charts and fingerprints could prove if Constanzo's death had been faked or if he was in fact deceased. Tests were run, and Ramirez soon assured the public that the cult leader had been killed. The relief was tangible.

"When you get right down to it," the agent said in making the announcement, "Constanzo was a killer, he was a madman, and he proved it right up to the end. We had to be sure he was dead."

In response to their son's demise, Mark Kilroy's parents, James and Helen, created a nonprofit antidrug foundation in his name.

While in custody, Aldrete later said that she was tortured by the *federales*—blindfolded, stripped, hung upside down, burned and beaten, her toenails yanked out, her body damaged so badly that she could never have children. (The *federales* denied all this.) She was given at least thirty years in prison, but if that sentence runs out, she could still be prosecuted for the murder of Mark Kilroy, a case that has never come to court.

12

MARSHALL APPLEWHITE AND HEAVEN'S GATE

Cult leaders are often people who find something they strongly believe in for their own personal identity or sanity or salvation but then want or expect others to embrace the same set of convictions—and with the same fervor. It isn't enough for them to find great meaning in what many see as eccentric ideas or religious systems. They have to take their disciples down with them.

Marshall Herff Applewhite was born on May 17, 1931, in Spur, Texas, the son of a Presbyterian minister. Marshall grew up with the stigma of being a PK ("Preacher's Kid") whose family moved from town to town around the Lone Star State every two or three years. From an early age, he was an overachiever in school, a natural leader, and almost always on the honor roll. Heavily influenced by his father's religious work, the young man considered becoming a minister; however, his future appeared to lie in music rather than the pulpit. After graduating in 1952 from Austin College, he got married and served in the Army Signal Corps. With a rich baritone voice and a commanding theatrical presence, he performed in musicals in Texas and Colorado before taking off for New York City to find a life onstage. As with countless would-be stars and starlets before him, his talent didn't rise to that level.

His acting chops weren't up to Broadway's standards but were good enough to make him a gifted public speaker. Initially, he used those skills in the classroom as an assistant professor and choirmaster at the University of Alabama and then when he headed up the music department at the University of St. Thomas, a Catholic school in Houston. He also landed fifteen roles with that city's grand opera. He was building a musical career, but trouble brewed underneath every advance he made in academia.

By the late 1960s, Applewhite's struggles with his sexuality were beginning to surface. Many years later, the *Washington Post* would report that Applewhite had been fired from his job at the University of St. Thomas because of an affair with a male student. He had a wife and two children, but the couple divorced in 1968. Two years later, Applewhite left teaching altogether in the midst of something like a nervous breakdown. Rather than accepting his apparent sexual inclinations, he fought against them until he was unable to cope.

According to his sister, Louise Winant, Applewhite's sufferings caused him to be admitted to a Houston hospital in 1972, where he had a near-death experience. (Others would allege that he'd gone into the facility in the hopes that the psychiatric staff could "cure" him of being gay.) This experience expanded his view of reality and left him open and ready for something more. That soon appeared in the person of a nurse,

Bonnie Lou Nettles, forty-four and married, who told him that he had survived for a reason: to use his multiple gifts to help others who were struggling. Nettles had developed a passionate interest in religion that went beyond Christianity or the Bible and reached into more unconventional spiritual disciplines, some with science fictional overtones.

Nettles studied the Book of Revelations, which mentioned "the Two" who were believed to have been placed on earth for a special mission. As she got to know Applewhite, she said that fate had brought them together as the Two who would go forward and do God's work. In the biblical rendering of the story, the Two were prophets who would be killed by a beast from the bottomless pit but then resurrected before ascending into heaven.

Applewhite and Nettles became members of a small group with similar beliefs and also became a couple, but he claimed that their relationship was platonic. This arrangement seemed to work well for them. It gave her a partner in her spiritual mission and gave him a personal life without the need to engage in sex with a woman or a man. The pair began living together and going through a series of name changes. For a while they called themselves "Bo" and "Peep" and then switched to "Ti" and "Do." (The latter was his name and was pronounced "Doe.") When Applewhite eventually found himself unable to stifle his sexual urges, he found another and final answer to his problem: he had himself castrated.

When studying aberrant behavior, researchers often say that one person alone with strange ideas or criminal tendencies will never act out those impulses on his or her own. But when that individual comes together with another like-minded person (think Bonnie and Clyde of movie fame or Dick Hickock and Perry Smith of the notorious *In Cold Blood* murders), the dynamics shift. It's almost as if a third entity comes into being who will do things that the other two never would by themselves. Applewhite and Nettles fit the description well, a classic case of bad chemistry. She had the need to be important, and he had serious religious and sexual challenges that she would help him resolve. She wanted, at least in her own mind, to do something good for people, and he had a wonderful voice and stage appeal. She had the original concepts that they would develop together, using his charisma as a springboard. It would prove a deadly combination.

Applewhite and Nettles began wandering around the Southwest spreading their teachings. Like his father, Marshall went from town to town, but with a far different mentality than the older man's. The couple had convinced themselves that because they were answering the call from the Book of Revelations, they were above human laws. In 1974, they committed credit card fraud and then Applewhite rented a car in Saint Louis and failed to return it. He did six months in prison, and in the long tradition of the incarcerated he passed the time by immersing himself in religious study to forge a better understanding of the work he and Nettles hoped to do after his release. The pair had come to embrace the notion of a "Level Above Human," something akin to heaven, from which messengers were sent to earth to assist others in reaching the "Next Level." The duo were certain they were such messengers, and to help others reach that Next Level they could teach them how to stand aside from all that was human in preparation to ascend—with the help of a UFO. Only a chosen few would make that journey, and Applewhite and Nettles would decide who did and did not make the cut.

Their beliefs, which amounted to the creation of their own cosmology, eventually were collected in a self-published book. Their story went like this: 2,000 years ago, those in the Kingdom Level Above Human had sent a "Representative" (Jesus) to earth to instruct people on how to enter the "true" Kingdom of God. Things had gone awry, and the powers that be at that time had come together to kill that individual. Over centuries, humanity had turned his once-pure message into "watered-down Country Club religion." During that time of darkness, people had become lost and society degraded. But a new opportunity had arisen in the 1970s after the Kingdom Level had dispatched two "Older Members" to occupy human bodies ("vehicles") and offer the teachings again.

It doesn't seem coincidental that Applewhite and Nettles put forth this message at a moment in American history characterized by confusion, doubt, and the breakdown of many conventional ideas. Young people had spent the last decade or so rebelling against all kinds of authority and questioning almost everything, including the value of the nuclear family. The duo was there to offer them a new kind of family, and some were willing to listen to their dreams of the future. The teachings also gave them an absolute set of answers to life's mysteries and a clear chain of command.

One part of the book read, "The only way an individual can grow in the Next Level is to learn to be dependent on his Older Member as that source of unlimited growth and knowledge. So, any younger member in good standing, forever remains totally dependent upon (and looks to) his Older Member for all things."

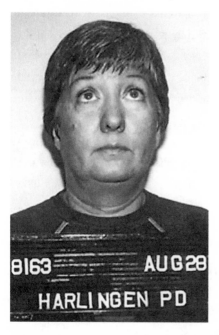

8163 — AUG 28

HARLINGEN PD

The couple cut off all ties with their families and encouraged their followers to do the same thing. This caused distress among their relatives, but how could people stop other adults from doing what they wanted? By September 1975, in Waldport, Oregon, Applewhite and Nettles had worked with the group Human Individual Metamorphosis to create a flyer

BONNIE LOU NETTLES IN A HARLINGEN, TEXAS, POLICE MUG SHOT FROM HER 1974 ARREST WITH MARSHALL APPLEWHITE FOR AUTO THEFT.

for a talk featuring "two individuals [who] say they were sent from the level above human, and will return to that level in a space ship (UFO) within the next few months." The duo promoted the idea of "TELAH, The Evolutionary Level Above Human" and attracted an audience of around 150. The event was unusual enough to be covered in a *New York Times* article, and soon afterward twenty to thirty people drove off with Applewhite and Nettles to Grand Junction, Colorado, where they were supposed to be visited by aliens.

Those activities gained national attention and prompted Walter Cronkite of the *CBS Evening News* to say on the air, "A score of persons … have disappeared. It's a mystery whether they've been taken on a so-called trip to eternity—or simply been taken."

The spaceship didn't materialize in Grand Junction, but the couple's reputation was growing and they became the subject of a 1976 book: *UFO Missionaries Extraordinary*. They sent their acolytes out to recruit new members and soon had as many as 200 followers. As they continued traveling, they demanded that all their adherents live a Spartan life of strict discipline, sleeping at campsites and experimenting with unusual diets and sexual habits. They banned smoking, alcohol, and sex, with Applewhite encouraging the males to imitate him and get castrated to eliminate "human mammalian behavior." A few of the men agreed to have the operation done in Mexico. All the disciples had to wear short hair and baggy clothing in a further effort to mask their gender and sexuality. They were to shun fast food and soft drinks and do three-month-long bodily cleansings by drinking a cocktail made of lemonade, cayenne pepper, and maple syrup. They watched and rewatched *Star Trek*, *Star Wars*, and *Close Encounters of the Third Kind*, borrowing some of the language from those hit films for their own purposes.

Applewhite and Nettles systematically eliminated all of those from the group but the most obedient as though they were employing a handbook on how to succeed in building a cult. Some followers fell away, but others stayed on. Those who weren't committed to grappling with the difficulties of their own identities but were drawn to taking on new ones offered by someone else gravitated toward the group and its ideas. The body, the cult leaders said, was merely a vessel to lead you to the next plane of existence, and if you didn't take this chance to ascend, you'd be left behind to fight the demons soon coming to invade the earth.

After a brief flurry of regional and national publicity in the mid-1970s, including a February 1976 article in the *New York Times Magazine*, the cult basically went underground to hone its tactics and message. The group would later describe the years 1975 to 1992 on its website: "We were very much 'lifted out' of this world—literally. In 1988, however, we did write the '*88 Update*, including, quite appropriately, some updated thinking. We also took this opportunity to set the record straight with a written account of our history, refuting many of the false reports and outright lies widely circulated and published by the media back in 1975. We sent it out far and wide for 'those who had ears to hear.' But it was clearly part of the Next Level's design to keep us protected and secluded a while longer, so we remained hidden and virtually unfindable for several more years."

By the mid-1980s, Applewhite's followers had become less itinerant, settling into houses or apartments and holding jobs, usually with false names. In 1985 the group was temporarily staggered when Nettles died of cancer. Applewhite had lost not just his partner but the one who had inspired him to take on the otherworldly cause. He had to decide whether he could carry out the mission alone, a mission refined down to this: "To be saved from Lucifer, human beings must give up all earthly pleasures."

After grieving and adjusting to Nettles's absence, Applewhite chose to continue with his core group. They were entering a new phase, driven in part by the arrival of novel technology as they kept up with the ever-expanding realm of modern media. In the late 1980s they released a number of satellite-broadcast videos titled *Beyond Human (The Last Call)* that offered more information about the Next Level and their vision of the future. They were hardly alone, as many Americans and those beyond the United States were embarking on their own spiritual quests, with New Age lingo and movements reaching into the country's mainstream. Yet none would take the same path as that promoted by Applewhite, which offered a blend of Christianity and alternative spiritual searching. Applewhite was being positioned as the Second Coming of Christ, and he advocated that everyone within range of his teaching should prepare for the imminent End Times. For good measure, he threw in some thoughts that could have come straight out of the hippie counterculture of the 1960s. In one initiation tape, he said that "parents do not possess the offspring they have. It's a very evil thing for them to think they're theirs, that they are products of theirs, property of theirs."

Applewhite's ideas were about to connect with one of the major technological breakthroughs of the late twentieth century. In the mid-'90s the Internet was just coming online in terms of public mass consumption, and Applewhite's group had a tech-savvy contingent that included web designers. The cult became one of the first to use cyberspace to recruit new followers and launch its own cyberbusiness. They were soon managing a successful computer outfit—one client was the San Diego Polo Club—and their headquarters and living quarters were very different from tent-and-camp living. The official name they went by now was Heaven's Gate.

Heaven's Gate's members were very conscious about what they were doing and kept a running account of their own developments as a group in part because they didn't feel the American media could portray their journey accurately. The Heaven's Gate website gave this narrative of what happened next:

> In the early 1990's, we began to get clear signals that our
> "classroom time" *per se* was nearly over, but that some
> involvement with the public was about to begin. So, we

started the painful and arduous task of trying to figure out how to re-interface, communicate, with a human civilization which by this time had become quite foreign to where our thinking had evolved. Nevertheless, in early 1992, we had our "coming out." . . . We corresponded for a brief period with those who opted to write to us. And a very interesting phenomenon occurred. Although we thought we were presenting our information to the "public at large," much to our surprise, those who watched and responded were almost entirely our own "lost sheep"— that is, crew members who had previously dropped away, having been overcome in earlier years by the temptations of an increasingly decadent civilization. They now were desperately seeking a way to reconnect. And they did. . . .

Heaven's Gate reached out on conventional media platforms for more people to join it for the next leg of its mission:

On May 27, 1993, we took a much more overt step toward the conclusion of our task. We published a 1/3-page ad/statement in both the national and international editions of *USA TODAY*, entitled *'UFO Cult' Resurfaces with Final Offer*. . . . This ad/statement, with slight variations, entitled *Last Chance To Advance Beyond Human* . . . was then reprinted in alternative newspapers, weekly newspapers, and various magazines around the country as well as overseas. . . . During the months that followed, we maintained an ongoing correspondence with, as well as provided video tapes and written materials to, those who wrote to us with sincere interest.

In January of 1994 . . . we sold all of our worldly possessions except for a few cars and changes of clothing, and set out cross-country holding free public meetings from coast to coast for 9 months. . . . In addition, we did countless newspaper, radio, and TV interviews. It became clear to us, during the course of these meetings, that our primary purpose for being out there at this particular time, was *not* to relate to the public in general, but to locate our additional crew members, whom we now refer to as the "second wave." Their addition to our class in 1994 nearly doubled our numbers. . . . We realized that this was all part of a greater plan that was unfolding according to the design of those in the Next Level responsible for this current civilization "experiment." What some might call the "second rapture" or snatching away, found all of us, both the first and the second wave, removed from the world, entering into what we would describe as an accelerated version of the "metamorphic classroom," lasting over a year before our once again "coming out."

It was time for them to explain their intentions and strategies by using the next wave of communications technology:

Then on September 25–26, 1995, from a secluded location, we issued a statement that went out—"on line"— around the globe, for our sixth public interaction. The statement entitled "*Undercover 'Jesus' Surfaces Before Departure*" was posted to the World Wide Web and to 95 UseNET newsgroups on the Internet, potentially reaching millions simultaneously. And in keeping with our policy of "speaking in tongues," on October 11, 1995, we posted a higher, more generic translation, entitled *"95 Statement by an E.T. Presently Incarnate."* The response was extremely animated and somewhat mixed. However, the loudest voices were those expressing ridicule, hostility, or both—so quick to judge that which they could not comprehend. This was the signal to us to begin our preparations to return "home." The weeds have taken over the garden and truly disturbed its usefulness beyond repair—it is time for the civilization to be recycled— "spaded under."

And so this brings us before the public once again, with our *"farewell legacy."* At the time of this writing, we do not yet know the extent of this seventh, and we suspect final, public involvement. . . . Nothing is predetermined. The response of the world to the Next Level will be monitored very carefully. What happens next remains in the balance. It has been given that what you do with this—how *you* respond to us—is strictly up to you.

This last message was somewhat ambiguous. The Heaven's Gate website didn't promote suicide per se but rather a "willful exit" to "entering the Kingdom of Heaven. . . . We have thoroughly discussed this topic [of willful exit of the body under such conditions] and have mentally prepared ourselves for this possibility as can be seen in a few of our statements. However, this act certainly does not need serious consideration at this time and hopefully will not in the future. The true meaning of suicide is to turn against the next level when it is being offered."

Within two years, scientists announced that Comet Hale-Bopp would pass close to the earth in 1997. Applewhite, who now called himself "Do" or "Ti," took this as a sign that his cult's long-promoted prophecy was about to become real. He believed that a spaceship was trailing the comet and that it would take his band of true believers off the planet and deliver them to the Next Level.

Heaven's Gate soon posted this about the coming of the Comet Hale-Bopp and a UFO:

> Whether Hale-Bopp has a "companion" or not is irrelevant from our perspective. However, its arrival is joyously very significant to us at "Heaven's Gate." The joy is that our Older Member in the Evolutionary Level Above Human (the "Kingdom of Heaven") has made it clear to us that Hale-Bopp's approach is the "marker" we've been waiting for—the time for the arrival of the spacecraft from the Level Above Human to take us home to "Their World"—in the literal Heavens. Our 22 years of classroom here on planet Earth is finally coming to conclusion—"graduation" from the Human Evolutionary Level. We are happily prepared to leave "this world" and go with Ti's crew.
>
> If you study the material on this website you will hopefully understand our joy and what our purpose here on Earth has been. You may even find your "boarding pass" to leave with us during this brief "window."
>
> We are so very thankful that we have been recipients of this opportunity to prepare for membership in Their Kingdom, and to experience Their boundless Caring and Nurturing.

Certain that the "marker" was there to instruct the group on what to do now, Heaven's Gate made its next move. They rented for $7,000 a month a cream-colored Spanish-style mansion twenty miles north of

San Diego in the upscale neighborhood of Rancho Santa Fe, California, far removed from the humbler addresses of their past. Rancho Santa Fe was known for its wooded, hilly landscape filled with horse barns, fine restaurants, and golf courses as well as for tight housing regulations. The area controlled the color of paint used on fences, roofing designs, and even the lightbulbs that illuminated the expensive real estate: the average price of a local home in the mid-'90s was just under $2 million. Celebrities such as actor Victor Mature, sportscaster Dick Enberg, and diet maven Jenny Craig had residences there.

Rancho Santa Fe quickly took note of the cultists, because they all wore the same clothing and because their shunning of suntanning made their skin extremely pale, something that stood out in southern California. The group hunkered down in the seven-bedroom, nine-bathroom house, which was outfitted with the bare-bones accommodations of cheap plastic chairs, bunk beds, low-grade office furniture, around two dozen computers, and food purchased in bulk. In addition to banning sex, the group appeared to have taken a vow of silence, at least with outsiders, casting a veil of secrecy over its activities inside the mansion. They communicated with outsiders largely through their website and an online business called "Higher Source."

"Individually and collectively," the Higher Source site said, "we have focused on outgrowing the artificial limitations this society has programmed all of us to accept in personal conduct and task efficiency . . . we can produce at a level of efficiency and quality unequalled in the computer industry."

In the near future, commentators across the country would attempt to explain the appeal of a group like Heaven's Gate. In the *Journal of Computer-Mediated Communication*, Wendy Gale Robinson, a professor of religion at Duke University, wrote: "Freedom from the physical body and the free . . . [rein] given to the imagination in cyberspace . . . *could* have contributed to the cult members' decision to go to the next, if illogical, step. . . . It's within the realm of possibility that Applewhite's ministry plus cyber-culture was a toxic mix."

In early 1997, as Hale-Bopp came nearer to the earth, Heaven's Gate made plans for its Last Supper. Late that March, they gathered at a Marie Callender's restaurant in Carlsbad, and everyone ordered the same thing: dinner salads with tomato vinegar dressing, turkey pot pies, and iced tea, followed by cheesecake with blueberries. The waiter who served them would recall that the diners seemed quite upbeat that evening and showed no signs of discontent or depression. Several days afterward, when Hale-Bopp came closest to the earth, Applewhite took the final step of his mission.

On March 26, the bodies of twenty-one women and eighteen men, including Applewhite, were discovered at the Rancho Santa Fe address. All the dead were laid out in the bunk beds, wearing black track suits and black-and-white Nike Decade sneakers, their heads covered with bags and their bodies draped in purple shrouds. Each had a five-dollar bill and three quarters in his or her pocket—apparently the fare needed for intergalactic travel. On their all-black outfits was a patch reading "Heaven's Gate Away Team."

In a videotape later broadcast by the CBS network and its affiliates, a white-haired man thought to be Applewhite said, "You can follow us but you cannot stay here."

The police, led by Deputy Robert Brunk and Laura Gacek, were the first to enter the home through an unlocked door after responding to a call to check on the house. They immediately smelled an odor they had been trained to identify: corpses. As they moved from one room to the next, they found ten bodies before calling for backup because of the magnitude of what they were witnessing. They eventually would learn that every cult member had consumed a toxic mixture of phenobarbital, hydrocodone, and applesauce, washing it all down with vodka. A group of eight had helped with the first round of suicides before taking their own lives in a pattern called "the Routine." The police who found the bodies had rarely witnessed such a peaceful scene of mass death.

Describing the final Heaven's Gate ritual, CNN wrote, "Then a second group of 15 would die, also assisted by eight people. Given that 39 victims were found, that would have left a final group of nine."

The deaths set off alarms at the highest levels of the American government, in part because since 1994 more than seventy members of another sect, the Order of the Solar Temple, had killed themselves in Canada and Europe, also believing that they could escape a corrupt world and achieve a higher state of being.

Speaking from the White House in the wake of the Rancho Santa Fe tragedy, President Bill Clinton told reporters that the event was "heart-breaking, sickening. . . . It's important that we get as many facts as we can about this and to try to determine what, in fact, motivated those people and what all of us can do to make sure there aren't other people thinking the same way out there."

The police set up a toll-free number for friends and next of kin to the dead and logged nearly 1,500 calls in two days. One victim was Thomas Nichols, whose sister, Nichelle Nichols, had played Lieutenant Uhura in the original *Star Trek* series. Others among the deceased included two African Americans and one Hispanic; the rest were Caucasian. Their ages ranged from the twenties to seventy-two, and various forms of identification indicated that they came from Texas, Washington State, Colorado, Arizona, New Mexico, Florida, Minnesota, and California. Some of them had prerecorded "exit videos" to explain their actions and encourage others to follow their lead.

This wasn't suicide, they claimed, because once they had removed themselves from their worldly vessels, or "containers," the spaceship traveling in Hale-Bopp's wake would carry them away from this planet and into the realm of ascension. Their messages provided little comfort to the loved ones they had left behind, who were faced with trying to comprehend and articulate to themselves and others what had happened. In May 1998, two more Heaven's Gate members attempted suicide at an Encinitas, California motel, utilizing the same method of death. Wayne Cooke perished there, but Chuck Humphrey survived and was hospitalized; nine months later, using carbon monoxide and a sealed tent, he killed himself.

In the aftermath of the deaths, the Heaven's Gate website posted: "'Away Team' Returns to Level Above Human in Distant Space . . . [by] the time you receive this, we'll be gone—several dozen of us . . . we have now exited the bodies that we were wearing for our earthly task . . . task completed."

Sometime later, the Heaven's Gate's webpage's administration would send a message to the Reddit.com blog about what those who had passed were trying to accomplish with their teachings: "The information must be available to mankind, in preparation for their return. We don't know when that will be but those who are interested will find the information."

INTERIOR OF THE SAN DIEGO MANSION WHERE THE HEAVEN'S GATE CULT MEMBERS COMMITTED SUICIDE.

The Heaven's Gate website remains active, with the domain name and server regularly renewed by an anonymous source. And there are still believers. After the suicides, Rio DiAngelo, the last known cult survivor, had kept the faith. "I can say with absolute, undeniable certainty," he told CNN, "that 'Do' [Applewhite] was a second coming of Jesus."

In May 2012, CBS Las Vegas contacted the site to find out information about the status of Heaven's Gate fifteen years after the deaths. Whoever received and responded to the inquiry (the writers were anonymous) would say only that the website was still run by the TELAH Foundation, with its total of two members. Those two told CBS Las Vegas: "The Group left us to take care of the website, book and the tapes that they wanted to speak for them. . . . [But] very few people ask for the book or tapes, so very little is given out."

The TELAH Foundation called those who committed suicide "the finest and most caring individuals that were on this planet."

The reaching out to the Heaven's Gate website and TELAH Foundation in the year 2012 wasn't purely coincidental in light of what some thought would occur seven months later. According to the ancient Mayan calendar, the end of humanity on earth was scheduled to come on December 21, 2012—based on the close of their Long Count calendar, which had run about 5,125 years. All over the world, people were talking about that date and anticipating the event (or nonevent), depending on what did or didn't happen that day.

When CBS Las Vegas raised this issue with the TELAH Foundation, the organization's representative shrugged it off. "Our own opinion," the spokesperson said, "is that it is a bunch of nonsense. The world will still be here on December 22."

13

CHRIS KORDA AND THE CHURCH OF EUTHANASIA

Recent decades have seen the rise of "identity politics," in which one's political leanings are closely tied to one's personal identification with race, gender, sexual orientation, or a particular cause. This has led to a wide variety of groups that build their political or social convictions around a single overriding issue: they're prolife or prochoice, believers or nonbelievers in climate change, vaxxers or antivaxxers; they're transgender advocates, voting rights proponents, and so on. Only one group has embraced the politics of utter self-destruction.

Chris Korda was born a man in 1962 but would transform into a transgender software developer, a musician, and a DJ with a deep attachment to the Dadaist movement that surfaced in Europe in 1914 after the start of World War I. Before hostilities broke out, the Continent had seen a hundred years of relative peace, and the twentieth century had been ushered in with a spirit of optimism. Significant strides had been made in science (Einstein), psychology (Freud), and economic reform (Marx), along with advances in the arts and other fields. It seemed that the early 1900s, like the century that had recently ended, would build on all this progress. Fourteen years later, the bloodshed sweeping across Europe had just begun, but it profoundly affected the countries fighting the war. Some of the new technologies—tanks, flamethrowers, poison gas—were being used to kill both soldiers and civilians. The world, or at least Europe, had never seen such widespread slaughter.

Tragic or apocalyptic eras produce bizarre and/or desperate responses and equally bizarre individuals. Dadaism was an artistic response to the horrors engulfing Europe as combatants stood in trenches month after month and year after year and killed one another in a war that seemed to have no end. Many artists, seeing the war as absurd, tried to channel that absurdity into their painting and writing. They did so, as one Dadaist put it, "to destroy the hoaxes of reason and to discover an unreasoned order."

The movement first took root in Switzerland in 1915 before spreading to New York and then to Paris, where it flourished. Antiviolent and antinationalist, Dadaism was based on rejecting logic in favor of irrationality or outright nonsense.

Andre Breton, a founder of surrealism and a fellow traveler with the Dadaists, famously said, "Reason can only solve problems of secondary importance." The Dadaist poet Tristan Tzara described the movement's origins as "not the beginnings of art, but of disgust."

The end of the twentieth century, mirroring the beginning, would produce an event the planet had never seen before. When Chris Korda was ten, he read an article in the *New York Times* about climate change.

He interpreted it to mean that global warming was irreversible and the human race was doomed unless radical action was taken immediately. Twenty years later, inspired by this challenge as well as the Dadaists, he founded the Church of Euthanasia (CoE), which promoted mass suicide. The idea for the CoE came to him in a dream in which he was, according to the church's website, "confronted [by] an alien intelligence known as The Being who speaks for the inhabitants of Earth in other dimensions. The Being warned that our planet's ecosystem is failing, and that our leaders deny this. The Being asked why our leaders lie to us, and why so many of us believe these lies."

CoE contended that all aspects of the environmental crisis—climate change, topsoil erosion, poisoning of the water and atmosphere, reduction of biodiversity—were caused by human overpopulation. The church's platform was built on four pillars: suicide, abortion, sodomy, and cannibalism. All were voluntary forms of depopulation, mostly through not breeding. CoE was also strictly vegetarian, but if one insisted on eating flesh, the church advised, he or she should resort to cannibalism to get rid of more human beings.

That was what the church supported, yet it opposed all types of involuntary population reduction, such as murder, conventional or biological warfare, and the dissemination of airborne diseases. Its core mission was to take action to change the debate about creating social progress. It hoped to do that by disrupting everyday experience, provoking dissonance, and promoting critical thinking.

As the 1990s unfolded, Korda began identifying as transgender. "I believe," he/she said in 1999, "that cross-dressing is the balancing of male and female aspects within a person, within a person's psyche, within their soul, if you will. And everyone has these male and female aspects. I mean, in most cases, they are grossly out of balance due to the extreme gender socialization that we're exposed to as children. Men are forced into extreme male gender roles, women are forced into extreme female gender roles."

The church's first and only commandment was "Thou shall not procreate."

By that point CoE had come up with the slogan that would become its trademark: "Save the Planet, Kill Yourself."

At the 1992 Democratic national convention in New York City, Korda handed out stickers reading "Save the Planet, Kill Yourself" to convention delegates and began putting them on police cars. That phrase became the title of Korda's 1994 EP recording released on Kevorkian Records, named after the infamous Dr. Jack Kevorkian, America's euthanasia champion who was then assisting people with their suicides. To Korda, he was "a saint."

Also in 1992, Delaware became the first state to recognize Korda's organization as a church and offer it tax-exempt status. CoE's guerrilla tactics were soon to deepen as it spread its message. In September 1993, people driving on the Massachusetts Turnpike saw that a Museum of Science in Boston billboard had been covered by a ten-by-ten-foot black banner with five words painted boldly in white: "Save the Planet, Kill Yourself." The same month, CoE joined a march at Boston's World Population Day event, where Korda led a dozen members of the congregation through the streets while carrying a proabortion symbol: a stick with a bloody baby doll tied to a torn American flag. Other CoE marchers held up an oversized fake RU-486 abortifacient pill that they passed from one to another as they chanted, "Save the planet! Kill yourself!"

When those running the parade saw what CoE was doing, they kicked them out.

Rather than pull back, Korda took more and more outrageous actions, turning up the heat on procreating and childbearing, and holding counterprotests against antiabortion activists. The CoE cult gathered around a Boston abortion clinic with signs that read "Make Love, Not Babies," "No Kid, No Labor," "Sperm-Free C—for the Earth," "Depressed?

Commit Spermicide," "Love the Earth, Tie Your Tubes," "Fetuses Are for Scraping," "Feeling Maternal? Adopt!" and, to drive the point home with finality, "Fuck Breeding."

From 1994 to 1997, CoE recruited new members and backed up its street tactics with the publication of a provocative journal, *Snuff It*, that carried messages such as "The octopus wraps his tentacles around the Earth and feeds hungrily. He rips deep holes in her flesh, and sucks up her sweet essences, water and oil and gas."

By 1995, the church had expanded its campaign by purchasing a billboard with a 900 number for a "Suicide Assistance Hot-Line," along with the message: "Helping you every step of the way! Thousands helped! How about you?"

The hotline featured a recording offering detailed suicide instructions, but the phone company refused to activate the number. The church turned to cyberspace, where its website gave explicit guidelines for killing oneself. Although no one had done that at CoE's behest yet, the church was sued by the parents of children who were considering suicide. Then a Missouri woman was found dead with a printout from the CoE site lying next to her. When Jennifer Joyce, Saint Louis's lead prosecutor, threatened the church with voluntary manslaughter charges, Korda took down the instructions.

CoE continued protesting antiabortionists after an apprentice hairdresser named John Salvi III shot and killed a receptionist at a Planned Parenthood clinic in the Boston suburb of Brookline and then murdered another receptionist at Brookline's Preterm Health Services. In 1996,

CoE confronted antiabortion groups in front of the same clinic with the sign "Eat a Queer Fetus for Jesus."

The next year, CoE launched a fake organization, the Boston Fertility Task Force, to manipulate prolife activists into attending a faux protest at a local sperm bank. Korda had promised the protesters that Courtney Love would show up at the demonstration and get inseminated. In anticipation of this, nuns came to the location with their rosary beads and teenagers gathered to see the former wife of Kurt Cobain (the lead singer of Nirvana, who had some standing with the CoE because of his 1994 suicide). Love never arrived, but at a climactic moment in the day's events Korda unveiled a two-story penis puppet that dashed toward the sperm bank and "ejaculated" in front of the building. The rabid antiabortion group Operation Rescue put the church on its official enemies list and devoted a full page to its followers, including photos.

In October 1997, CoE decided to take free speech a bit further by holding a "fetus barbecue" at one of the nation's biggest prolife events: the Walk for Life on Boston Common. On hand was Cardinal Law, who was about to be implicated in hiding sex abuse in the Catholic Church. CoE members carried signs reading "Pedophile Priests for Life," and things veered toward chaos when an enraged park commissioner grabbed a camera strap and nearly strangled a photographer snapping pictures of the CoE.

Two years later, Korda expanded on his/her musical career with a techno album *Six Billion Humans Can't Be Wrong*, which was released on the Kevorkian label. A sample of the lyrics from "Fleshdance" reads as follows:

> *Eat eat eat eat eat eat eat eat*
> *Flesh flesh flesh flesh flesh flesh flesh flesh.*
> *Cow chicken pig human, cow chicken pig human.*
> *What's the difference?*

Korda's American mainstream debut came when the CoE appeared on the *Jerry Springer Show*. The episode was titled "I Want to Join a Suicide Cult," during which Springer begged a woman not to join the church. Also on the program was the extreme antiabortionist Neal Horsley, who had created a list of murdered abortion doctors with a line drawn through each name. He was known for giving out personal information about the doctors who remained alive. The broadcast was what one might have expected: Springer, unchained, criticizing Korda and the church for their support of cannibalism and offering instructions for "butchering a human carcass."

The church turned to eco-activism by building a raft to cross the Charles River during Boston's WBOS EarthFest festival. On the craft was an eighteen-by-five-foot banner with the familiar slogan "Save the Planet, Kill Yourself" waving in the wind as the crowd listened to songs from a Korda CD. The police quickly pulled the raft to shore and shut down the music.

In 2000, CoE attended Boston's BIO 2000 conference, a rapidly growing gathering for biotechnology companies, academic institutions, state biotech groups, and similar organizations across America and abroad. BIO 2000 drew protesters who felt that those institutions were dangerous and responsible for killing people and animals through science. Church members attended, holding signs that read "Human Extinction While We Still Can." According to Korda, the demonstrators beat up his/her followers. With the coming of the new millennium, he/she had received enough hate mail and death threats from both the right and the left to start taking them seriously. It was time to end the church's public events, but there would be other provocations.

At the end of 2001, Korda came out with a music video titled "I Like to Watch," a mishmash of sports images, porn clips, and footage of the 9/11 attacks that he/she claimed had aroused him/her sexually. The attacks showed Americans dying, which was in line with what he/she believed was necessary to save the planet. However, it was the kind of provocation that could prompt a hostile response, and Korda gradually dropped out of sight, leaving many questions unanswered.

Was he/she actually serious about any of these issues, or just trying to get attention through performance art? Was CoE all a big joke? Or was it an attempt to reduce reality to absurdity as Korda's heroes in the Dadaist movement had done nearly a century earlier to get people to look at life from a different angle, which might lead to different ways of thinking and acting? Whatever the answers may be, the 6,000-word "Antihumanism" manifesto Korda left us to ponder is a humorless tract bent on getting rid of human beings. Because we're unfit for life, it argues, we humans need to be eliminated. Nevertheless, the manifesto is fully supportive of non-human life. The section of the rambling screed labeled "Solutions" offers ways for exterminating people, but Korda does concede that certain types of "behavior modification" might render extinction unnecessary. The manifesto resembles an overstuffed novel produced by an overheated mind.

In an interview with the journalist Lex Marburger posted on the church's website, Korda came close to revealing the secrets of that mind: "We're attempting to wake people up out of a hypnotic trance induced by the Spectacle. It's only when they wake up, that they'll be able to perceive their own relationship to the earth in anything other than the terms defined by the consumer economy. If we achieve that goal, then it won't be necessary to kill myself. . . . I may kill myself, or I may not. . . . For the moment, I continue to be able to do more good by staying alive. . . ."

From the beginning of CoE, the dark-haired, cross-dressing Korda never broke character in his/her writing and music and seemed to believe in what he/she was doing. He/she addressed issues ranging from AIDS to nuclear physics, but in the end Korda returned to the cult's core belief: "Don't procreate."

The group has gone dormant, with its 501(c)(3) status lapsed for failure to bring in money, but in 2019 archivists put together a collection of CoE's artifacts to be installed in a Paris art space. Korda had made it to the home of the Dadaists and done so on his/her own terms. The exhibition featured video footage of the church's protests and original memorabilia, plus a clip from the *Jerry Springer Show*, a fitting close to the CoE.

We haven't solved our environmental issues, so there's no telling how people will look back on our time as climate change intensifies, the polar ice caps continue to melt, species face elimination (3 billion birds have vanished from the planet since 1970), our oceans fill with plastic, storms or droughts rage across the earth, populations grow, and water rises all around us. Radical (*i.e.,* root) problems spur the need for action and thinking outside the lines, which is often the first step in finding answers people never imagined were there. One thing is for sure: nobody went further afield in this direction than Chris Korda and his/her band of followers. They lived what they believed in.

14

DAVID KORESH AND THE BRANCH DAVIDIANS

If the Bible is true, then I'm Christ.

—David Koresh

Early in 1993, eighty armed agents of the Bureau of Alcohol, Tobacco, and Firearms raided the Branch Davidian compound at the Mount Carmel Center ranch in Axtell, Texas, thirteen miles northeast of Waco. They were attempting to serve a search-and-arrest warrant on the community's leader, David Koresh, on suspicion of violating federal firearms rules. In the ensuing gun battle, four ATF agents and six members of the compound were killed but nothing was resolved. The FBI was called in and took up posts around the property. Trained negotiators arrived on the scene, and for the next fifty-one days the two sides talked, sometimes around the clock. Pieces of their dialogue were recorded, released to the media, and became public around the world. During those discussions, Koresh tried to explain the thoughts and convictions of his religious community, but in the end he failed and something tragic came to their retreat.

In their own minds, the Branch Davidians were trying to do something new or fresh and off the grid of mainstream American religion and life. One follower had come all the way from Australia to join them. "If people read this account," wrote Clive Doyle in *A Journey to Waco,* "they will at least gain a different perspective on who David Koresh was, where he was coming from, who we were, and why we believe the way we do. Most people think 'cult' about us and think we are people who were brainwashed and deceived. They think our church members don't know what they're doing or where they're going. Hopefully, my story can open their eyes."

From a theological perspective, the Branch Davidians were millennialists who embraced the idea of the Second Coming of Christ and the beginning of a divine kingdom at the turn of the new millennium. They were an offshoot of a religious cult founded in 1959 by Ben Roden, which itself was an offshoot of the Davidian Seventh-day Adventist Church founded by Victor Houteff in the 1930s. By the 1960s, Roden had taken over the Branch Davidians' original settlement at Mount Carmel, named after a coastal mountain range in northern Israel. (In Hebrew the word "*carmel*" means "fresh" or "vineyard.") At the compound and far beyond its confines, speculation about the Second Coming, or the Eschaton—when God decreed the fate of all people on earth on the basis of the good and evil they had done in their lives—was rampant and had been around for decades. It appeared in books and sermons and discussions held by countless evangelical Christians. Some people took these prophecies more seriously than others.

One who did was Vernon Wayne Howell. Born in Houston in 1959 to a fourteen-year-old single mother, he came a bit late to the Jesus movement in America and the sense that something major was going to happen—something *had* to happen—as the twentieth century, with all its fire and fury, its world wars and cataclysmic upheavals, was coming to a close at the end of second millennium. Surely the prophecies from the Bible and other sources were intended for this moment, this "now" in the history of humankind. If the Bible was true, didn't one have to believe in these imminent events so long spoken of and written about?

A seeker from an early age, Howell arrived at Mount Carmel in a yellow Buick at age twenty-two, having lost faith in the Seventh-day Adventist religion of his youth. He was good with his hands, able to dismantle and rebuild guns and cars, and to most people he came across as gentle and kind, with a quick smile and waves of dark hair. Adding to his appeal, he was musical—he had played in a rock band and still dressed in the requisite clothes of rockers: T-shirts, sneakers, and blue jeans. More than anything, though, he excelled at memorizing and quoting Scripture. It came to him naturally, flowing from not just his lips but his spirit as he spoke to those around him at the compound, which had around 150 members. He saw himself and hoped that one day the Branch Davidians would see him as their own modern-day prophet.

In his book, Doyle wrote of those who traveled to their community and met Howell (not yet known as David Koresh): "A lot of them came with their heads in the clouds or with cameras, thinking they were tourists, if it was their first time. David straightened them out pretty quick," telling them, "You should come here to learn, that's why you came. If you want to do those other things, you might as well leave now and go have your fun. . . . But if you are here to study, you need to get your priorities straight."

When Roden died in 1978, his wife, Lois, ran the sect. Three years later Vernon Wayne Howell arrived at the compound. He became involved with Lois Roden and wanted to have a child with her who would be the Chosen One and start a new lineage of world leaders, but she was in her late sixties. When she died, her son George became the sect's prophet and leader. He and Howell struggled for supremacy, and the latter won over the majority of those in the community.

In a desperate effort to regain his standing, George Roden exhumed a corpse to show his superior spiritual powers and then challenged Howell to raise the dead. Roden's actions were illegal, and Howell attempted to file charges against him for corpse abuse as the conflict intensified. In late November 1987, Howell and seven male followers, dressed in camouflage and armed with two 12-gauge shotguns, two .22-caliber rifles, five .223-caliber semiautomatic assault rifles, and 400 rounds of ammunition, stormed their opponents at Mount Carmel and shot Roden in the hands and chest. The eight attackers were tried for attempted murder. Seven were acquitted, and Howell's case ended in a mistrial after he testified that he went to the compound looking for evidence of Roden's abuse of a corpse.

Within the next three years, Howell had changed his name to David Koresh and become the Branch Davidian leader. His new name evoked the biblical King David and Cyrus the Great. ("*Koresh*" is Hebrew for "Cyrus.") Like many millennialists before him, he was fascinated by the Book of Revelation, especially the sections about the seven seals: God had a scroll, locked by seven seals, that foretold the end of time. The Bible poses the questions of who is worthy to gain access to the scroll and loosen the seals, and the answer is the Lamb. The follow-up question is: Who is the Lamb? The Lamb is the one who reveals what is written on the scrolls and what will cause the end of time. As the leader of the Branch Davidians, Koresh was convinced he knew the identity of the Lamb.

He arrived at this thought by studying certain biblical passages that he felt applied to himself. He focused on Isaiah 48:14, which reads, "The LORD has loved him . . . [the] arm of Yahweh" who will destroy Babylon. The passage continues, "I have spoken, yea, I have called him: I have brought him, and he shall make his way prosperous . . . and now the Lord GOD and his Spirit hath sent me."

He also studied Psalm 80:17: "Let thy hand be upon the man of thy right hand, upon the son of man whom thou madest strong for thyself." This wasn't a description of Jesus, the head of the Branch Davidians taught his followers, but of *him*, David Koresh. He was the new Messiah, the one to lead them forward through the end of days, the one with special powers who deserved special treatment in the form of multiple wives, some reportedly as young as twelve or thirteen, when the legal age of marriage with parental consent in Texas was fourteen. After all, hadn't Psalm 45 spoken of a God-anointed king with many princess wives?

In the three years after Koresh took on his new name, his power within the cult increased and so did his battles with the authorities. When they arrived at the compound in late February 1993, suspecting him of violating federal firearms rules, he was ready for the kind of struggle that had been forecast for when the End Times neared. With ten people—four federal agents and half a dozen Branch Davidians—dead, the siege began. On the perimeter of the complex, the FBI put together what was probably the largest military force ever assembled against a civilian suspect: two Abrams tanks, four combat-engineering vehicles, ten Bradley tanks, and 668 agents, plus six U.S. Customs officers, fifteen U.S. Army personnel, thirteen members of the Texas National Guard, thirty-one Texas Rangers, 131 Texas Department of Public Safety officers, seventeen McLennan County sheriff's officers, and eighteen Waco police officers—a total of 899 people. The authorities viewed this as a hostage situation and hoped to wait it out and over time expose what they saw as Koresh's lies and pretensions—to the point where he would seek a peaceful outcome. Koresh obviously had a different perspective, convinced that he wasn't holding people at the compound against their will. For fifty-one days, the feds continued to wait and hope, believing that patience would pay off.

This did not produce results, and so the FBI decided that the stand-off was "non-negotiable." Pieces of dialogue between government officials and Koresh from this period, demonstrating the gulf between the two sides, were later released to the press and public. In the first contact Koresh had with an authority figure during the initial ATF assault, when people were wounded and dying and the gunfire on the compound was ongoing, he spoke with Larry Lynch in the local sheriff's office, and an FBI agent. Koresh, not surprisingly, wanted to discuss the fine points of the seven seals:

> *Koresh:* In the prophecies—
> *Lynch:* All right.
> *Koresh:* it says—
> *Lynch:* Let me, can I interrupt you for a minute?
> *Koresh:* Sure.
> *Lynch:* All right, we can talk theology. But right now—
> *Koresh:* No, this is life. This is life and death!
> *Lynch:* Okay.
> *Koresh:* Theology—
> *Lynch:* That's what I'm talking about.
> *Koresh:* is life and death . . .
> *FBI:* Now listen. Let's get back to the point in hand. This
> ah—you know—the writing of the seals. Okay. You've
> got to do that in there, and it's gonna take you *x* amount
> of time. But—just tell me this, David—are you saying
> that when you finish that manuscript—
> *Koresh:* Then I'm not bound any longer.

FBI: No. But see, that doesn't answer the question.

Koresh: Then I'll be out—yes—definitely.

FBI: I know you'll be out. But that could mean a lot of things, David.

Koresh: I'll be in custody in the jailhouse . . .

FBI: I know—I know that some point in time that's true. But I'm getting from you—I'm asking you, "When that is finished, are you telling me that you are coming out the next day, or two hours after you send that out or what?"

Sect member Steve Schneider was captured on audio speaking with an FBI negotiator about an undercover ATF agent who was using the name Robert Gonzalez. The ATF thought the Branch Davidians, who sold weapons at gun shows, had converted semiautomatic firearms to automatic without proper permits, which was one of the reasons for their going to the compound in the first place. Gonzalez's job was to infiltrate the Davidian community and look for evidence. He didn't find any, and that made everything to come more difficult for the government to explain. The Davidians were very upset with the feds when they realized that Gonzalez was not who he had told them he was. Schneider and a negotiator talked about how the sect felt they had been lied to and how this had left them with a sense of betrayal. The conversation, though brief, revealed much about how the cult members saw their mission in the world and naively thought outsiders would look upon them as they tried to spread the word of God. Here's a devoted evangelist speaking to a hardened FBI agent about what happened after Gonzalez had blown his cover:

FBI: Why didn't you have a confrontation [with Gonzalez] and say look, I just . . . don't appreciate you being here?

Schneider: Well . . . because here's a possible guy, here's a soul maybe, here's someone like myself—

FBI: Yeah. But he wasn't there to have his soul saved, right?

Schneider: Well, who knows, though? You never can tell.

FBI: Wait a minute. I know ... I worked undercover years and years ago and I wasn't there to have somebody save my soul ...

Schneider: I realize that. . . . [But] still, we love people so much, you give them the opportunity. . . . Even if it's one out of a million, even if it's that, whatever it might be, he's still a person that was made, created by an authority above himself and we loved the guy. I mean ... we spent enough time with him where we really do appreciate the man's character and personality.

The FBI looked upon the Davidians somewhat as they did upon Jim Jones's Peoples Temple cult in Guyana (see Chapter 6), which in 1978 had ended with a mass suicide that left 918 commune members dead,

SIEGE OF THE BRANCH DAVIDIAN RELIGIOUS SECT RANCH IN WACO, TEXAS, MARCH 1993.

including 304 children. For some analysts looking back on what was about to happen at the compound near Waco, this was a flaw in the government's thinking: the Branch Davidians were more conventionally religious, and their members probably would not have taken their own lives under orders from a dictator like Jones. Another segment of dialogue between Koresh and the FBI underscored the differences in how the government perceived Koresh's leadership and how he looked at his own position within the community. He clearly did not see himself as all-powerful:

> *FBI:* What I'm saying is that if you could make an agreement with your people that they're walking out of there and you could—
>
> *Koresh:* I am not going to tell them what to do. I never have and never will. I show them out of a book what God teaches. Then it's for them to decide.
>
> *FBI:* David, these kids need their parents, and we want everybody to be safe. How about the women? Can— will you let them come out of there? . . .
>
> *Koresh:* Yeah, but the thing of it is that if they wanted to, they, they could.
>
> *FBI:* Well, I, I think they feel like they can't because you don't want them to.
>
> *Koresh:* No, no, no, no. Let's stop that now.

As the siege continued, two FBI agents were caught revealing their true feelings about Koresh, calling his theology "Bible-babble" and referring to the sect leader as a "fanatic," "egotistical," "self-centered liar," "phony messiah," "con man," "child molester," and "cheap thug who interprets the Bible through the barrel of a gun." They also labeled him "delusional." Patience was running out on all sides. In doing research for an essay published in *Armageddon in Waco*, the religious scholar Nancy Ammerman later spoke with FBI hostage negotiators involved in the siege and wrote about how they could not take the Davidians' religious beliefs seriously: "For these men, David Koresh was a sociopath, and his followers were hostages. Religion was a convenient cover for Koresh's desire to control his followers and monopolize all the rewards for himself."

When the Bible scholar James Tabor heard Koresh talking on CNN about the seven seals, he reached out to fellow scholar Phillip Arnold and they went to the FBI. "It became clear to me," Tabor later wrote in an essay, "that neither the officials in charge nor the media who were sensationally reporting the sexual escapades of David Koresh had a clue about the biblical world which this group inhabited. I realized that in order to deal with David Koresh, and to have any chance for a peaceful resolution of the Waco situation, one would have to understand and make use of these biblical texts. . . . Might they [the Branch Davidians] not provoke a violent end to things simply because they felt it was the predetermined will of God, moving things along to the sixth seal, which was the great Judgment Day of God?"

Tabor and Arnold recorded a long discussion, offering their own reading of the Book of Revelation, and sent it to Koresh. He listened and was thrilled that someone was taking his convictions to heart.

"I am presently being permitted to document in structured form the decoded messages of the seven seals," he wrote back. "Upon the completion of this task, I will be freed of my waiting period. . . . As soon as I can see that people like Jim Tabor and Phil Arnold have a copy, I will come out and then you can do your thing with this beast."

This brought on rejoicing within the compound because the sect believed that the siege was about to end. But the FBI kept questioning Koresh about his real intentions and his next move. As the days and weeks went by, those in the compound asked the FBI to bring in milk for their children. The bureau considered the proposal but wanted some of the youngsters released first:

> *FBI:* We got the milk for you ... we'll bring the milk down.
> We'll drop it off. ... In return, we want four of your kids
> to come up, and we're going to give you the milk for the
> kids.
>
> *Kathy S. (sect member):* That doesn't make any sense.
>
> *FBI:* Listen. I'll, I'll get the milk to you for two kids.
>
> [*Kathy S.* responded badly to this ploy.]
>
> *FBI:* Kathy, perhaps we're wasting each other's time.
> All right? Put somebody else on.
>
> *Kathy S.:* I mean, all you want, all you want to do is
> bargain?
>
> *FBI:* Kathy!
>
> *Kathy S.:* Are you going to bargain with human lives?
>
> *FBI:* Kathy! I've told you what we'll do and, and if
> that's not agreeable to you, perhaps we're wasting
> one another's time. All right? ... Why don't you put
> somebody else on, please?
>
> *Kathy S.:* Look ... there are babies here that need the milk.
> Are you that inhumane that you can't just send us the
> milk for not sending out kids, or sending out David,
> or sending out women?
>
> *FBI:* Our concern, our concern is for those children
> first and foremost and the rest of you also. All right?
> The children—
>
> *Kathy S.:* So, your concern is that these babies get fed the
> milk they need?
>
> *FBI:* Kathy.
>
> *Kathy S.:* It doesn't sound like you are concerned.

During the siege, Koresh made a video of himself and his family. Sitting beside him was a young woman, and they were both holding small children. Koresh introduced those children and others to everyone watching while returning to one of his favorite subjects in the Bible: "These children that I have are for a reason, and unless we really have the ear and the eyes to open ourselves up and understand the prophecies in a lot of the Seven Seals the explanation would seem almost foolish."

Koresh tells viewers that a boy with long blond hair in the picture frame is Cyrus. Then there's a girl named Holly, a boy named Bobby, and several toddlers and babies, along with a pair of young women who appear to be teenagers. "This is my family," Koresh says, "and no one is going to come in on top of my family and start pushing my family around. It is not going to happen." He dons aviator sunglasses and adds, "You come pointing guns in the direction of my wives and my kids, damn it. I'm going to meet you at the door every time."

By then the agents had put up spotlights around the property and giant speakers that broadcast around the clock Tibetan monks chanting, telephones ringing, Christmas carols, the sounds of rabbits being killed, Nancy Sinatra singing "These Boots Are Made for Walking," and reveille, all of it making it far harder for Koresh's followers to get any sleep.

As the siege unfolded over weeks, Attorney General Janet Reno, the nation's top legal official, was the ultimate authority in the situation, the one who had to make the final decision. Reno came into office on March 12, a couple of weeks into the standoff, and the president would later say that she was under "enormous pressure from the FBI" to let them end the siege.

With some reluctance, after fifty-one days of talking and with no resolution in sight, she approved a plan to fire CS (tear) gas into Mount Carmel to force out the sect members. At a few minutes past 6 a.m. on April 19, 1993, FBI agents penetrated the walls with two specially equipped tanks with mechanical arms and deposited 400 containers of gas into spaces lit by Coleman lanterns and candles. Chunks of concrete began falling on those crouching inside. The feds had with them arrest and search warrants for Koresh and the Branch Davidians for illegally stockpiling weapons and on the suspicion of child abuse inside the compound. Gunfire broke out, and Koresh called 911:

> *911 Operator:* 911.
> *Koresh:* Hello?
> *911 Operator:* Yes?
> *Koresh:* This is Dave Koresh.
> *911 Operator:* This is who, sir?
> *Koresh:* David Koresh, Mount Carmel Center. We're being shot all up out here.
> *911 Operator:* Okay. Where are you?
> *Koresh:* Where am I? I'm at Mount Carmel Center!
> *911 Operator:* Okay, hang on just a second.
> *Koresh:* All right.
> *Deputy Sheriff:* Yeah, this is Lynch.
> *Koresh:* Hey, Lynch?
> *Deputy Sheriff:* Yeah?
> *Koresh:* This is David Koresh—
> *Deputy Sheriff:* Okay, David.
> *Koresh:* —the notorious. Why'd you go and do that for? You brought a bunch of guys out here and—

Changing direction, Koresh suddenly turned to biblical teaching.

> *Koresh:* There are seven seals.
> *Deputy Sheriff:* All right . . .

From there it descended into Koresh's preaching.

Outside the compound, the FBI's loudspeakers boomed, "David, you have had your fifteen minutes of fame. [Koresh] is finished. He is no longer the Messiah."

FBI agents were supposed to use their weapons only to return incoming fire; when the Branch Davidians began shooting at them, the feds increased the amount of gas filtering into the compound. Six hours after they had begun this process, flames erupted at three locations. Audio recordings from inside the compound suggest that Koresh's followers, acting on his orders, started the fires.

> *1st Davidian:* [surveillance tape] Start the fire?
>
> *2nd Davidian:* Got some fuel around here?
>
> *3rd Davidian:* Right here.
>
> *4th Davidian:* [surveillance tape] Did you pour it yet?
>
> *5th Davidian:* Huh?
>
> *4th Davidian:* Did you pour it yet?
>
> *5th Davidian:* I haven't yet.
>
> *6th Davidian:* David said pour it, right?
>
> *5th Davidian:* Did he? Do you want it poured?
>
> *6th Davidian:* Come on. Let's pour it.
>
> *5th Davidian:* Do you want it poured already?
>
> *7th Davidian:* We want some fuel.
>
> *5th Davidian:* I've got some here.
>
> *8th Davidian:* We should have gotten some more hay
>   in here.
>
> *9th Davidian:* I know.

It was too dangerous, officials believed, for firefighters to enter as flames consumed the compound. Nine sect members escaped, but investigators later found seventy-six bodies inside Mount Carmel, including twenty-five children. Koresh had fatal gunshot wounds, and that told the feds that he had died by suicide or murder-suicide. Others died from falling rubble or by suffocation from the fire.

The end of the standoff was national and international news for weeks, with government officials quickly coming under severe criticism for their handling of the siege. Reno tried to fend it off by taking responsibility for the raid, but that was not effective when no evidence of child abuse was found in the compound. The government attempted to justify its actions by stating that the Branch Davidians had started the fires but acknowledged that some of the gas they had used was indeed flammable under the right conditions. Reno was motivated to appoint the former senator John Danforth, an ordained Episcopal priest and establishment Republican, to investigate the siege.

When laying out his report to a special Senate panel in July 2000, Danforth recalled President Clinton's words from seven years earlier, after the Waco disaster: "I think when people are intent on burning themselves up, there's not much you can do about it."

FLAMES ENGULF THE BRANCH DAVIDIAN COMPOUND IN WACO, TEXAS, ON APRIL 19, 1993.

Danforth's views, unlike those of many others, were not ambiguous. In the preface to the report, he wrote, "Make no mistake: the bad acts alleged in this case are among the most serious charges that can be leveled against a government—that its agents deliberately set fire to a building full of people, that they pinned children in the burning building with gunfire, that they illegally employed the armed forces in these actions and that they then lied about their conduct."

In conclusion, he absolved the government of starting fires and shooting into the compound. The government, he wrote, did not improperly use the military or "engage in a massive conspiracy and cover-up. . . . There is no evidence of any wrongdoing on the part of Attorney General Reno, the present and former director of the FBI, other high officials of the United States, or the individual members of the FBI Hostage Rescue Team who fired three pyrotechnic tear gas rounds on April 19, 1993. . . .

"Responsibility for the tragedy at Waco rests with certain of the Branch Davidians and their leader, David Koresh, who shot and killed four ATF agents, wounded 20 others, shot at FBI agents trying to insert tear gas into the complex, burned down the complex, and shot at least 20 of their own people, including five children. . . .

"Ample forums exist to nurture our need to place blame on government. Sensational films construct dark theories out of little or no evidence and gain ready audiences for their message. Civil trial lawyers, both in the public and private sectors, carry the duty of zealous representation to extremes. The media, in the name of 'balance,' gives equal treatment to both outrageous and serious claims. Congressional committees and special counsels conduct their own lengthy investigations, lending further credence to the idea that there are bad acts to investigate. There is even pressure on them to find some bad act to justify their effort and expense. Add to all of this the longstanding public cynicism about government and its actions, and the result is a nearly universal readiness to believe that the government must have done something wrong. . . .

"In today's world, it is perhaps understandable that government officials are reluctant to make full disclosures of information for fear that the result of candor will be personal or professional ruin. Any misstep yields howls of indignation, calls for resignations, and still more investigations."

Despite everything Danforth believed and later wrote, the damage to the government's credibility, at least in some people's eyes, had been done. Reports of a growing militia movement spread across the nation, in part because of what had happened at Waco. On April 19, 1995, the second anniversary of the end of the siege, Timothy McVeigh, who had studied a white supremacist novel called *The Turner Diaries*—about a revolutionary named Earl Turner who blows up a federal building—drove a truck loaded with 4,800 pounds of fuel oil and aluminum nitrate to the Alfred P. Murrah Federal Building in Oklahoma City. The detonation killed 168 people and wounded 859.

A 2001 book co-authored by Second Amendment lawyer David Hardy, *This Is Not an Assault: Penetrating the Web of Official Lies Regarding the Waco Incident*, outlined his years of trying to learn more about what had happened on April 19, 1993. As a former U.S. Interior Department attorney, he used a freedom of information request to access an ATF "report of investigation" on two undercover agents who had gone hunting with Koresh eight days before the fires started and could have arrested him then. His revelations, which began coming out in 1999, were instrumental in Janet Reno's appointing Senator Danforth to open an official inquiry into misconduct during the siege. Hardy and others felt that the senator had covered up or at least whitewashed the reality at the compound in April 1993.

In retrospect, some who had been in power back then in Washington, D.C., changed their minds about the event or at least questioned themselves and their decisions. "We should have waited them out," Bill Clinton said at Hofstra University during a 2005 retrospective on his administration. He went on to talk about the instructions he had given to Reno as the siege lengthened into mid-April and then the decision to send in the FBI. "I am responsible for that," he said at Hofstra, "because I told her, if that's what they want to do, and she thought it was right. . . . It was a mistake and I'm responsible. And that's not one of those you get A for effort on."

Reno was attorney general till the end of Clinton's second term, the longest-serving AG of the twentieth century. "We'll never know whether it was a mistake or not, in one sense," she told NPR before leaving office. "But knowing what I do, I would not do it again. I would try to figure another way."

After the raid, *A Journey to Waco* author Clive Doyle stayed with the Branch Davidian principles. A new group, Branch, The Lord Our Righteousness, built a memorial for those lost in the siege and took over the land where the compound had been, hoping to heal what had taken place on the property. Doyle eventually left the new group but held on to his loyalty to his former leader and to, as he told the *New York Times* in 2007, "the true church."

Koresh left behind many quotes, one of which reflected what first had drawn him to the Branch Davidians and later caused him to encourage his followers to ride out the government's raid: "These people remain here because I have thoroughly opened to them the seven seals."

15

DAVID BERG AND THE CHILDREN OF GOD

We're even going to have sex in Heaven! How about that? Isn't that wonderful? Love all the girls you want to and all the handsome boys you want to and love all you want to and never get tired, never be impotent, never have a headache, never get hungry, never get sleepy, no pains, no VD, no nothin' except joy and praise and Hallelujah and lots of fun with your Bridegroom and all your friends and loved ones and the Family of God, His Family of Love, His children of God in Heaven when Jesus comes!

—David Berg

In the 1960s, David Berg traveled to churches with his children preaching, singing hymns, and spreading the word of the Bible as he interpreted it. Hoping to build a significant following, he promoted the idea of an imminent evangelical Christian uprising and made a reference to a popular rock band and current TV show. On the horizon, he said, there was "a teenage witnessing revolution to prove that Christ is more than the Monkeys [sic]." A revival was coming that would flow from one end of America to the other and beyond. This was, as things turned out, one of the very few prophecies Berg made that came true.

He had begun his life's work with the Christian and Missionary Alliance and in 1967 became the leader of an Assemblies of God Teen Challenge chapter in Huntington Beach, California, renaming it the "Light Club" and its members "Lightclubbers." Few were paying attention to him or his message until he hit upon an idea to lure the young people who he said were ready for the Christian message. He opened a coffee shop, brought in rock music, handed out free peanut butter sandwiches, and delivered his religious offerings from there. His timing was perfect because those activities were coinciding with the hippie movement, which was fundamentally driven by the power of new music coming out of the twenty-something generation. Guitars and evangelism were gaining ground together. Berg capitalized on that and on the growing communal lifestyle in southern California. He could look like a hippie himself. In a 1979 newsletter, he recalled having an epiphany about increasing his following: "I saw something was really happening and was really going to explode! I just knew it! I saw the Lord was really doing something! That's when I began to come down and teach in my dark glasses, beret, baggy pants, old torn jacket and tennis shoes."

Rumors filled the air of an imminent apocalypse, of Jesus returning to earth to hold all accountable for their lies and sins and of what would happen to those left behind when the Rapture came and the worthy ascended to heaven. While Berg ran the coffee shop, thousands upon thousands of young people heard those stories and started to drift toward evangelical Christianity, demonstrating that Berg's instincts had been right. They became known as "Jesus People," a loose collection of unconventional pastors, recent recruits to the Christian faith, and others determined to bring the Gospel to the younger generation and those in the counterculture.

As they drifted in their search for spirituality, Berg was there to connect with some of them, attracting a crowd and setting himself up as the "Endtime Prophet," the one to lead them forward as the world neared its last days. In 1969, he claimed that God had told him about an imminent earthquake that would cause part of California to crumble into the ocean. It didn't happen, but that didn't faze his growing band of converts, whom he now called the Children of God (COG). In the same year he took a second spouse, Maria, after receiving another message about the need to act out the Old Testament passage allowing multiple wives. It was the first hint of his adventurous sexual life to come.

As more and more people joined COG, Berg did what many other cult leaders do as part of their strategy for assuming control over their followers: he ordered new arrivals to cut off all contact with their families, give their possessions to COG, and go out into the streets and proselytize for their faith. In addition to spreading the word according to COG, they did something more alluring to the young: they sang together in public settings, and some of those drawn to COG recalled doing so because they first heard the music and couldn't help responding. When recruiting new members, COG adherents referred to the easy targets as "sheep" and to the harder ones as "wolves." The sheep were quickly steered toward Berg and his teachings, followed by COG indoctrination and a set of rules that would grow more rigid over time. He was preparing all of them for the demands that would hit one of the most vulnerable areas for many human beings: their sexuality.

Berg traveled around the country with his new "family" and soon had nearly 200 followers. He had renamed himself "Moses Berg," and his goal wasn't simply to build a membership in California but to create COG "colonies" throughout America, if not in other countries. He continued using the tool of prophecy, proclaiming that a comet was about to hit the United States and destroy everything in its path. That didn't happen either, but he kept making predictions about future disasters.

In 1970, COG returned to southern California and put together a series of communes, each one usually populated by twelve adults and their children. Berg had gone into isolation and communicated with his people through writings called "MO Letters." He referred to them as "literature" and labeled this kind of witnessing "litnessing." He sent out the letters in exchange for donations, writing more than 2,500 of them. The language and tone of his writing were dramatically changed from his earlier teachings. In one letter, "A Shepherd-Time Story," he spoke of his "happy folds" and how COG members protected small lambs that "laugh and sing and dance and play and fuck and bear lots of little lambs! And the shepherds like it!"

It was the first indication of his deeper intentions as the leader of a cult based on his views of the Christian religion. In 1984 his daughter, Deborah, would expose detailed COG secrets by saying that her father had attempted on multiple occasions to have sex with her and also had been in a sexual relationship with Deborah's sister, Faith. By the late '70s, Berg was openly advocating "raising children the natural way" and "sexual sharing" to his flock and their offspring.

"God," he wrote in a letter, "created boys and girls able to have children by about 12 years of age." Another proclaimed: "We have a sexy God and a sexy religion with a very sexy leader with an extremely sexy young following! So if you don't like sex, you better get out while you can." A photo he released showed a mother having oral sex with a young boy; another image depicted an adult woman and a toddler naked in bed, her fingers by his penis. "Well," the caption read, "they *told* us to go to bed!"

In the letters, he spelled out COG's core beliefs and guidelines, the things that he thought distinguished it from all other religious sects. First and foremost was that every Christian denomination besides COG was false. Furthermore, not just COG members or other Christians but humanity itself would one day be saved and enter the kingdom of heaven. He believed that it was good to masturbate while imagining having sex with Jesus, who, according to Berg's doctrine, had had sex with both Martha and Mary from the Gospels. COG followers were instructed to reject "the System," meaning all forms of government and all of society, which was on the verge of self-destruction. Also, Berg encouraged his followers to think of themselves as superior to those outside the cult. He wrote: "God is a racist! He has a special elite race of supermen who are going to live above all others in the Holy City, the magical, mystical, marvelous, mysterious Space City!"

COG believed in exorcisms to rid people of evil spirits and in speaking with the dead. Birth control was banished so that the group could produce more children who would become Endtime soldiers for the battles ahead. They were to rely on two sources for all faith and instruction and decision-making—the Bible and Berg's writings—but if one had to choose, Berg generally was considered the final authority. Jesus, according to Berg's teachings, had been conceived through intercourse between Mary and the angel Gabriel. At the core, COG members should be devoted to sexual exploration. "Heaven is here to stay and sex is here to stay!" he wrote. "We'll be able to enjoy many of these so-called fleshly pleasures on the other side, like Jesus did!"

With his flowing beard, ragged clothes, and vision of the End Times, Berg promoted himself as the final prophet on earth before Armageddon. The human race was facing its last war, and only the strongest, most disciplined, and most committed to Berg would survive. Because of this, he was dedicated to punishing anyone who refused to follow his commands. Stories eventually would emerge from those who left the group of COG children beaten till they were severely bruised and of Berg using a coat hanger for the job. Missing your quota of fund-raising for a single day meant no dinner that evening. Children were forced to sing outside until midnight, even in rainstorms, to raise enough money before being allowed to go to bed.

Convinced that the mass suicides at Jonestown in 1978 would give these kinds of alternative religious groups a bad name, Berg changed COG to the "Family of Love." This also was done because COG leaders' "abuses of authority" had begun leaking out to the public. To stave off more scrutiny, Berg replaced his elders, deacons, and apostles with a democratic structure, and every commune became autonomous. Before that happened, he came up with a fund-raising tactic called "flirty fishing": even if they were married, females needed to have sex with men as a way of converting them. Based on Jesus's statement "Follow Me, and I will make you fishers of men" (Matthew 4:19), women were told to go into bars, find single men or those in small packs, and become intimate with them as quickly as possible; after a successful seduction, the men would be brought into the COG fold. (Years later, when the media learned of this recruiting technique, they would refer to the women as "Hookers for Jesus.") In his 1979 annual report, Berg stated that his "FFers" (flirty fishers) had "witnessed to over a quarter of a million souls, loved over 25,000 of them, and won about 19,000 to the Lord." Untold numbers of "Jesus Babies" came from these unions until COG decided to pull back from flirty fishing because of the AIDS epidemic. "It was religious prostitution," Berg's daughter Deborah said of the FF strategy in her exposé. "I had to quit looking at the man as my father but as the leader of a worldwide movement that was destroying lives."

In addition to the FF technique, the cult was most successful when recruiting teen dropouts and those trying to escape mainstream American society. In the late 1970s, COG had more than 130 communities in places as diverse as Staten Island and Tucson, with outposts around the world. In excess of 10,000 followers were dwelling in 1,642 homes, or "communes," with four to five families per home.

Berg continued to issue prophecies, one of which was that a comet would ram into the United States and destroy all life. To plan for this, he organized the "Great Escape," motivating a number of followers to resettle in various European countries, India, South America, and Australia. The comet never arrived, and a number of his other prophecies failed to come true: a mid-1980s War of Armageddon, with America and Israel vanquished by the USSR; an Egyptian socialist becoming the country's dictator in 1986; and in 1993 the return of Jesus Christ to earth, at which point all the saved would ascend to heaven as Christ ruled the planet for the next 1,000 years with the ongoing help of the Family of Love. The false warnings did not keep the cult from expanding. But as it grew, so did the number of those who escaped from it and who were starting to reveal its inner workings and secrets.

One who eventually came forward was Ricky Rodriguez, born in 1975 to one of Berg's wives. Renaming him "Davidito," Berg had proclaimed him the sect's next leader. In early childhood, Rodriguez had witnessed those around him having sex and had had his genitals fondled. These kinds of activities were described and illustrated in *The Davidito Book,* which Berg published as a guide for raising children. He encouraged young boys to explore their sexuality freely, although some would later say they were coerced into doing what Berg wanted.

In 2000, Rodriguez escaped from the cult, and on January 8, 2005, he made a recording in which he said, "There's this need that I have. It's not a want. It's a need for revenge. It's a need for justice, because I can't go on like this." The next night, according to the authorities who later investigated Rodriguez's actions, he went the apartment of Angela Smith, one of his former nannies, and stabbed her to death. Then he drove to Blythe, California, and killed himself with a single gunshot to the head.

As youngsters, celebrity actors such as Oscar-winner Joaquin Phoenix, River Phoenix, and Rose McGowan were all part of Berg's cult. McGowan lived until age ten in Italy, where her father headed a Children of God chapter. The family of Fleetwood Mac guitarist Jeremy Spencer also had associations with the group. In 1991, River Phoenix told *Details* magazine that he was four when he initially had sex at COG. On Halloween 1993, River died of a drug overdose at age twenty-three.

Years later, Joaquin Phoenix told *Entertainment Online* about the ease with which people can be manipulated into joining a cult: "I think my parents thought they'd found a community that shared their ideals. Cults rarely advertise themselves as such. It's usually someone saying, 'We're like-minded people. This is a community,' but I think the moment my parents realized there was something more to it, they got out."

The BBC would report that former COG member Verity Carter had alleged that she was abused from age four by her father and other

YOUTHFUL MEMBERS OF THE "CHILDREN OF GOD" SING BEFORE SITTING DOWN FOR LUNCH, FEBRUARY 2, 1971.

cult members. In February 2018, Alexander Watt was convicted after admitting to four charges of sexually abusing Carter and another child on the east coast of Scotland in the 1980s. She also said she was repeatedly whipped and beaten for small transgressions such as bed wetting. Others inside the cult said that this infraction could lead to a child being thrown out of a window.

The kids' routines rarely changed, with days starting at 7 a.m., when they were ordered to pray on their knees. After breakfast and more prayer, they were sent out in the streets to beg, their only contact with outsiders. Afternoons were devoted to exercise in preparation for serving as one of God's army when the world ended. When Verity reached fifteen, feeling that death was preferable to staying in COG, she was able to escape the cult and live on her own despite suffering from substance abuse and thoughts of suicide.

As the 1980s unfolded, bad publicity caused Berg and his organization to attempt to change the Family of Love's image. By 1989, it stated publicly that any sexual activity involving minors was strictly forbidden and would lead to excommunication. As Berg neared death after having fled to Portugal to avoid being investigated further, the Family of Love made a concerted effort to separate itself from his sexual commands so that it would be seen as a legitimate religious sect. It launched a marketing campaign, and during the 1992 Christmas season several of its young members sang for Barbara Bush at the White House. That wasn't enough to stop impending allegations that some of the households were engaging in illicit sexual behavior involving children.

In 1993, CNN talk show host Larry King asked ex-COG member Ricky Dupuy how he became aware that those practices existed inside the cult. "Because," Dupuy replied, "I was ordered in the group to have sex with a ten-year-old by the leadership of the group."

"Did you?" King asked.

"Yes. It was to get me in so deep that I would be afraid to ever come out and speak against the group."

After Berg's death at age seventy-five in 1994, his widow, Karen Zerby, along with her new husband, Steve Kelly, took over. In time they made a concerted effort to change the direction and image of the group. They called that change "the Reboot," and it brought forth an entirely new set of possibilities. In February 2009, they overturned a number of Berg's previous prophecies by announcing that the world would not be ending after all, at least for a while, and so their followers could relax and begin to enjoy a life with a future. Many of the younger members had never lived with this thought. Those in the organization no longer had to live in communes or commit themselves 100 percent to serving the group. They were now free to send their children to conventional schools, hold regular jobs, and have relationships with those outside the cult, an activity that had been anathema. Not everyone was happy with the new rules, as they seemed to undercut what Berg had created and stood for. Overall, the Reboot seemed effective for preserving COG.

Despite the arrest of some of its leaders on child sex-abuse charges over the last three decades—including in Mexico and the United Kingdom—the organization, now known as Family International, still claims to have more than 2,500 members in eighty countries. It branded itself as having wholesome family values while acknowledging that some of its previous followers had misinterpreted the church's original teachings. Parts of David Berg's writings do not, Family International assures the public, reflect their policies and beliefs and should not reflect poorly on the current leaders. The predicted disasters of the apocalypse didn't come to punish those left behind except for the ones ensnared in the projections of a sex-crazed despot.

16

BOB MATHEWS AND
THE ORDER

At 9 p.m. on June 18, 1984, Alan Berg and his ex-wife, Judith, were driving back to his Denver condo from dinner in the suburbs. Berg was by far the most controversial radio talk show host the city had ever seen but also the most beloved in some ways. He liked to say on the air that he was addicted to certain things—cigarettes, coffee, and, in his past, alcohol—and he knew how to addict people to his program. He had won the award for being the "most disliked" and "most liked" local media personality in the same year. Funny, outrageous, irreverent, and confrontational, he would take on any subject, starting with religion and racism, two hot-button topics that never went out of style. After bouncing around several smaller Denver stations, he had landed a gig at KOA, the flagship radio outlet not just for Colorado but for the Rocky Mountain West. At night people could pick up Berg's program in Los Angeles, his scratchy voice reaching tens of thousands of listeners and callers.

As he pulled up in front of his town house and left the engine of his Volkswagen Beetle running, Berg and Judith did what they had been doing for decades—try to make a decision about their relationship, discussing whether she should come in and spend the night with him. For five minutes they went back and forth, kicking around the pros and cons, before he put the car in gear and drove her across town to her car at a shopping mall's parking lot. He then headed back home, lighting one more cigarette as he parked in his driveway and turned off the engine.

As the tall, very lean, well-dressed, and heavily bearded Berg stepped from the vehicle, a dozen bullets hit him in the face and the torso. Sprayed from a semiautomatic Ingram MAC-10 machine pistol, they killed him instantly. A passerby soon found him in a pool of blood, and word went out over Denver and national media: controversial Alan Berg had been murdered at his address in what was being framed as the first assassination of an American broadcaster. In another part of the city, Judith arrived at the house where she was staying that night and saw her hosts watching a breaking news report. She looked on in horror and shock at the repeatedly played images of her former husband lying dead on the pavement in front of his residence. If she had decided to go into the town house with him, she realized, she too would be dead.

Denver law enforcement immediately opened a homicide investigation, operating on the assumption that Berg had finally angered the wrong person on the radio, enraging some individual to the point of violence. Not long after the murder, a reporter asked one of the head detectives if he had any leads on the killer.

The officer nodded at the Denver phone book on his desk. "Everyone in there is a suspect," he said. "Berg pissed off a lot of people."

Four months to the day after the shooting—October 18, 1984—police raided the home of Gary Yarbrough of Sandpoint, Idaho. The initial murder investigation had expanded far beyond Denver and Colorado because other crimes had been happening throughout the West—robbery, counterfeiting, another murder or two, and the heist of a Brink's truck near Ukiah, California. Various police departments and federal agents were spread over the United States, looking not for one perpetrator but for a group of them in what had become the largest probe into domestic terrorism in American history.

During the search of Yarbrough's premises, officers went upstairs to an opening that led to a small space and opened the door. They were startled by what was facing them: a shrine to Adolf Hitler surrounded by black crepe paper and candles. Moving farther inside, they found neo-Nazi literature, multiple weapons, hand grenades, 100 sticks of dynamite, 110 blasting caps, 6,000 rounds of ammunition, police scanners, and a semiautomatic Ingram MAC-10 with a silencer. After sending it in for ballistics testing, they soon were able to prove that it was the gun that had killed Alan Berg.

They took Yarbrough into custody, a victory for the feds, although the man they were most intent on catching was not Yarbrough but the one who had masterminded the group and the crimes it had been committing over the last year. He was a short, dark-haired, dark-eyed dynamic figure named Bob Mathews, the leader of a cadre called The Order that in the fall of 1983 had come into being as a handful of men stood in the woods in the Northwest and pledged their undying loyalty to one another and their cause. They believed it was time to stop talking about a white-power revolution and the cleansing of the United States of all their enemies—African Americans, feminists, Jews, other minorities, gays, liberal judges, and the like—and take action. It was time for what people on the radical right called "the propaganda of the deed"—to put down the books and the speeches and pick up guns and shoot at selected people. They would start with that talk show host down in Denver who had been taking on racists on his program for years. Silencing him would be the first step in unleashing their armed rebellion. Once their leader had commanded the action, the deed was soon done, and the photo of Berg sprawled out dead by his Volkswagen became one of the iconic pictures of the far right and a source of propaganda for decades to come.

Born in Marfa, Texas, on January 16, 1953, Robert Jay Mathews was the youngest of three boys born to Johnny and Una Mathews. The family was highly respected and held important jobs in the community. Bob's father, of Scottish descent, became the mayor of Marfa, the president of the Chamber of Commerce, and a Methodist church official. Una was the den mother of the local Cub Scout troop. As a child, Bob showed no particular passions until he was old enough to start reading about history and politics after the family had moved to Phoenix. Something in his studies compelled him—at only eleven—to join the far-right John Birch Society, which advocated small government and was fiercely anti-communist. The youngster had extreme views on the Soviets, but he was even more engaged with the issue of race. He had always wanted to have lighter skin than he did and was very sensitive about its color. Any suggestion that he was something other than Anglo annoyed him, and as he got older, the annoyance hardened into anger and then rage.

In high school, he was baptized into the Church of Jesus Christ of Latter-day Saints and began recruiting young Mormon men into his militia group, the Sons of Liberty. He realized that he could motivate others to rally around his beliefs and organize them into a group. He could give fiery speeches that people responded to, and he wasn't afraid to cross the line into criminal behavior. When he got involved in the tax resistance movement, he filled out an employer's Form W-4 and claimed ten dependents, leading to his arrest for tax fraud. After serving six months of probation, he had grown tired of leading the Sons of Liberty and was ready for something new. In 1974, he resettled in Metaline Falls,

Washington, where he and his father purchased sixty wooded acres to build a home. Two years after arriving in Metaline Falls, he married Debbie McGarity, raised Scottish Galloway cattle, and tried to live a normal life but couldn't suppress his deeper impulses and inevitably was drawn to an organization one state to the east.

The Aryan Nations compound in northern Idaho was surrounded by a chain-link fence and held a watchtower, armed guards, a rifle range, German shepherds, and Doberman pinschers. On a wooden shed two words were boldly painted in red and blue letters: "Whites Only." The group's world headquarters, twenty acres near the Coeur d'Alene National Forest, was known by its inhabitants as the "Heavenly Reich." Others called it "God's Country," with its stunning hills, towering evergreens, and pristine lakes, the beauty of the landscape standing in sharp contrast to the brutality of the beliefs expressed inside the compound. Aryan Nations was just outside Hayden Lake in Kootenai County. The town had 60,000 inhabitants, only 50 of whom were Jewish and 20 of whom were African American—exactly the kind of demographic Mathews was looking for.

Inside the compound, Reverend Richard Butler preached Christian Identity, which contended that Jews were not the Chosen People of the Old Testament but wicked impostors born from the coupling of Eve and Satan. The real Chosen People, Butler thundered from his pulpit on Sunday mornings, were just like him: Anglo-Saxons and Scandinavians from England, Ireland, Scotland, Germany, Sweden, Norway, and the United States. African Americans were subhuman "mud people," and the mixing of the races was the essence of evil. At the Aryan Nations school, children were taught the four "R's": readin', 'ritin', 'rithmetic, and race.

When the sun went down, Butler's troops gathered in the darkness and, shoulder to shoulder, burned large crosses, sending flames high into the night sky. They chanted slogans, with loaded guns in their hands and mounting violence in their words. They railed against the "other"—the black other, the Jewish other, the Hispanic other, the Asian other, and the Caucasian other who did not accept their views. They mailed Aryan Nations literature to white inmates in jails across the nation, recruiting among the poor and the incarcerated as well as disgruntled veterans of the Vietnam War. After being released, some of the prisoners came north to visit the man behind the pamphlets.

Butler brought in David Lane from Denver, who had argued about race on the radio with Alan Berg. He also brought in Bruce Pierce from Kentucky, an emotionally troubled volatile high school dropout who came to Aryan Nations looking for political guidance and a spiritual teacher. Then he brought in Bob Mathews, who shared the beliefs of the others but was different from the rest. He was beyond weary of all the theories and windy speeches about white power and Christian Identity, about how someday things would change. He believed that day had arrived.

Everyone assembled at the Aryan Nations compound had one thing in common: a book they had been studying for the last few years. Published in 1978, *The Turner Diaries* had been written by William Pierce, a physicist who had begun his career at the Los Alamos National Laboratory in New Mexico. In the 1960s, he became a professor at the University of Oregon before going to work for George Lincoln Rockwell, the head of the American Nazi Party. *The Turner Diaries* sold 350,000 copies, quickly establishing itself as *the* classic of hate fiction and fantasy. Other racist organizations, such as the Ku Klux Klan and Posse Comitatus, had been around a long time, supporting white nationalism, opposition to immigration, and occasional outbursts of violence against African Americans. They were antiminority but generally advocated the separation of the races, not the extermination of people who were not of their ethnic background. *The Turner Diaries* made no attempt to disguise its true purpose and intention.

In the novel, a handful of white men, led by Earl Turner, form a hard-core group of revolutionaries called The Order who make a commitment to one another to change the ethnic face of America. They don't merely talk about race wars and getting rid of nonwhites, feminists, gays, and liberal judges—they act on their convictions. They begin executing their enemies, and on the infamous "Day of the Rope," they kill 60 million of their fellow citizens before their goal is achieved and their victory is complete.

While William Pierce had written and Richard Butler had preached for years about returning the United States to some imagined "purified state," Butler in particular didn't want anyone breaking the law on his property. Inside the compound, he was quick to remind outsiders that he was merely exercising his right to free speech and practicing the religion of his choice, both of which were protected under the First Amendment of the Constitution. Chanting anti-Semitic slogans in the dark and shooting at six-pointed stars was one thing; actually killing someone was something else. It wasn't his fault, he said, that a decade after his arrival in Idaho, the state's human rights commission reported that racial harassment cases during the last three years had increased by 550 percent. He wasn't responsible for those painted swastikas showing up in Kootenai County or that anti-Semitic slogan at a Hayden Lake restaurant owned by sixty-two-year-old Sid Rosen. Butler wasn't to blame when Connie Fort, a local white woman married to a black man, got hate mail and death threats.

The young white supremacists who gathered around Butler had plenty of fervor and racial hatred, but they lacked two things: organization and a leader. Bob Mathews didn't care about skirting legal issues and wasn't concerned about taking risks. He had worked in a mine and elsewhere as a laborer and saw no future there. There had to be easier ways to get hold of cash that could be used to start a revolt, and he knew how to motivate others to get it. One thing virtually all cult leaders can be defined by is their ability to make those who had never engaged in serious criminal behavior do so at their command. They will follow wherever the leader goes, whether that leads to prison or to a graveyard. Mathews had conceived an idea so bold and outlandish that no one dared to think that it might actually be put into action: Why couldn't his small band of men bring *The Turner Diaries* to life and turn the fictional Order's plan for cleaning up America into a reality?

In September 1983, at a makeshift barracks he had built on his land in Metaline, he and eight others founded their own Order. This included a neighbor, Ken Loff, and associates from Aryan Nations and the National Alliance: Randy Duey, Dan Bauer, Bruce Pierce, Denver Parmenter, Richard Kemp, Bill Soderquist, and David Lane, who had quarreled with Alan Berg about race on the radio. Mathews had grandiose plans for their future, but first they had to raise money for the cause. Using *The Turner Diaries* as their blueprint, they robbed an adult bookstore in Spokane, leaving with $369.10. They counterfeited $50 bills and hit a bank north of Seattle, netting around $26,000. More robberies generated $43,000, with some of the stolen money going to North Carolina's White Patriot Party and other white nationalist groups. The core members of The Order called themselves the Silent Brotherhood— *Brüder Schweigen* was how they said it to each other in German. They swore eternal loyalty to the group and vowed that they would choose death over revealing its innermost secrets and crimes.

With *The Turner Diaries* as their model, they put together a list of assassination targets. One was TV producer Norman Lear (*All in the Family, The Jeffersons*) and another was former secretary of state Henry Kissinger, but they decided to start with someone whose profile was not that high nationally. It would be a sort of test run for murders later on and for building up to their own Day of the Rope, when they would wipe out more of the population. As they searched for their initial target, David Lane told them about a Denver talk show host who was always calling out people with The Order's views, putting them down, and trying to make them look bad to his audience. Lane had tangled with him and held a festering grudge. Why not start there? They had met a woman in Wyoming, Jean Craig, who could travel to Denver and conduct surveillance on where Berg lived and worked, his daily schedule, and when he would be most vulnerable to attack. Craig undertook the mission and reported back to Mathews: Berg tended to eat out at night and return home around nine, and the street he lived on was relatively quiet and dark. His pattern was to pull into the small driveway in front of his town house and walk the few steps to his door. That would be the best time to strike.

In mid-June, Mathews, Lane, Pierce, and a fourth Order member, Richard Scutari, rode into Denver on the evening of the eighteenth and parked near Berg's address. Although Mathews had set the game plan for this and future crimes, he didn't get out of the car and approach Berg himself. Like Richard Butler before him, he wouldn't pull the trigger on the chosen target. For that, he used Bruce Pierce, who had not only a visceral hatred of minorities but a history of mental instability. In the coming years, that dynamic would play itself out over and again in murders undertaken for political reasons. Our culture eventually developed a name for what Mathews had done with Pierce: "trolling for assassins."

Pierce advanced and opened fire on Berg, who died with a lit cigarette between his fingers. The men fled and the next morning made a point of getting that day's newspapers to read the headlines about the murder of the talk show host. They believed they really had done something to start a white-power revolution, just as William Pierce had prescribed in *The Turner Diaries*. Bigger plans loomed, but they needed more money and looked around for a huge score.

About a month after the gunning down of the talk show host, a dozen men carried out a successful robbery of a Brink's truck outside Ukiah, California, stealing more than $3,600,000. The operation had gone smoothly, but at the end Mathews had dropped a handgun on the floor of the truck and forgotten to retrieve it. The authorities took the gun into evidence and began tracing it back to a member of The Order. It was their first break in connecting a series of crimes that had occurred over the western United States in the last few months. That led them toward the Aryan Nations compound. Butler denied any involvement in those activities, but the investigation was spreading far beyond northern Idaho.

Nineteen eighty-four, the year made famous by George Orwell's novel, turned out to be the year of The Order. Its members, a score of men and one woman, would commit 240 crimes, counterfeit untold thousands of dollars, steal more than $4 million, kill five people, and force the federal government to launch a vast probe into domestic terrorism. A handful of racists under the guidance of one man who had set out to kill individuals and undermine democracy would unleash nationwide destruction.

The revolution was succeeding until another recruit, Tom Martinez, was busted for passing The Order's counterfeit currency in the Philadelphia area. Taken into custody, he chose not to be quiet as the Silent Brotherhood had promised one another they would be, but to talk. He told the FBI about the group's crimes and Bob Mathews, and the feds closed in on the leader during a massive manhunt. Martinez's betrayals, along with Mathews's loss of the gun in the Ukiah robbery, were enough to help government agents understand that they were chasing a cadre of white-power terrorists. Their investigation led them to Sandpoint, Idaho, and the home of Gary Yarbrough. That in turn led them to his shrine to Adolf Hitler and the gun that had murdered Alan Berg. The Order soon split up and went on the run.

After a shootout in Portland in which he suffered a hand wound, Mathews fled to a safe house on Whidbey Island, north of Seattle. From there, the thirty-one-year-old wrote a lengthy screed declaring war on the United States and trying to rationalize The Order's crimes. He explained why he had "quit being the hunted and become the hunter," ending with "I am not going into hiding, rather I will press the FBI and let them know what it is like to become the hunted. Doing so it is only logical to assume that my days on this planet are rapidly drawing to a close. Even so, I have no fear. For the reality of my life is death, and the worst the enemy can do to me is shorten my tour of duty in this world. I will leave knowing that I have made the ultimate sacrifice to ensure the future of my children."

The American government had trailed Mathews to the safe house. Surrounded by federal agents, he remained defiant, armed, and dangerous. On December 8, 1984, after repeated attempts by the feds to make him surrender, he stopped talking and picked up a gun. The FBI lobbed scores of smoke grenades and a stun grenade into the residence, but Mathews put on a gas mask and began shooting. When agents tried to enter the property, he held them off. That night, as a helicopter flew overhead, he attempted to bring it down from an upstairs window. From the helicopter, the FBI dropped three M79 Starburst flares into the house, detonating a box of hand grenades and other ammunition. For as long as he could, Mathews continued firing an assault rifle at the agents while the house around him burned. This went on and on, with the trapped man firing off more than 100 rounds without hitting anyone. Then silence settled over the residence and the gunfire ended.

When the flames were extinguished, agents went into the residence and saw the charred remains of a body on the floor, a pistol gripped in its hand. As the feds reported the killing of The Order's leader, rumors immediately started to spread on the far right that Mathews wasn't really dead but had escaped from the house and was on the lam in the northwestern woods or some other locale. His cohorts were hiding him, having sworn to keep him alive to spur the revolution onward. However, dental records proved otherwise, showing that the body inside the house was indeed that of Bob Mathews, burned beyond facial recognition but not beyond identification through these records. Mathews had died not from bullets but from smoke inhalation and burns. His family retrieved his remains and cremated them, scattering his ashes on his land in Metaline Falls.

The FBI's search for those still on the run intensified. David Lane was arrested in Winston-Salem, North Carolina, and Bruce Pierce was taken into custody in Rossville, Georgia, after leading agents from one end of the country to the other. All the surviving Order members were soon rounded up and pressured to talk about their criminal spree. Roughly half of them broke their code of silence by agreeing to cooperate with the government and testify against the other half in a federal trial that opened in Seattle in September 1985. The defendants were not prosecuted for specific offenses but under the 1970 Racketeer Influenced and Corrupt Organizations (RICO) Act, which was designed originally to fight organized crime.

Despite having railed against the government for the last few years and attacked its institutions and agents, the defendants all were provided

FBI AGENTS SIFT THROUGH DEBRIS OF A HOME THAT BURNED TO THE GROUND ON WHIDBEY ISLAND, NORTH OF SEATTLE, WASHINGTON, AFTER A THIRTY-FIVE-HOUR STANDOFF WITH NEO-NAZI ROBERT J. MATHEWS IN DECEMBER 1984.

with able counsel free of charge. Each was found guilty and given a lengthy sentence, some running to forty and sixty years. Other legal proceedings followed. In all there were eight trials, with more than seventy-five people convicted of crimes connected to The Order, including civil rights violations, robbery, conspiracy, transporting stolen money, and murder.

The story of The Order did not end with Mathews's death and the sentencing of the defendants, and has not yet ended today. The Order had functioned mostly in isolation from other racist organizations, afraid even to use the phone. What they talked and dreamed about in the mid-1980s was that one day in the not-too-distant future, they would have access to personal computers that could link all the white nationalists together not just across the country but around the world; they would trade information and plot more terrorist actions while staying anonymous online. The Order never saw this development, but those who came after it to carry on Mathews's vision would.

The Turner Diaries had an ongoing life as well. A young man who had been a veteran of the Gulf War, Timothy McVeigh, had read the book and sold it at gun shows around the Midwest. He was already strongly antigovernment, but his convictions took a more serious turn after the 1993 siege at David Koresh's Branch Davidian compound in Waco, Texas, which had left eighty dead, including Koresh and numerous children (see Chapter 14). McVeigh wanted to launch his own revolution and focused on the part in *The Turner Diaries* about The Order building a bomb for use at a federal location and detonating it at nine in the morning. On April 19, 1995, two years to the day after Koresh and the others perished at Waco, McVeigh set off a truckload of explosives in front of the Alfred P. Murrah Federal Building in Oklahoma City, leaving 168 dead. A photocopied segment of William Pierce's book was found in the vehicle McVeigh had driven to the site of the devastation. Facing more than 160 state offenses and 11 federal ones, he was convicted in 1997 in Denver on all counts and sentenced to death. Like Mathews, McVeigh had been willing to trade his life for his beliefs. Four years later he was executed by lethal injection in Terre Haute, Indiana.

By then, white nationalists everywhere were connected through the Internet. They had their own websites, hate music, and writings. They shared information about bombing bridges and igniting gas in urban sewers to bring a major city to a halt. They had what Mathews had envisioned: an electronic network for spewing bigotry, seeking new members, and plotting violence. High-tech rage and racist propaganda had arrived. All they needed was something to set them aflame.

The early November night in 2008 when President Barack Obama was elected to the Oval Office as America's first African-American chief executive, far-right computer networks blew up with fear, anger, and paranoia until they crashed. White nationalists would use Obama's rise to power to find recruits online to join the movement and take part in whatever was being planned.

In February 2009, as the Obamas settled into the White House, the Southern Poverty Law Center in Montgomery, Alabama, issued its latest *Intelligence Report*, detailing the growth of hate groups in the United States. Since 2000, the numbers had surged by more than 50 percent and were increasing once again. In 2000, there had been 602 reported hate groups. At the end of 2008, there were 926. Said Mark Potok, head of the Southern Poverty Law Center, when looking over those numbers:

"We saw seven or eight straight years of hate-group growth driven by immigration, until early 2009. With the falling economy and the rise of Obama, new issues came into play. David Duke [the white nationalist and former grand wizard of the Knights of the Ku Klux Klan, former Republican Louisiana state representative, and former presidential candidate] wrote an essay before the election, and all the racial violence starts. What we have here is a perfect storm for these hate groups to grow.

"The enemy in the White House has a black face and that brings together a lot of different aspects of the movement. They can all agree on at least one thing—the country's going to hell in a hand basket and the black guy is leading us there. The militias are back in the woods training again, carrying their guns and doing maneuvers. We've just had a whole new security makeover at our office because we're getting a lot more threats."

By 2018, hate groups operating across the United States rose to a record high of 1,020, increasing for the fourth straight year. According to FBI statistics, hate crimes had increased by 30 percent in the three-year period ending in 2017. The leaders of those groups engaged in some of the same tactics Bob Mathews had used in enlisting Bruce Pierce to kill Alan Berg: trolling for assassins among the mentally ill.

James A. Fields, Jr., never met his father, who was killed in a traffic accident caused by a drunk driver before the boy was born. Another car wreck left his mother, Samantha Bloom, paralyzed below the waist. Growing up in northern Kentucky, James was a loner who developed a fascination with Adolf Hitler and the Third Reich. In high school, he wrote a three-page paper praising Nazi ideology and the armed forces commanded by Hitler. He had hoped to join the Army but was rejected because he was schizophrenic and took antipsychotic drugs. In the eighth and ninth grades, Fields had displayed a history of violent abuse toward his disabled mother; the police were summoned to his home four times. The 911 dispatcher on one of his mother's calls wrote the following in capital letters:

> 13 YO MALE TOOK CALLER'S PHONE SMACKED
> CALLER IN THE HEAD.... IS THE SON.... PUT
> HIS HANDS OVER HER MOUTH.... ON MEDS
> TO CONTROL TEMPER.... STARTED BECAUSE
> CALLER TOLD HIM TO STOP PLAYING VIDEO
> GAMES TOLD HER THAT HE WOULD BEAT
> HER UP WAS RESTRAINING CALLER EARLIER
> SAYS SHE IS AFRAID OF HIM....

After another outburst, Fields was arrested and sent to a juvenile detention center.

By August 2017, the twenty-year-old Fields was working as a security guard in Ohio when he heard about an upcoming rally in Charlottesville, Virginia. Right-wing groups had organized the event to make a statement against the removal of a statue of Confederate General Robert E. Lee. Fields drove to Virginia in a souped-up 2010 Dodge Challenger with tinted windows and spiked wheels. Arriving on a Saturday afternoon, he located the rally and steered his vehicle toward a pedestrian mall, ramming into another car. He aimed the Dodge at the crowd and sent bodies sprawling, killing Heather Heyer, a thirty-two-year-old counterprotester, and injuring nineteen others. The white nationalists and the alt-right, as some of the groups were now called, instantly tried to dissociate themselves from Fields. In 2018, the Southern Poverty Law Center reported that those groups and their fellow travelers were connected to the murder of forty-three Americans and the injuring of sixty-seven more.

On October 27, 2018, forty-six-year-old Robert Gregory Bowers entered the Tree of Life (or L'Simcha Congregation) synagogue in Pittsburgh's Squirrel Hill neighborhood during Shabbat morning services. As they proceeded, Bowes opened fire, murdering eleven and injuring six more—the deadliest attack ever on the Jewish community in the United States. Arrested and charged with sixty-three federal crimes, Bowers pleaded not guilty. Before the attack, he had posted anti-Semitic content on the social network Gab, attacking HIAS (the Hebrew Immigrant Aid Society), which Tree of Life supported. In a reference to the current Central American immigrants trying to enter the United States on its southern border, he had written, "HIAS likes to bring invaders in that kill our people. I can't sit by and watch my people get slaughtered. Screw your optics, I'm going in."

Bowers too had struggled with emotional and mental challenges. His parents were divorced when he was a year old, and his father committed suicide at age twenty-seven, when the boy was six. He was raised by his maternal grandparents because of his mother's health problems. He dropped out of high school, becoming more and more remote except for his cyberconnections with those who shared his view of Jews and other minorities.

The white nationalist movement Bob Mathews had longed for when leading The Order took a few more decades and some new technology to arrive in America. Although it has far more members now, no one with quite his mixture of charisma and commitment to an organized violent white supremacist revolution—ridding the United States of its diversity and opportunities for people of all backgrounds, races, genders, and other inherent human differences—has replaced him. He had become a martyr to the faithful, someone who would do whatever was necessary to eliminate the enemy and rebuild America from scratch, just the way William Pierce and Earl Turner wanted it, with only white people populating the country. Mathews planted and passed on the seed of hate.

The godfather of today's radical right, he set the tone for the racist future, leaving behind many sons and a few daughters who felt as he did and proving one thing above all: a small cult of committed terrorists driven by a maniacal leader can create extreme suffering that will resonate for generations.

17

JEONG MYEONG-SEOK AND PROVIDENCE

It felt like a commune. We got up at the same time, ate together and there were people from all walks of life— smart, loving, spiritual people. I worked and gave the church money, but the group marriage ceremony at Madison Square Garden was for me the beginning of the end. My arranged marriage was supposed to expunge karma from my lineage and make this a purified relationship with one's spouse. After a while, I realized I didn't want to be married to the woman they'd arranged for me and

*then met another woman and broke my vows. I began to
think that the Reverend Sun Myung Moon was a meg-
alomaniac, especially when we had to sit through these
four-hour speeches in which he railed on and on about
morals. . . .*

—James Townsend, on the Unification Church

History has seen good cults and bad ones, plus a few in between. Some
people think of the Reverend Sun Myung Moon's "Moonies" as a cult
but one that, according to many of its members and ex-members, tried
to accomplish beneficial things. In the process of doing so, it spun off a
bastard son in South Korea who attempted to imitate many of its ideas,
but not with the same intentions.

Only later in life, after proclaiming himself the Messiah, did Jeong
Myeong-seok (sometimes Jung Myung Seak) say that his birthplace,
Wolmyeong-dong in South Chungcheong Province in South Korea, was
sacred. By then it had become very important to him that his background
appear special. He was born into poverty on March 16, 1945, the third of
his family's seven children, and from an early age he sought to rise above
his upbringing. In the late 1940s, his village had not yet been exposed to
the Gospels, but that changed when he went to a Christian elementary
school and began to accept Jesus as his savior. Missionaries handed out
free Bibles to every household in Wolmyeong-dong, and Jeong started
reading the Scriptures. He was soon praying not just for salvation but for
Jesus to help him escape his meager circumstances and find a rewarding
path forward.

As a teenager he joined the Unification Church and embraced the
teachings of Reverend Sun Myung Moon, at least for a while. However,
he chafed at the church's policy of arranged marriage. Jeong wanted to
be free to choose his own wife (or perhaps more than one wife). That

impulse seemed innocent enough in the beginning and became the motivation for his next move. Once again, as in many cults, sex and religion were about to collide and leave victims everywhere.

In 1978, Jeong broke away from the Unification Church and founded a sect called Providence, which he sometimes referred to as Jesus Morning Star (JMS are Jeong's initials) or the Christian Gospel Mission or the Bright Moon Church. He had a knack for generating business and used it. Providence was successful and pulled him out of poverty, quickly spreading across South Korea, with 240 branches in that country alone. It would eventually claim to have 100,000 to 150,000 members in 300 affiliated churches in the United States, Australia, Germany, the United Kingdom, South Africa, Taiwan, and Japan. Jeong had taken some of the Reverend Moon's concepts while developing his own set of teachings based on thirty core lessons and principles. One was that 2,000 years ago, when Jesus was crucified, his message and work were left unfinished; therefore, the modern world demanded not just a new interpretation of the Gospel but a new "Lord" to go along with it.

Another of Jeong's principles was that only a contemporary messiah could lead people into heaven. To attain membership in Providence, one had to affirm that Jeong had special powers and was in fact that new messiah. A third principle required that his followers accept the idea that he would rule them through inspired revelation. Those divine revelations allowed him to give new meaning to terms such as "resurrection" and "born again" as well as novel reinterpretations of biblical passages. As the Messiah, only Jeong could receive "Jesus's spirit, power, mission and heart."

When laying out his principles, Jeong hoped that his new church would be affiliated with the Methodist branch of Christianity, but the more the Methodists learned about Jeong's beliefs and practices, the more unsettled they were, and they backed away and expelled him from their religion. Their instincts would prove to be sound.

From the start, Jeong knew who he wanted in his congregation. He placed emphasis not just on bringing women into the flock but on recruiting young and attractive ones, the taller the better. Those within Providence were sent out to hunt for good-looking women, often locating them on college campuses and in shopping centers, where they were given a welcoming talk and asked to consider joining. The sect sold new followers on what it openly called "heavenly deception"—offering potential recruits sports programs, Bible study sessions, or modeling jobs to draw them in. Sometimes they lured people with the promise of watching a performance of tae kwon do, the traditional Korean martial art. Things soon turned sexually abusive for the women. Female members were instructed that they were now God's—and by extension Jeong's—spiritual brides and that he could have as many as he wanted.

As with other budding cults, this one insisted that new followers cut their ties with family and friends while living on communal property with other sect members, all of whom were under the sway of Jeong's teachings. Some JMS events involved sleep deprivation designed to wear down the participants and undermine their critical thinking skills. If they managed to fall asleep, they were subjected to 4 a.m. church services and weekend ones that might go on all day or all night. These were effective cult strategies but were legal. However, Providence began veering toward criminal behavior when stories leaked out about JMS and its leader placing more and more emphasis on sex and complete submission to Jeong's salacious desires.

For women to achieve "purification," Jeong maintained, they needed to have intercourse with their messiah. The Taiwan media started to investigate and criticize Providence as Jeong came under more pressure. In 1999, he fled South Korea for Hong Kong amid rape accusations from a variety of women and rumors that he had molested scores of Taiwanese college students. Two years later, the Korean government charged him with sexual assault, but none of this altered his behavior. According to the Japanese newspaper *Asahi Shimbun,* more than 100 women said they had been sexually abused by Jeong during his "religious purification" rituals. In Hong Kong, when South Korean women came to visit him, he raped them.

EXODUS, a South Korean (and later international) nongovernmental organization that rescues men, women, and children from sexual enslavement, stepped in to help the victims and held a press conference on the spread of Jeong's influence and alleged crimes. In 2003, he fled again, this time to mainland China, with both EXODUS and Interpol (an international police organization headquartered in Lyon, France, that coordinates police cooperation around the world) in pursuit. At that time Jeong was believed to be holed up in one of his four lavish homes in Anshan in the Chinese province of Liaoning. His minions were both protecting him and trying to find more women for his pleasure.

Tarnished by bad publicity and the widening search for its fugitive leader, Providence tried to prop up its faltering image by posting counterstories about the sect on its website:

"God's purpose of creating human beings is so that we can live loving God as our Bridegroom, our Counterpart of love. . . .

"Despite being born in a time of great poverty in South Korea, Pastor Jung Myung Seok developed a profound love for the Lord, starting an ascetic life of prayer from young. Through deep prayers, he came to learn the deep profound Word from the Lord and realized the grief of God's unfulfilled love towards all of mankind. He preaches the message of loving the Holy Trinity like a bridegroom as the top priority of one's life and loving other lives with the same heart as God."

By that point, the outside world was immune to such propaganda and the authorities continued to close in on Jeong.

In 2003, the Australian Peter Daley came to South Korea to teach English at Keimyung University. He heard about Providence and began a secret probe into the sect. He was invited to an event at the cult compound when Jeong was no longer there but others were operating much as before. What Daley witnessed led him to conclude that Jeong was "a serial rapist" after he found videos in which four or five naked women were dancing and chanting "Seonsaengnim [teacher], we love you!" Another video showed a woman licking a picture of Jeong and then placing it near her genitals. Daley created a website to expose Jeong and his followers, an effort that would cause the English professor to be harassed and taken to court by the sect.

"If you look at all their [JMS] events and all their propaganda and material through the lens of a serial rapist," Daley told SBS, Australia's multicultural and multilingual broadcast outlet, "it all makes sense. When I first heard about them in Australia, it was quite a shock because I encountered them on this mountain in the middle of South Korea, it was just so far removed from my experience of growing up in Australia . . . they seemed like galaxies apart."

While in hiding, Jeong continued his sexual predation as the police kept up their pursuit. In April 2006, four South Korean women publicly accused him of rape; for their media announcement, they cried and wore sunglasses, hats, and masks over their mouths to cover their faces and conceal their identities, as they feared retaliation. The former leader of EXODUS, Gim Du-hyeong, spoke about tracking Jeong Myeong-seok through various countries over the years, always one step behind. Gim explained how Jeong used the idea of "salvation through intercourse" to rape women in Korea, Taiwan, Malaysia, Japan, and Hong Kong. Gim said that based on anecdotal evidence, Jeong had lately had group sex with more than fifty women who had been taken in by his ruse of watching tae kwon do. One woman, according to Gim, had been badly injured during the orgy. Jeong's actions had become so egregious that they had spawned a new organization to help find him and assist those trying to get away from the sect.

In May 2007, Jeong was arrested in northeast China and returned to South Korea. His trial began in February 2008, with former sect members revealing how attractive young women who had been given to Jeong as "gifts" were forced into having intercourse with him. During the trial, Jeong steadfastly maintained that he had done nothing wrong in the practice of his religion, but there was too much evidence suggesting otherwise. The sixty-three-year-old was found guilty and sentenced to six years for molestation and rape. Not many were satisfied with that outcome.

In the aftermath of the verdict, an official with the Seoul district court said, "We expect both sides to appeal." He meant that the prosecution probably would ask for a longer sentence and the defense would seek to overturn the conviction. His prediction was accurate. In April 2009, the supreme court of South Korea extended Jeong's sentence by four years, giving him a full decade in prison.

Behind bars, Jeong stayed in contact with his flock, asking female sect members and new female recruits to send him pictures of themselves dressed in bridal wear. Some complied.

An ex-JMS member known only as "Liz" appeared on Australia's SBS to talk about how she had been recruited by Providence and her state of mind when it had come into her life. Her words could have been spoken by countless others who had almost unconsciously fallen into an involvement with cults: "At times I felt suicidal, at times I felt completely just like road kill, I guess, just run over, used by someone else for their own purposes and then just cast aside."

In 2011, she had been shopping in Australia's Canberra Centre when a Korean woman approached her and asked if she would fill out a survey. "I didn't think I was joining anything," Liz said. "They said they were doing a Christian art show and so they emailed me some pictures and it looked wonderful, it looked awesome, so I said I'd meet up with them and chat with them about maybe participating."

She was soon a new recruit, praying to images of both Jesus and Jeong and wearing a necklace as a symbol of devotion to the founder. After Jeong's arrest, she said, sect members were at pains to describe how this had happened. They "told us that he was in prison because . . . he was being persecuted and falsely accused. They said we are in the position of brides towards God and we are also in the position of brides towards Jeong, the leader, because he represents God."

Liz was encouraged to write intimate letters to the imprisoned leader, and she did. He wrote her back, and on the air she said, "He would say things like, 'Women are much more beautiful when they are naked' and he said my white skin arouses him."

She told Reuters News Service about her trips to see Jeong after his arrest: "We got a fifteen-minute visit with him. He knew me by name when I stepped into the room, so he had obviously seen my photos and he told me through letters that he would stroke our photos on the wall of his cell."

Then Cult Information and Family Support, another group helping people escape from the sect, came onto the scene. It had been founded by Ros Hodgkins after her daughter was ensnared in a cult and she wanted to learn more about how these organizations function and draw unsuspecting people into their religious practices. In 2013, the parents of two young women reached out to her, distressed over their daughters joining

JMS. Hodgkins looked into the sect and attended one of its Bible studies, shocked at what she was seeing and hearing.

Hodgkins has interviewed hundreds of people who have left cults, and in media interviews she has said one thing that resonates through all the investigations into cults conducted by law enforcement, civilian groups, and the general public. It can stand as a statement for the entire cult phenomenon and a warning to those who may still be trying to get loved ones out of danger engendered by false promises, criminal leaders, and the allure of finding a different and more glorious life by letting others take control of one's own.

The biggest misconception that people have about cults, Hodgkins has said, is that "some crazy people" get into them. Over recent decades, so have a lot of seemingly normal or formerly normal people who were searching for something to lead them toward a better and more fulfilling existence. Wasn't that what Jeong was doing as a boy in Wolmyeongdong and when he left the church of the Reverend Sun Myung Moon to start his own congregation?

There's an ongoing historical debate over whether P. T. Barnum was the first to say "There's a sucker born every minute," but not much debate over the accuracy of the saying.

18

WARREN JEFFS
AND THE FLDS

In the 1890s, the leaders of the Utah Territory wanted to become an American state, but the U.S. government forbade that unless they would meet one simple condition: give up the practice of polygamy, which had begun with the founder of the Mormon religion, Joseph Smith, in the 1830s. In 1844, Smith was arrested in Nauvoo, Illinois, and an enraged mob—200 men with their faces painted black—stormed the jail and murdered him for his polygamist beliefs and practices. Another strong leader, Brigham Young, emerged as the next head of the Church of Jesus Christ of Latter-day Saints, and he too lived out the "sacred principle," marrying as many as fifty women. To get farther away from America's established order, Young and his followers marched across the Midwest in wintertime, on foot and in covered wagons, with many dying along the way, until they reached the Great Salt Lake. No sooner had the Mormons resettled in the West than the U.S. government began trying to end their polygamous practices. In the 1850s, President James Buchanan ordered one-fifth of the nation's military to invade the region and wipe out plural marriage, but force failed to accomplish that goal.

In 1896, the Mormon hierarchy gave up polygamy and Utah became a state. Not everyone was happy about it, and the hard-core polygamists felt betrayed: How could the LDS Church have caved in so easily, denying the core tenet that most distinguished Mormonism from all other Christian denominations? Why had Joseph Smith's "one true faith" bowed to a secular authority? Four hundred rebels broke away from LDS headquarters in Salt Lake City and moved south to what would become the border between Utah and Arizona, just below Zion National Park and roughly 100 miles northwest of the Grand Canyon. They called their new home Short Creek or just "The Crick." Down there they would live as they wanted to, away from the heathen (or "apostates") running both the LDS Church and law enforcement agencies. Far from everyone else—living free and practicing their religion in a spectacular, wide-open landscape of red dirt, jackrabbits, and stray dogs—they would flourish.

For the next thirty years the outside world left them alone until Arizona Governor Howard Pyle declared that polygamy was "the foulest conspiracy you could possibly imagine. . . . In the evidence the State has accumulated there are multiple instances of statutory rape, adultery, bigamy, open and notorious cohabitation, contributing to the delinquency of minors, marrying the spouse of another . . . along with various instances of income tax evasion, failure to comply with Arizona's corporation laws, misappropriation of school funds, improper use of school facilities and falsification of public records. . . ."

At 4 a.m. on Sunday, July 26, 1953, Governor Pyle sent more than 120 officers to Short Creek, where they barged into homes and bedrooms, shining lights into the eyes of sleeping families, dragging the men out at gunpoint, and taking them to jail. The national press descended on the town, snapping photos of women and children crying as their families were ripped apart. The images filtered out across the United States, and Pyle's grand plan to rout the polygamists backfired, generating an outpouring of sympathy for those caught in the raid. The men soon were reunited with their wives and kids, and Pyle lost his bid for reelection. A very clear message had been sent to the region's politicians and law enforcement: hands off the polygamists. For the next five decades no one in authority touched the twin border towns now called Colorado City, Arizona, and Hildale, Utah, population around 6,000 to 8,000. No matter what one thought of polygamy, the risk of policing the FLDS (Fundamentalist Latter-day Saints) was too great. The men of Short Creek were free to do almost anything they wanted. Some had thirty to forty wives, and some had more, with scores of children, and there were rumors of underage marriages, forced marriages, incest, and inbreeding that produced deformed children.

A Priesthood Council of seven males ran the sect and shared the duties. One of the men was called the Prophet, but nobody was allowed too much power or permitted to become a dictator. Thus, they avoided the dangers of one-man rule. From 1954 to 1986 Leroy Johnson was the Prophet; when he died, Rulon Jeffs, who lived outside Salt Lake City, took on that mantle. He had scores of wives and many children, but his favorite child was the tall, skinny, awkward-looking Warren, who was born in 1956. After graduating in the top 3 percent of his high school class, Warren worked briefly in his father's accounting business. In 1973, when Rulon opened Alta Academy, a private school on his compound, the seventeen-year-old Jeffs became a teacher in math, science, and—most important—FLDS Priesthood history. He was certain that Joseph

Smith had discovered the "one true faith" and closely identified with the struggles of the Mormon founder. He grew up in the shadow of the 1953 raid and detested the outside world.

Alta became Warren's laboratory for controlling and punishing human behavior. For years he had been reading about the rise of Adolf Hitler and Nazi Germany, paying close attention to the relationship between sex and power. Be prepared to defend our way of life, he told the boys at school. Keep sweet and obedient in all things, he emphasized to the girls—keep sweet in thoughts and deeds, stay true to our faith, and one day you'll be blessed by living the polygamous lifestyle. And remember: all marital unions have to be arranged by the leader.

"The Prophet," he taught, "doesn't make mistakes as far as marriages are concerned.... If ever a marriage fails, it's not the Prophet's fault. It's the people who lived it wrong.... You are the children of Zion today, and you are offered to live it [plural marriage] no matter what the world thinks. This law is the greatest and most holy law that will exalt men and women."

FLDS women wore long pastel-colored dresses and kept their waist-length hair in braids or buns. Both sexes donned sacred long underwear beneath their clothing even in the hottest desert months. At Alta, Warren kept boys and girls segregated from one another, their bodies covered from neck to toe. Their skin was never to be exposed to the sun so that they would remain as white as possible. Race was part of the educational process; teachers tried to use textbooks without pictures of African Americans, Mexicans, or anyone else with dark skin. If they couldn't find such books, they went through others and meticulously cut out images of people of color. (The official LDS church refused to accept blacks as priests until 1978.) Rulon Jeffs once declared that the penalty for being homosexual or for an FLDS worshipper marrying an African American was "death on the spot."

Warren shared his ideas on this subject with his students, delivered in his flat, soft, droning, almost hypnotic voice: "You see some classes of the human family that are black, uncouth, or rude and filthy, uncomely, dis-agreeable and low in their habits; wild and seemingly deprived of nearly all the blessings of the intelligence that is usually bestowed upon mankind."

He began each school day with a one-hour devotional filled with ser-mons, hymns, and Scripture readings—but not the Pledge of Allegiance. At Alta, the authority of the federal government was nothing compared with God's authority—or his own—as Jeffs constantly enforced his brand of discipline. Sloppy handwriting or a casual remark led to ver-bal humiliation from the principal. An untucked shirttail brought on a whack with a yardstick or a belt whipping. If a girl's skirt was too short or she smiled at a boy, she could be suspended. Jeffs like to make the students stand in the classroom and flex their buttock muscles in front of others. Sometimes he shocked the class by grabbing a first- or second-grade boy by the ankles, flipping him upside down, and saying, "I'm shaking the evil out of him!" From moment to moment, Warren was their best friend or flew into a rage, keeping everyone off balance. A snowball fight could lead to expulsion. He interrogated youngsters about their parents, gath-ering information to be used later on. The mothers and fathers assumed that someone, most likely Rulon, would step in and stop Warren, but that didn't happen. Rulon was also vengeful, embracing "blood atone-ment" for his enemies:

"I could refer you to plenty of instances where men have been righ-teously slain for their sins. I have seen scores and hundreds of people for whom there would have been a chance (in the last resurrection there will be) if their lives had been taken and their blood spilled on the ground as a smoking incense to the Almighty. . . . This is loving our neighbor as our-selves; if he needs help, help him; and if he wants salvation and it is neces-sary to spill his blood on the earth in order that he may be saved, spill it."

In school, Warren didn't just teach but bluntly demonstrated what it means for girls and women to keep sweet. His first wife, Annette, was Alta's home economics instructor, and one morning in the meeting hall

Warren grabbed her long braided hair, twisting it slowly around his hand and then tightening his grip until she dropped to the floor, her face crimson and contorting in pain. But she made no sound or movement in protest. Finally, he let go and quietly left the room with no explanation to the students or apology to his wife, who stood up, straightened her hair, and went back to teaching and "keeping sweet."

Contact between Alta boys and girls was off limits: Warren told the opposite sexes to treat each other as if they were "snakes." Yet he didn't forgo physical interactions himself. In 2004, one of his ex-students filed a civil lawsuit against him for his actions at the school. For decades Brent Jeffs (many in the insular community shared the same surnames) had kept quiet about his experience at the academy, but that hadn't stopped the recurring nightmares or waking up screaming in the darkness, "Don't hurt me! Don't hurt me!" In his suit, Brent alleged that when he was five years old, Warren and two of his brothers, Blaine and Leslie Jeffs, slipped away during church services and took him into a bathroom, where they sodomized him. According to Brent, the three adults told him that this ritual was God's will and the way for him to become a man. Before Brent had worked up the courage to file the suit, one of his brothers supporting his accounts, Clayne Jeffs, shot himself in the head. The suicide was a major motivation for Brent to take legal action.

Others had already stepped forward to confront Jeffs and the FLDS. Laura Chapman's father, a prominent member of the church, had sexually violated her at an early age before placing her in an arranged teenage marriage. By 1998, she had escaped the sect and become an antipolygamy activist, taking her concerns to the steps of the Utah state courthouse in Salt Lake City and demanding that Governor Mike Leavitt investigate the FLDS as a criminal organization. Just one example of their actions was driving underage girls from the border towns to Caliente, Nevada, for secret wedding ceremonies conducted in an FLDS-owned motel. The transporting of minors across state lines for sexual purposes was a violation of the Mann Act, but no one in law enforcement seemed concerned. The governor assured Laura that the church had the right to do what it was doing under the protection of the First Amendment to the U.S. Constitution. Six years later, Chapman addressed an international audience at the United Nations.

"In recent months," she said, "the United States has championed the cause of women's human rights in Afghanistan and condemned religious fundamentalism in other countries. Yet in the U.S. itself, religious fundamentalists are allowed to violate women's human rights with impunity.

"Media and activist sources have documented a pattern of human rights abuses in polygamous families in Utah and neighboring states. Women and girls are subjected to violence, sexual abuse, incest, child marriage, trafficking, and coerced or forced marriage. Many live in closed religious communities where they are denied education and access to information from the outside world. Although both international human rights law and U.S. law prohibit these abuses, local and national officials have failed to ensure that these legal guarantees are observed in practice."

The sect wasn't worried about any of this in the late 1990s because Rulon and other church leaders felt certain that the world would end on June 12, 1999. Before this, the Jeffs clan had moved down to the border towns to enforce their leadership at close range. The world didn't end that June, but Rulon was in his eighties and failing (although he told the faithful that he would live to at least 350). After the death of the Prophet, the next senior man on the Priesthood Council usually became the new leader; but as Rulon slipped into near senility, Warren took over his daily duties one by one, assuming the Prophet's role in everything but name. With Rulon fading, his son began making more and more outrageous demands on worshippers. One-man rule had arrived.

Warren ordered families to cut off all ties with modern media—to get rid of television sets, satellite dishes, newspapers, magazines, and Internet connections. Radios were allowed but not movies. He banned anything with the color red, children's videos, and musical recordings except for songs he had written and performed. He scheduled closed-door meetings with parents, criticizing their clothing, dress, and attitudes, castigating them for an unsnapped button or an out-of-place lock of hair. Men were told to be obedient, and women were instructed to keep their children in check and their homes spotless. He sent gangs of young men, called "Uncle Warren's Sons of Helaman," into the houses of potential offenders, which they inspected for neatness, dust, and questionable behavior.

Warren encouraged children to rat out their parents for minor rule violations, banished traditional FLDS holidays and dancing, and forbade swimming and other water sports. He made business owners turn their assets over to him and give the church the money they had placed in 401(k) accounts. He forced youngsters to stop playing basketball and told people not to leave town to eat in restaurants, which he considered a waste of time and money. Parents were ordered to throw away their Bibles and Book of Mormon storybooks (Warren was particularly disturbed by Dr. Seuss books depicting animals with human characteristics). When a family's dog attacked a two-year-old boy inside the city limits, Jeffs commanded his minions to round up all the canines in town, take them to a ditch outside Colorado City, and execute them. He sold off all the animals in the town's small, quaint zoo.

In August 2000, Warren ordered FLDS parents to pull their kids out of the public schools serving Colorado City and Hildale, ending the children's interaction with outside teachers and classmates from nearby Centennial Park. Enrollment at Phelps Elementary School dropped from 350 to 16. The FLDS tried home schooling, leaving the boys and girls more isolated and falling further behind in their education.

Then Warren began tearing families apart. He told some of the most successful and respected men in the congregation to write down a list of their sins, give it to him, and then go away and repent. They did as they were asked, and while they were gone, he took their wives and children and distributed them to men who were in his favor. When the banned men tried to come back to the church and their homes, they were excommunicated for good without a hearing or redress of any kind. More suicides of despairing men would soon follow. For decades, the FLDS had been taught to fear the outside world because it probably would attack them as Arizona officials had done in 1953. While looking for an enemy to strike from without, most townspeople didn't recognize the monster growing within.

"Unlike Warren," says FLDS historian Ben Bistline, "Rulon had some compassion and forgiveness for people who weren't his relatives. He'd ask you to confess your sins, then forgive you, re-baptize you, let you come back into the church, and you'd feel good about all this. It was genuine. Warren had none of these qualities—no feelings at all about what he was doing or asking others to do. Just a massive ego."

"Looking back," says Richard Holm, whom Jeffs threw out of the church, "I can see that all these feelings of nervousness and uncertainty were building up in town throughout the 1990s. Everyone was being closely observed and judged and tested for our loyalty to the Jeffs, but we didn't really understand that at the time. We were not used to dealing with power-hungry mongrels. We might have thought that something bad could happen to someone else in the church, but it wouldn't happen to me."

When Rulon died in September 2002, Warren assumed full power. In August 2003, the new Prophet named twelve men, including Holm, as "high priests" in the church. During priesthood meetings, Jeffs turned to each man and in a very quiet voice said, "Draw in, brethren, draw in. The Lord is now choosing his people and his leaders."

"What he meant," Holm says, "was that he wanted us to come in and kiss his ass, throw our money and our daughters at him in the hope that we'd be allowed to have a new wife or build a new home. Many went along with this. Almost all of the high priests had given Warren a daughter to marry to someone else. Those were the men who'd be rewarded later, but I hadn't done this for him. I didn't really understand how extreme he was. At that time, I don't think anybody did."

Holm had made a fortune in construction, which the FLDS excelled at; most of the local men and boys worked at one of the sect's lucrative building companies. Some of those companies were owned and run by the church, which had long ignored child labor laws. In the early 2000s, the economy of the Southwest was booming and building skills were in high demand. Each morning, boys as young as ten or eleven were hauled to construction sites and expected to put in eight or nine hours of work alongside their fathers. The temperature in July in nearby Mesquite, Nevada, the locale for some of the building, was searing enough to bend the heads of palm trees until they were touching the ground. During the hottest months, the workers wore long sleeves, their arms and legs fully covered from the sun.

"Slave labor" was how some referred to this arrangement for the boys. They weren't paid but provided extra hands and extra profits for the bosses, a critical factor for the FLDS in underbidding other companies to get the jobs, including government contracts. Although the FLDS hated the American power structure, the sect loved finding ways to take its money—a strategy it referred to as "bleeding the beast." They bled benefits from every angle: through welfare payments, health insurance payouts, and business contracts for publicly financed work projects. NewEra Manufacturing, an FLDS-run outfit, had a Department of Defense contract for aircraft wheel and brake manufacturing worth $1.2 million. JNJ Engineering had an $11.3 million deal with the Las Vegas Valley Water District. A third FLDS company, Paragon Contractors Corporation, was fined more than $10,000 by the U.S. Department of Labor for employing boys twelve to fifteen years old and not paying them.

An inherent problem with polygamy is that if one man has twenty-five wives, there aren't enough women to go around. This results in an excess of single young men in their physical and sexual prime. In many cultures, men without women—young men drifting together in packs out of loneliness, boredom, a lack of identity, or a sense of adventure—increase the potential for trouble. Jeffs's solution was simply to get rid of the young males, hundreds of them, perhaps a thousand. He ordered wave after wave of teenagers and slightly older men to leave the community for smoking, drinking beer, or partying northwest of town at a spot called the "Edge of the World." They were excommunicated for watching movies, talking to girls, kissing in public, or having a bad attitude and left to fend for themselves on the streets of St. George, Salt Lake City, and Las Vegas. Known collectively as the "lost boys," they crowded together in tiny apartments called "Butt Huts," sleeping on couches and floors if they bothered sleeping at all. Some turned to using or selling drugs or prostitution. One young man got high at a party and shot his girlfriend to death in front of others.

As Jeffs had taught long ago at Alta Academy, the Prophet had the ultimate power over who got married and to whom. In 2001, he advised fourteen-year-old Elissa Wall to marry her nineteen-year-old cousin, Allen Steed, whom she disliked. Elissa begged Warren to let her out of the arrangement, but he refused. She went along with the wedding and for the next few years lived in misery. Jeffs didn't know it at the time, but he had pushed the wrong girl beyond her capacity to keep sweet.

In early 2004, after the authorities had ignored the rule of law in the border towns for fifty years, Mohave County, Arizona, sent former Denver police officer Gary Engels into the community to investigate underage marriage, incest, polygamy, and other illegal practices. Instantly, he became the most hated man in town—followed everywhere by intimidating locals, his office burglarized, his position on the border too dangerous for him to sleep there at night (he drove twenty-two miles every evening to get some rest in Hurricane, Utah). Mormons aren't supposed to drink, but Engels liked wine and so did some of the men Jeffs had thrown out of the church, whom he began to cultivate. One was

Richard Holm, who knew the FLDS inside and out and who soon connected with Engels and, over wine, told him the sect's most explosive secrets. He introduced Engels to Elissa Wall, and she became the first girl in the FLDS to file criminal charges against Jeffs for "accomplice to rape" for forcing her to marry and have sex with her husband.

With the law closing in, Jeffs went on the lam while demanding more and more money from his followers. Late at night, he would circle back to the twin towns, his minions escorting him in to perform underage marriages in hidden locations. For the true believers, those nocturnal comings and goings only added to his legend, with the flock looking upon him as invincible, a god in flight, a true outlaw Prophet. He had created FLDS outposts in South Dakota and Colorado and "hiding houses" around the Southwest, where he had stashed groups of his wives. From time to time, he would do a drive-by to replenish his cash supply, deliver a sermon, and have sex.

A few years earlier, Jeffs had realized that his days on the border were numbered, and so he sent a group of men to west Texas to buy 1,691 acres

WARREN JEFFS WANTED POSTER.

FBI TEN MOST WANTED FUGITIVE

 Name: Warren Steed Jeffs
Date of Birth: December 3, 1955

near Eldorado to restart the FLDS from scratch. The men built massive houses and a school, installed irrigation systems, and planted vegetables, erecting a pure white limestone temple meant to rival the one of the LDS in Salt Lake City; the whole operation was valued at more than $20 million. Jeffs called this ranch Yearning for Zion, where the sect was now to "be fruitful and multiply" to increase the population. The authorities knew of the ranch and unsuccessfully chased Jeffs as he moved about the country. They offered a $10,000 reward for anyone with information leading to his arrest. When that failed to produce results, the FBI stepped in in the spring of 2006 and upped the reward to $50,000, putting Jeffs on its Ten Most Wanted list. Since the feds had created the list in 1950, 94 percent of those placed on it had been caught. The authorities were confident that they would catch Jeffs but fearful that the FLDS might have stockpiled arms at the edge of town. They wanted to avoid the sort of standoff they had experienced with David Koresh and the Branch Davidians in Waco thirteen years earlier (see Chapter 14).

For months, Jeffs continued to evade detection, moving in and out of Texas, the border towns, and farther afield, switching cars and phones when he made stops until he was riding through the summer desert nights in a red Escalade—the color he once had banned. By the evening of August 28, 2006, he had been a fugitive for more than two years, zigzagging up to Canada and down to Mexico and taking a side trip to Florida to visit Disney World. As Gary Engels intensified his investigation, private investigator Sam Brower tailed Jeffs everywhere. Elaine Tyler, who ran the Hope Organization outside St. George for the increasing number of women who were finding the courage to escape the FLDS, provided them with clothing, furniture, utensils, and other necessities of life. The feds raised the reward for the fugitive's capture to $100,000. Night after night, Jeffs's picture had appeared on national and international television, alerting viewers to be on the lookout for his lean body and long face. Four months had passed without a single sighting of the man or a decent lead.

On the night of the twenty-eighth, as the red Escalade passed by him in near darkness just outside Las Vegas, Trooper Eddie Dutchover noticed its temporary license plate. It was partially obscured—a minor violation—but in light of all the warnings that were coming out of the Homeland Security Department, one couldn't be too careful. The officer hesitated: Should he stop the car and correct the problem or let it slide? It was the sort of split-second call a patrolman has to make every day. Instinctively, he pulled out behind the Escalade, moving in closer and then lighting it up on the highway. At 9:04 p.m., the Cadillac came to a stop on the I-15 shoulder. Dutchover stepped out and approached the driver's side in routine fashion, but he had been trained to be ready for anything. He saw one man driving, who turned out to be one of Jeffs's brothers. He saw two people in the backseat, one a tall man eating a salad. In recent weeks, Warren had gotten cocky and lazy, neglecting to put on his wig and the other disguises he usually wore. Dutchover recognized Warren and placed him under arrest.

Jeffs had never been in custody before, let alone locked in a cell. He did very badly in jail, ramming his head against the walls and trying to kill himself more than once. Elissa Wall testified at his 2007 trial, and for anyone skeptical about the damage cults can do to the young, especially regarding sexual assault, her courtroom words shattered the doubts. The sobbing, the choking, the shaking, and the agony of recollection—it was almost too much to witness. Jeffs was convicted on two counts of rape as an accomplice and received a sentence of ten years to life.

After the verdict, Elissa Wall stood next to her lawyer on the courthouse steps and quoted Emily Dickinson: "Opinion is a fleeting thing, but truth outlasts the sun." She talked about the profound difficulties of leaving a cult in which oneself and one's family have been raised. She addressed both her mother, Sharon Wall, and her other relatives, all of whom had remained inside the FLDS:

"When I was young, my mother taught me that evil flourishes when good men do nothing. This has not been easy. The easy thing would have been to do nothing, but I have followed my heart and spoken the truth. . . . Mother, I love you and my sisters unconditionally, and will go to the ends of the earth for you. I understand and respect your convictions but I will never give up on you. When you are ready, I am here.

"I have very tender feelings for the FLDS people. There is so much good in them. I pray they will find the strength to step back, re-examine what they have been told to believe and follow their hearts. This trial has not been about religion or a vendetta. It was simply about child abuse and preventing further abuse. I hope that all FLDS girls and women will understand that, no matter what anyone may say, we are created equal.

"You do not have to surrender your rights or your spiritual sovereignty. I know how hard it is, but please stand up and fight for your voice and power of choice. I will continue to fight for you. . . ."

In 2009, while incarcerated in Arizona, Jeffs, who had gone on a hunger strike, had to be force-fed to stay alive. During a severe depression, he confessed to another brother that he wasn't the Prophet and never had been—he was just an impostor. That did nothing to soften the charges against him. In 2010, his conviction was overturned by Utah's supreme court because of flawed jury instructions, but he already had been extradited to Texas to await his next trial.

In April 2008, authorities in the Lone Star State had raided the YFZ Ranch, leading to the removal of 439 boys and girls from the property and unleashing the largest child custody case in American history—all based on the fear of rampant underage marriage and pregnancy at the compound. As with the 1953 raid on Short Creek, the children soon would be returned to their families, but investigators had retrieved evidence of Jeffs's crimes in Texas. Rooms inside the temple included a "sacred bed" and were used for his liaisons with young girls; photos discovered during the raid showed him passionately kissing twelve- and thirteen-year-old girls, presumably his new brides. He was found guilty of sexual assault of a child (for sex with a fifteen-year-old he had married) and aggravated sexual assault against a child (for sex with a twelve-year-old he had married). He was sentenced to life in prison plus twenty years.

The FLDS had been scattering across the West, infiltrating small towns and hoping to gain power by assuming important positions or running for office in those communities. The accumulation of the sect's criminal acts motivated Senate Majority Leader Harry Reid, the highest-ranking Mormon in U.S. history, to call for a federal investigation of the FLDS. The church and its religious community, so secretive for so long while hiding in plain sight in the Southwest, had come under a national spotlight that would have been unimaginable only a few years earlier. Various governmental agencies would continue to probe the FLDS, and an accountant out of Salt Lake City gradually would break apart the trust that had ruled the border towns and let people own their own homes and run their own businesses. Change was coming, driven primarily by a group of courageous young women determined to stop the reign of terror the church and Jeffs in particular had imposed on them since 1942. While they did so, Jeffs tried to continue running what remained of his FLDS followers from a Texas prison. Between bouts of what his lawyers called "mental breakdowns," he sent out directives, but many had stopped listening and were learning how to live their own lives without the commandments of a prophet. The outlaw had ended up alone, away from his people, hanging on to the religion of his long-dead father.

19

THE COLUMBINE MASS-SHOOTING CULT

Every day, news broadcasts stories of students shooting students or going on killing sprees. It is just as easy to bring a loaded handgun to school as it is to bring a calculator.

—Eric Harris

Despite the piercing cold and damp of an evening in late April 1999, many people had driven out to Columbine High School in southwestern Denver to view the crime scene. They stood next to a chain-link fence that kept them from getting too close to the facility and watched hundreds upon hundreds of teenagers and adults kneel down in the spring mud and burst into tears, grabbing onto one another for support or clutching the fence, swaying, and wailing in anguish. Several days earlier, two Columbine students, Eric Harris and Dylan Klebold, had walked into the suburban school wearing black trench coats and opened fire with shotguns and semiautomatic weapons, wounding twenty-three students and killing twelve teenagers, one teacher, and themselves.

A man cried and held a basketball, leaning over and setting it down gently in the mud. A woman mumbled a prayer and placed a yellow rose in a square hole in the fence. Nobody said anything or made eye contact; the shame of what had happened was too deep to be put into words or even glances. The emotion of the moment—a combination of intimate horror and surprise—was overwhelming. Everyone's expression said the same thing: these were our kids who did this, the ones we thought we knew, as were the kids who died. We can no longer pretend that as a community or a society we're safe or innocent or better than any other group of people.

The country had seen numerous school shootings—in Mississippi, Arkansas, and Oregon, among other places—but this one was special or at least especially horrifying and it became the template for future similar acts. Earlier school shootings had been brief, but Columbine had unfolded over more than seventeen minutes and left behind iconic images that stir visceral emotions no matter how many times one has seen them. People had watched on live TV as students ran out of the building with their hands on their heads as SWAT teams charged with guns at the ready and as a bloody young man crawled from a broken window. Some of those trapped inside the school had cell phones and called their parents or media outlets and were interviewed as the massacre was carried out.

Harris and Klebold had engineered the deadliest school shooting in the nation's history, but from their perspective it was a colossal bust.

They had built ninety-five bombs and planted most of them around Columbine. These included forty-eight carbon dioxide bombs (known as "crickets"), eleven 1½-gallon propane containers, seven incendiary devices with forty-plus gallons of flammable liquids, and two duffel bag bombs with twenty-pound liquefied petroleum gas tanks. One cricket was attached to a quart of homemade napalm.

Some of the bombs were intended to detonate inside the school cafeteria at 11:20 a.m, during the height of lunch hour. Hundreds of kids would die while eating, and when those who survived went running outside to escape the fireballs and mayhem, the duo would gun them down one by one. The bombs and bullets were supposed to kill 500 people, if not more. But the explosives failed to go off and the plan went awry, and so the young men entered the school and began shooting, ending their own lives after taking those of thirteen others.

"Thank God, these people weren't good bomb makers," Pete Mang, the deputy director of the Colorado Bureau of Investigation, later told the *Denver Post*.

"As bad as this was," added Chuck Burdick, the operations chief of the Littleton Fire Department, "we were so very, very lucky. It could have been so much worse."

The purpose of this bloodbath, as revealed on a videotape discovered after the killers' deaths, was not subtle. Harris and Klebold had wanted to "kick-start a revolution" against their enemies: "niggers, spics, Jews, gays, fucking whites . . . humanity." They had taken Adolf Hitler as one of their heroes, and their day of infamy at the school—April 20, 1999—was Hitler's 110th birthday.

Initially, the Columbine massacre was widely viewed as a killing spree by a couple of late adolescent boys who had given in to their random violent impulses. The aching question—*Why* would they do such a thing?—lingered long after the wilted flowers honoring the dead had been hauled away. Why would two intelligent young men from solid, middle-class families (Klebold drove a BMW, after all) have chosen to engage in mass murder and destroy themselves in the process? How could this have occurred in the upwardly mobile suburb of Littleton, Colorado, and at a good institution like Columbine high School? What was the message the boys were sending—the point of the event?

It was anything but a random act of violence and was designed to be the single largest act of domestic terrorism in American history, dwarfing Timothy McVeigh's 1995 bombing of the Alfred P. Murrah Federal Building in Oklahoma City, which ended 168 lives. Unlike McVeigh, Harris and Klebold knew some of their victims and chose to die with them. They believed so strongly in their cause that they made no attempt to hide their involvement or get away with their crimes.

One counselor of the survivors and the victims' families was Dr. Frank Ochberg, a Michigan psychiatrist who specializes in post-traumatic stress. According to Dr. Ochberg, Eric Harris was simply the "Mozart of psychopaths, the kind of person who comes along only every two or three hundred years." Except that both before and after Columbine, this kind of Mozart was showing up everywhere across America and opening fire in schools, churches, shopping malls, and many other public places. In April 2000, a year after Columbine, the *New York Times* published the results of a study of 102 rampage killers who had murdered 425 people during the last several decades. The *Times's* survey, which included the Columbine massacre and was the largest database yet compiled on the subject, began like this: "They are not drunk or high on drugs. They are not racists or Satanists, or addicted to violent video games, movies or music. . . . They give lots of warning and even tell people explicitly what they plan to do. . . . They do not try to get away."

In a videotape made with a camcorder borrowed from Columbine High, the two young men sat in Harris's bedroom about a month before the rampage, passing a bottle of whiskey back and forth and talking about their upcoming day of infamy. Several aspects of the tape were startling.

They debated which famous movie director would film their story: Quentin Tarantino or Steven Spielberg. Beyond all that was their calmness and lucidity. They understood what they were about to do and were ready to accept the consequences. They wanted to make a statement about their lives and the social conditions at their school. They had expected that the adult realm of teachers and administrators at Columbine would have protected them from the bullying they complained of, but that hadn't happened, and so something else would. It was the thoughtfulness and deliberateness they showed on the tape that would attract other young people to their ways long after they were dead. The boys' twisted and horrific plan wasn't just personal but something larger, something that wanted humanity to be different from what it is—if not change for the better. This is the wellspring from which the "cult of Columbine" was created.

In the video, the boys delivered a lengthy apology to their parents for what was coming, and their words revealed a complexity of thinking and feeling that fit no prescribed mold having to do with child abuse or other forms of deprivation leading to violence. They could as easily have been getting high and talking about a fantasy event, but they weren't. Only slowly did a viewer of the tape realize the most startling thing of all: the boys' absolute madness was expressed as a normal response to their perceptions of the world around them.

"It fucking sucks to do this to them," Harris said of his mother and father. "They're going to be put through hell once we do this. There's nothing you guys could've done to prevent this."

Klebold told his own mother and father that they had been "great parents" who taught him "self-awareness, self-reliance. . . . I always appreciated that." Then he paused and said, "I'm sorry I have so much rage."

"My parents are the best fucking parents I have ever known," Harris said. "My dad is great. I wish I was a fucking sociopath so I didn't have any remorse, but I do." He spoke just as lovingly of his mother, adding, "I really am sorry about all this, but war's war."

The boys expressed their hatred toward many different groups and several individuals at their school who they felt had gotten away with bullying them for too long.

"You've given us shit for years," Klebold said of his classmates. "You're fucking going to pay for all the shit. We don't give a shit because we're going to die doing it."

The problem, Klebold indicated, was very widespread. It was in his eyes all of "humanity. Look at what you made. You're fucking shit, you humans, and you need to die."

"We need to die too," Harris said.

Without mentioning it directly, the tape conveys a more subtle message that would echo deep into the future: the boys and their fellow students might have been accomplished at science or math or English or many other subjects, but they had neither learned nor been taught much about managing their emotions—their anger and fear and their sense of being victimized at Columbine. It would take years and many more school shootings for the American educational system to consider this issue and, at least in some places, to introduce classes in conflict resolution or mindfulness or the simple discipline of knowing how to calm down instead of building on the rage until it has to explode.

After the massacre, others came forward to talk about the emotional atmosphere the boys had endured during their high school years.

"Everyone hates you," Brooks Brown, a former student at Columbine, would later say about the school on Oprah Winfrey's television program, referring to the cliques that had tormented him and other kids. "The people who made fun of me my whole life are still on top."

"It was relentless," Debra Sears told the *Denver Rocky Mountain News* when describing the bullying at Columbine. In the mid-'90s, Sears had withdrawn her stepsons from the school because of the harassment. "The constant threats walking through the halls. You had a whole legion of people that would tell you that just going to school was unbearable."

One young man, Evan Todd, a 255-pound defensive lineman on the football team, was wounded in the shooting. In a December 1999 issue of *Time* magazine, he characterized Harris and Klebold this way: "Columbine is a clean, good place except for those rejects. Most kids didn't want them there. They were into witchcraft. They were into voodoo dolls. Sure, we teased them. But what do you expect when kids come to school with weird hairdos and horns on their hats? It's not just jocks; the whole school's disgusted with them. They're a bunch of homos, grabbing each other's private parts. If you want to get rid of someone, usually you tease 'em. So the whole school would call them homos, and when they did something sick, we'd tell them, 'You're sick and you're wrong.'"

Gradually, the video and writings of Harris and Klebold would become public and reach young people everywhere. In the decades after Columbine, America would see not only the continuation of mass shootings but something else deeply disturbing: a group of young people who supported the shooters or saw them as martyrs, with some in that group carrying out their own carnage against their perceived enemies.

In May 2018 at Santa Fe High School, in Santa Fe, Texas, seventeen-year-old Dimitrios Pagourtzis walked into his school wearing a black trench coat and opened fire with a sawed-off shotgun—the same clothing and weaponry used at Columbine High nineteen years earlier. In bold letters his T-shirt read "Born to Kill," evoking the T-shirts donned by Harris and Klebold for their attack, which read "Wrath" and "Natural Selection." Pagourtzis had the same canisters of carbon dioxide gas and Molotov cocktails employed by the Columbine gunmen. His Facebook picture showed him in the trench coat. A small red-star medallion he wore on its collar featured the same communist hammer-and-sickle design that was seen on the boots of the Columbine shooters.

Adam Lanza, the 20-year-old assailant who in 2012 killed twenty-six people at Connecticut's Sandy Hook Elementary School, had put together a mass-murder spreadsheet and materials on Harris and Klebold

and what amounted to a copy of the official Columbine investigation. In his writings, Seung-Hui Cho, who in 2007 shot and killed thirty-two students at Virginia Tech, claimed to have been inspired by the Columbine duo and referred to them by their first names and as "martyrs" in a video recording he left behind before dying the day of his assault. "You had a hundred billion ways to have avoided today," he said on the video. "But you decided to spill my blood. You forced me into a corner and gave me only one option. Now you have blood on your hands that will never wash off."

In Parkland, Florida, on Valentine's Day 2018, nineteen-year-old Nikolas Cruz made a cellphone video before he went into Marjory Stoneman Douglas High School and killed seventeen while wounding seventeen more. "I'm going to be the next school shooter of 2018," he said. "My goal is at least 20 people, with an AR-15 and a couple tracer rounds. . . . It's going to be a big event. When you see me on the news you'll all know who I am." He laughed and sang out, "You're all going to die."

A cult was growing up around the events at Columbine, made up of those who had committed other mass shootings, attempted to do so, or just thought about it. On the Internet they were known as "Columbiners," and they discussed Harris and Klebold and their infamous crimes on social media groups, forums, and Tumblr blogs devoted to the duo. In many cases, they didn't merely remember the two but celebrated them. Young women fell in love with the boys and their deeds, blogging about their own anxiety and depression over rejection or bullying. Their fans uploaded tributes to the pair on YouTube and displayed images of the killers set to Marilyn Manson songs or poetry. They created their own language based on the dead boys' writings: "REB" (Harris's nickname), "VoDKa" (Klebold's nickname), "NBK" (Natural Born Killers), and "Natural Selection." Some saw the shooters as valiant rebels and the real victims of Columbine. In Iowa, seventeen-year-old Mellissa Andersen ran a Harris and Klebold "fan site." On Yahoo, discussion lists with names like "I love Eric and Dylan" have thousands of members.

The themes, words, and wounded feelings of Harris and Klebold surfaced again and again, creating a copycat syndrome with their actions serving as a blueprint and cult members professing their willingness to die to fulfill their mission. They read the same books as Harris and Klebold, wore the same clothing, and used the same tactics. Some went so far as to reach out to prior shooting victims before moving forward with their violent intentions. In February 2018, an eighteen-year-old Vermont man was arrested for planning a mass shooting at his former high school. The Parkland High School shooting had just happened, and he contacted a young female student there because, according to a police report, "he wanted to know how it made her feel and what it felt like being inside the school."

In Hillsborough, North Carolina, an eighteen-year-old-man sent an e-mail to Frank DeAngelis, the Columbine principal at the time of Harris and Klebold's attack, informing him of a school shooting that was about to happen in his state. "Dear Principal . . ." the teenager wrote. "I remember Columbine. It is time the world remembered it." DeAngelis and school administrators immediately reached out to the police, but it was too late: the e-mail writer had already killed his father before driving to Hillsborough's Orange High School and opening fire in a parking lot, wounding two students. For his day of infamy he also wore a black trench coat and carried a sawed-off shotgun that he had named Arlene, as one of the Columbine killers had done. The North Carolina shooter labeled his attack "Operation Columbine."

Sometime later, a sixteen-year-old Utah student who claimed to be an aspiring journalist came to Colorado to interview DeAngelis. Not long after his departure, the principal got a call from the police. The student had just been taken into custody in Utah and told the authorities questioning him that he was "fascinated" by Columbine. He was arrested for plotting with another student to detonate a bomb during a school assembly.

In the journal they kept before their attack, Harris and Klebold had written: "We'll never be forgotten" and "We'll be remembered forever."

According to the National Safety Center, in the handful of weeks after Columbine, 3,000 other high school students across the country concocted bomb threats or developed schemes intended to result in death. Upon hearing this statistic, one journalist reporting on the tragedy's aftermath for a national magazine said, "If I hear one more teenager say that he or she understands why those two kids did what they did, I'm going to scream."

As the mass shootings continued month by month and year by year, the confusion, mystery, and horror around them grew. For the crimes of burglary, assault, robbery, and theft, the United States had statistics similar to those of other developed countries. But America's gun homicide rate was about 11,000 a year—thirty times higher, for example, than France's or Australia's, according to the United Nations Office on Drugs and Crime, and twelve times higher than in most other comparable nations. Adam Lanza's December 2012 Newtown massacre initially was seen as the tipping point for the mass shooting phenomenon, when the nation would at last confront all the gun violence, take action against it, and start to lower the number of fatalities. In fact, in the fourteen months after Newtown, the country saw a school shooting an average of every ten days—eighty-eight more of them in less than the next two years. Instead of turning the trend around, Sandy Hook had made it worse.

Some of the school shooters would reveal to the police that they were competing with prior mass shooters in the hopes of killing the most people. Peter Langman, a psychologist and the author of *Why Kids Kill: Inside the Minds of School Shooters*, runs the website SchoolShooters.info. Using a diagram, he has tracked the Columbine influence on more than thirty other armed assaults at schools or other venues both in America and abroad. As on a corporate flowchart, the lines of the diagrams point to two people: Harris and Klebold.

In 2014, nineteen-year-old James Gamble and twenty-two-year-old Lindsay Souvannarath met online. He was unemployed, and she had just graduated from a liberal arts school in Iowa with thoughts of joining the Peace Corps. Each one alone probably would have gone in more conventional directions, but the excitement of talking honestly on the Internet caused them to reveal what they really wanted to do: plan a shopping mall massacre. (She was writing a novel featuring a mass murder.) They initially made contact through the Columbine community on Tumblr, and his blog included imagery of Nazis and the Columbine massacre. The vast physical distance between the two didn't dampen their desire to keep communicating. She was in America, and he lived almost 2,000 miles away in Canada, but what would happen if she arrived in Canada wearing a trench coat like Harris and Klebold?

"People," she wrote to James, "would be like OH GOD THERE'S TWO OF THEM NOW. What a great way to spend a day, just terrorizing normal/inferior people."

"I hope to do that on a major scale someday," he wrote back.

"Same."

Asked by someone on Tumblr whether he wore "boots like Dylan," James wrote back, "Indeed I do," and posted a photo of himself carrying a knife and a rifle.

Lindsay and James needed one more conspirator to set a plan in motion. In February 2015, Lindsay flew north to meet her like-minded friends. For the Valentine holiday, she and James were going to have sex, go into a mall, and kill as many people as they could and then shoot themselves just as Harris and Klebold had.

On February 12, the police in Halifax, Canada, were tipped off that three people—Lindsay Souvannarath, James Gamble, and Randall Shepherd—were conspiring to commit a mass killing at the Halifax Shopping Centre. Shepherd and Souvannarath were quickly arrested and would be convicted of conspiracy to commit murder. Gamble killed himself with a hunting rifle as the police closed in. Lindsay was sentenced to life in prison with no possibility of parole for ten years.

In mid-April 2019, as the twentieth anniversary of the Columbine massacre approached, tributes to the school, the teachers, the administration, the former principal, and the survivors were publicized. A memorial was planned for Saturday, April 20, at a park near where the tragedy had occurred. Three days before the scheduled event, Dean Phillips, the special agent in charge of the FBI's Denver field office, reported that law enforcement had found the body of an eighteen-year-old Florida woman named Sol Pais while searching near Mount Evans, a Rocky Mountain peak west of Denver. Columbine had been shut down a short time earlier because the authorities believed that Pais, who was headed to the school, was armed, dangerous, and a threat to bring violence back into its hallways. The warnings weren't limited to Columbine; more than a dozen Colorado school districts were also closed that Wednesday.

Pais's comments to others and social media posts had brought her to the attention of the FBI, which contacted authorities in Florida. At the start of the week of April 15, Florida law enforcement officials had warned the Denver FBI office about Pais. By Tuesday, Colorado officials had begun looking into remarks Pais had made in the past based on her "infatuation" with the Columbine massacre and the shooters. But now she had done more than just talk about all this; she was in Colorado. "We took it as a credible threat to the community," Phillips said later, "and potentially a threat to schools in the area, although non-specific to any particular school."

On April 15, 16, and 17, Pais purchased three one-way tickets to fly from Miami to Denver, raising even more suspicions. She used the initial ticket, arriving in Colorado on Monday, April 15, and went straight to a firearms outlet to buy a shotgun. The authorities started to track her after she rented a vehicle and drove up to the area around Mount Evans. As the weekend neared, numerous law enforcement agencies launched what they would call a "massive manhunt." It lasted for only two days. On Wednesday morning they located Pais not far from the Echo Lake Campground in the Arapaho National Forest, at the base of Mount Evans. She apparently had taken her life with the weapon she had just purchased.

On Thursday, Jason Glass, the superintendent of Jeffco Public Schools, which includes Columbine, told the press that students would return to classes that day "with heightened safety and security procedures, and ongoing vigilance in the days to come."

The anniversary event was still on, but "the shadow of Columbine looms pretty large here in Jeffco, as it does across the state and the country," said John McDonald, executive director of school safety and security at Jeffco Public Schools. "We know that Columbine continues to attract people from around the world. . . . If I have any message—we're not a place to come visit if you're not a student, if you don't have business there. We're not a tourist attraction, and we're not a place for you to come and gain inspiration."

That Saturday was warm and sunny as hundreds of people came out to remember the Columbine tragedy, renew acquaintances, and express sorrow for the deceased and gratitude for having survived the massacre. It was an intimate moment filled with hugs and tears but also with smiles and laughter. Only those who had been invited could get inside the ropes where the memorial was being conducted. Others had to stand in the distance, craning their necks to watch and listen as the words of memory and healing poured from loudspeakers and brought back haunting images of April 20, 1999, and the feelings that had accompanied them. Call it mass shame for what had come to the city of Denver and its environs. Call it the inability to look at another person on the street without wondering what he or she might be capable of. On that afternoon, no one could answer that most fundamental question: How could this have taken place in our community?

The reach of Harris and Klebold into America's future was surely more than they could have imagined in ways both good and bad. If a cult had developed around them and their killings, Columbine High now had what the *Washington Post* called "likely the most sophisticated school security system in the country," with its cameras, twenty-four-hour dispatch center, monitoring of social media accounts, and remote-control locks. People throughout the educational system had spent the last two decades trying to figure out what they could do better to prevent another mass shooting.

Six months later, in October 2019, the authorities discovered numerous guns, knives, and material on mass killings in another Florida home, this one belonging to twenty-seven-year-old Michelle Kolts of Wimauma, about thirty miles south of Tampa. The unemployed laborer was taken into custody and charged with twenty-four counts of building a destructive device with the intent of doing property damage or bodily harm. Like Sol Pais, she had become obsessed with two of the major criminal events in recent American history: the Columbine shootings and the Oklahoma City bombing. Her arrest came after her parents had found two dozen pipe bombs in her bedroom.

For the last year, according to Sheriff Chad Chronister of Hillsborough County, Kolts had been on the authorities' radar. In 2018, a printing company had contacted his department after Kolts had ordered work done for "anarchist instructions" and "several manifestoes."

At a press conference, the sheriff said, "She became consumed with the Columbine and Oklahoma killings. . . . While checking Michelle's bedroom, her parents found what appeared to be a significant amount of pipe bombs, other bomb-making materials and numerous weapons."

After the arrest, police had to evacuate Kolts's home and bring in a bomb squad in case any of the weapons required disarming. In the house were two hatchets, two BB-pellet-type rifles, six BB-pellet-type handguns, smokeless rifle powder, the twenty-four pipe bombs, smokeless pistol powder, fuse material, twenty-three different knives, and scores of DVDs and books about murder, mass killing, bomb making, and domestic terrorism.

"The amount of highly destructive materials we found in this home were astonishing," Sheriff Chronister said. "If used, these bombs could have caused catastrophic damage and harm to hundreds, even thousands of people."

Under interrogation, Kolts acknowledged that she had made the devices and planned to use them. "Who knows," Chronister added, "the amount of harm that could have been done, or how many lives could have been lost, had these parents not found the courage to call the sheriff's office and seek help?"

Across the United States, the mass shootings have gone on, as has the cult of Columbine, with its tendrils reaching out through the Internet and beyond. Based on statistics running through September 24, 2019, 334 mass shootings—defined here as one in which four or more people are killed or injured by gunfire—had occurred in less than the first nine months of 2019. That averages 1.24 mass shootings per day. In those 334 shootings, 1,347 people were injured and 377 died—a total of 1,684 victims.

As the sun was falling behind the Rocky Mountains on that cold, damp evening at Columbine soon after the shootings, a huge mound of earth jutted up to the west, perhaps a hundred feet in elevation. A large wooden cross rose above it, put there during the last few days and bold against the sky. Long lines of people were wending their way up the mound toward the cross as if drawn there by an invisible hand. The chilly wind blew over them, ruffling their hair and stretching out their clothes. They lowered their heads and marched upward through the dirt and mud, determined to reach the top. When they arrived at the summit, they raised their fingers and touched the cross, gazing down onto the high school, which was surrounded by thousands of bouquets of flowers, balloons, and handwritten messages to the dead.

Black clouds appeared overhead, churning and shifting in blue and gray patterns. They suddenly split apart, and shafts of light shot down, illuminating the mound and the cross and the people climbing toward it. Everything was lit with golden rays, and it was stunningly biblical, evoking the hill at Calvary outside Jerusalem where Jesus had been crucified. But here it shone on a parking lot filled with Red Cross and Salvation Army trucks.

In addition to everything else that dark legacy of what Harris and Klebold had wrought on April 20, 1999, it helped bring a novel saying to America, one that law enforcement now states over and over again, especially after another mass shooting erupts in a new place. They've put up signs with these six words on them and tried to make everyone aware of their significance and potential power:

"If you see something, say something."

The message from the police and other authorities is clear—be active, not reactive. Don't allow yourself to be a passive observer of the next mass killing if you've detected something, maybe the smallest thing, in someone you know or just met. Imagine that you can be a participant in this process, not just a victim, and that you can make a difference. Imagine stopping someone or more than one person from doing what Harris and Klebold did at Columbine in 1999—and what would have happened if just one person had taken that step.

SOURCES

1. KEITH RANIERE AND NXIVM

Berman, Sarah. "The Defense of NXIVM Leader Accused of Seeking Sex Slave: He's Not a Misogynist." *Vice*, June 19, 2019. https://www.vice.com/en_us/article/pajwgz/the-defense-of-nxivm-leader-accused-of-seeking-sex-slave-hes-not-a-misogynist

Berman, Sarah. "An Ex-Prosecutor Breaks Down the 'Sex Cult' Trafficking Case Against NXIVM Leader Keith Raniere." *Vice*, May 15, 2019. https://www.vice.com/en_us/article/ywy33b/an-ex-prosecutor-breaks-down-the-sex-cult-trafficking-case-against-nxivm-leader-keith-raniere

Berman, Sarah. "Everything You Need to Know About the NXIVM Sex Trafficking Trial." *Vice*, May 3, 2019. https://www.vice.com/en_ca/article/qv7kjp/everything-you-need-to-know-about-the-nxivm-sex-trafficking-trial-keith-raniere

Berman, Sarah. "How Three Teen Sisters Were Allegedly Groomed into NXIVM Leader Keith Raniere's 'Sex Cult.'" *Vice*, May 24, 2019. https://www.vice.com/en_us/article/7xgwqg/how-three-teen-sisters-were-allegedly-groomed-into-nxivm-leader-keith-ranieres-sex-cult

Berman, Sarah. "'I Was Gone from the World and Nobody Notice': One Woman's Story of Being Trapped by NXIVM." *Vice*, May 30, 2019. https://www.vice.com/en_us/article/evy58a/i-was-gone-from-the-world-and-nobody-noticed-one-womans-story-of-being-trapped-by-nxivm

Berman, Sarah. "Keith Raniere's 'Sex Cult' Was Powered by Gaslighting, Experts and Witnesses Testify." *Vice*, June 19, 2019. https://www.vice.com/en_us/article/7xgdq9/keith-ranieres-sex-cult-was-powered-by-gaslighting-experts-and-witnesses-testify

Berman, Sarah. NXIVM "'Sex Cult' Leader Keith Raniere Convicted of Sex Trafficking." *Vice* June 19, 2019. https://www.vice.com/en_ca/article/pajwk7/nxivm-sex-cult-leader-keith-raniere-convicted-of-sex-trafficking

Berman, Sarah. "The NXIVM 'Sex Cult' Story Keeps Getting More Disturbing." *Vice*, May 20, 2019. https://www.vice.com/en_us/article/evyb5j/the-nxivm-sex-cult-story-keeps-getting-more-disturbing

Berman, Sarah. "One Woman's Harrowing Journey from Aspiring Olympian to NXIVM Sex Slave." *Vice*, May 8, 2019. https://www.vice.com/en_us/article/neaenk/one-womans-harrowing-journey-from-aspiring-olympian-to-nxivm-sex-slave-trial

Berman, Sarah. "'Slave to NXIVM 'Sex Cult' Leader Pleads Guilty to Racketeering." *Vice*, March 29, 2019. https://www.vice.com/en_us/article/9kpp9p/slave-to-nxivm-sex-cult-leader-pleads-guilty-to-racketeering

Berman, Sarah. "Smallville' Actress Allison Mack Pleads Guilty to Racketeering.' *Vice*, April 8, 2019. https://www.vice.com/en_us/article/d3ma47/smallville-actress-allison-mack-pleads-guilty-to-racketeering-nxivm

Berman, Sarah. "We Watched the Lifetime NXIVM 'Sex Cult' Movie So You Don't Have To." *Vice*, September 26, 2019. https://www.vice.com/en_us/article/qvgzn3/we-fact-checked-lfetimes-escaping-the-nxivm-cult-movie

Berman, Sarah. "What It's Like to Be Surveilled and Sued by NXIVM." *Vice*, June 13, 2019. https://www.vice.com/en_ca/article/j5wk88/what-its-like-to-be-surveilled-and-sued-by-nxivm

Bowden, Ebony. "NXIVM Leader's Ex Claims He Stalked Her, Killed Her Dog: Report. "*New York Post*, September 24, 2019

Bowden, Ebony. "NXIVM Survivor Sarah Edmondson Breaks Silence on 'Dr. Oz.'" *New York Post*, September 17, 2019

Bruder, Jessica. "She Escaped From NXIVM. Now She's Written a Book About the Sex Cult." *New York Times*, September 17, 2019.

Denney, Andrew. Feds Set Sentencing Date for NXIVM Leader Keith Raniere. *New York Post*, October 4, 2019.

Denney, Andrew. "NXIVM Financier Clare Bronfman to Be Sentenced in January." *New York Post*, September 27, 2019.

Edmonson, Sarah. "How I Became a Top NXIVM Recruiter." *Vice*, October 4, 2019. https://www.vice.com/en_us/article/pa7qjy/how-i-became-nxivms-most-successful-recruiter

Fenton, Reuven and Emily Saul. "Seagram's Heiress Clare Bronfman Pays Feds $6M Over Role in NXIVM." *New York Post*, August 14, 2019.

"Former NXIVM Cult Member Branded During Secret Ritual Says Pain Was 'Horrific.'" *Inside Edition*, September 19, 2019. https://www.insideedition.com/former-nxivm-cult-member-branded-during-secret-ritual-says-pain-was-horrific-56081

Hastings, Deborah. "'Smallville' Actress Allison Mack Pleads Guilty to Charges in NXIVM Sex Cult Case." *Inside Edition*, April 8, 2019. https://www.insideedition.com/smallville-actress-allison-mack-pleads-guilty-charges-nxivm-sex-cult-case-52029

Jackson, Dory. "How Long Will Allison Mack Go to Jail? Everything We Know After Actor Pleads Guilty in NXIVM Case." *Newsweek*, April 8, 2019.

Knoll, Corina. From "'Smallville' to a Sex Cult: The Fall of the Actress Allison Mack." *New York Times*, May 13, 2019.

Meier, Barry. "Co-Founder of Cultlike Group Where Women Were Branded Pleads Guilty." *New York Times*, March 12, 2019.

Meier, Barry. "Once Idolized, Guru of NXIVM 'Sex Cult' to Stand Trial Alone." *New York Times*, May 1, 2019.

Meier, Barry and Colin Moynihan. "Clare Bronfman Pleads Guilty in NXIVM 'Sex Cult' Case, Leaving Leader to Stand Trial Alone." *New York Times*, April 19, 2019.

Moynihan, Colin. "Former Member of Sex Cult Describes How She Became 'Slave.'" *New York Times*, May 9, 2019.

Moynihan, Colin. "Former Sex Cult Official Describes Its 'Evil' Inner Workings." *New York Times*, May 7, 2019.

Moynihan, Colin. "In NXIVM Trial, a Woman Lured Into Sex With Cult Leader Describes His Harem." *New York Times*, May 23, 2019.

Moynihan, Colin. "NXIVM Branding Was Scripted by Sex Cult Leader to Be 'Like a Sacrifice.'" *New York Times*, May 26, 2019.

Moynihan, Colin. "NXIVM: How a Sex Cult Leader Seduced and Programmed His Followers." *New York Times*, June 14, 2019.

Moynihan, Colin. "NXIVM Trial: Cult Leader Forced Women to Starve Themselves to Be 'Wraith Thin,'" Witness Said. *New York Times*, May 13, 2019.

Moynihan, Colin. "NXIVM Trial: Naked Meetings and Photos for Sex Cult 'Grandmaster.'" *New York Times*, May 17, 2019.

Moynihan, Colin. "NXIVM Trial: Sex Cult Leader Confined Woman in a Room for 2 Years in Jealous Rage." *New York Times*, May 30, 2019.

Moynihan, Colin. "NXIVM Trial: Sex Cult Tried to Gather Intelligence on 'Enemies,' Including Schumer." *New York Times*, June 16, 2019.

Moynihan, Colin. "NXIVM Trial: Sex Cult Was Like 'Horror Movie' Prosecutor Says." *New York Times*, June 17, 2019.

Moynihan, Colin. "NXIVM Trial: Sex Cult's 'Grandmaster' Was Seen as "Some Kind of God." *New York Times*, May 11, 2019.

Moynihan, Colin. "NXIVM'S Keith Raniere Convicted in Trial Exposing Sex Cult's Inner Workings." *New York Times*, June 19, 2019.

Moynihan, Colin. "Sex Cult Used Spyware to Monitor Bronfman." *New York Times*, May 28, 2019.

Moynihan, Colin. "'Slave' Details Her Daily Life in Testimony at Sex Cult Founder's Trial." *New York Times*, May 28, 2019.

Moynihan, Colin and Emily Palmer. "NXIVM Trial: Allison Mack Lured Woman Into Sex Cult, She Says." *New York Times*, June 8, 2019.

Moynihan, Colin and Michael Gold. "Allison Mack of 'Smallville' Pleads Guilty in Case of NXIVM 'Sex Cult' Where Women Were Branded." *New York Times*, April 8, 2019.

Palmer, Emily. "What It Was Like to Report on the NXIVM Sex Cult Trial." *New York Times*, June 24, 2019.

Paybarah, Azi. "What Is NXIVM, and Who Is Keith Raniere?" *New York Times*, May 8, 2019.

Piccoli, Sean. "Seagram's Liquor Heiress Charged in NXIVM Sex-Trafficking Case." *New York Times*, July 24, 2018.

Prokos, Hayley. "'NXIVM' Leader Keith Raniere Guilty of Felony Charges: What Will His Sentence Be?" *Newsweek* June 6, 2019.

Saul, Emily. "Alleged Sex Cult Leader Was Really Focused on Penis Size." *New York Post*, June 5, 2019.

Saul, Emily. "Allison Mack Allegedly Starved 'Dynasty' Star's Daughter." *New York Post*, June 7, 2019.

Saul, Emily. "Allison Mack Said Sex with Cult Leader Would 'Heal' Molestation Trauma: Ex-NXIVM 'Slave.'" *New York Post*, June 11, 2019

Saul, Emily. "Allison Mack Told Alleged Sex Slave She Could Be 'Wonder Woman.'" *New York Post*, June 6, 2019.

Saul, Emily. "Allison Mack Was Ready to Testify Against NXIVM's Keith Raniere." *New York Post*, June 26, 2019.

Saul, Emily. "NXIVM Leader Liked 'Sex Slaves' Thin—but Pigged Out on Junk Food." *New York Post*, June 19, 2019.

Saul, Emily. "NXIVM Leader Wanted Branding Ceremonies to Be Like Human Sacrifices." *New York Post*, May 22, 2019

Saul, Emily. "NXIVM Leader Was 'Crime Boss' in Quiet Upstate Neighborhood: Prosecutor." *New York Post*, June 17, 2019

Saul, Emily. "NXIVM Zealot Offered Keith Raniere Teen Daughter As Virginal Sacrifice." *New York Post*, June 13, 2019.

Saul, Emily. "Seagram's Heiress Clare Bronfman Gives $14M to NXIVM Defense Fund." *New York Post*, June 11, 2019.

Saul, Emily and Lia Eustachewich. "NXIVM Leader Keith Raniere Found Guilty on All Counts in Sex Cult Trial." *New York Post*, June 19, 2019.

Saul, Emily and Lia Eustachewich. "NXIVM Leader Taught Disciples That Women Enjoyed Rape: Witness." *New York Post*, June 14, 2019.

Saul, Emily and Lia Eustachewich. "NXIVM 'Slave' Says Joining Sex Cult Derailed Her Life: 'It Was a Lie.'" *New York Post*, May 23, 2019.

Saul, Emily and Lia Eustachewich. "Courtroom Fills with Laughter Over NXIVM Leader's 'Bulls—t' Reputation." *New York Post*, June 6, 2019.

Saul, Emily and Kate Sheehy. "Ex-NXIVM Disciple: Torture Was a Way of Life." *New York Post*, May 20, 2019.

Saul, Emily and Kate Sheehy. "What It Feels Like to Get Branded by a Sex Cult." *New York Post*, May 20, 2019.

Saul, Emily and Max Jaeger. "NXIVM Leader Claimed Abortions Help Women 'Lose Weight and Get Fit': Witness." *New York Post*, May 28, 2019.

Sosa, Anabel and Ebony Bowden. "Inside the Alleged Cult That Has Been Quietly Operating in NY for Decades." *New York Post*, November 11, 2019.

Voytko, Lisette. "From Heiress To Felon: How Clare Bronfman Wound Up In 'Cult-Like' Group NXIVM." *Forbes*, June 6, 2019.

Voytko, Lisette. "NXIVM 'Crime Boss' Keith Raniere Convicted, Faces Possible Life Sentence." *Forbes*, June 19, 2019.

Voytko, Lisette. "NXIVM Leader's Text Messages With Sex 'Slave.'" *Forbes*, June 6, 2019.

Williams, Janice. "Allison Mack Forced NXIVM Sex Cult Members to Follow 500-Calorie-a-Day Diets, Witness Testifies." *Newsweek*, June 11, 2019.

Williams, Janice. "Did Allison Mack Try To Recruit 'Smallville' Castmate Alaina Huffman to NXIVM Sex Cult?" *Newsweek*, May 23, 2019.

Yakowicz, Will. "From Heiress To Felon: How Clare Bronfman Wound Up In 'Cult-Like' Group NXIVM." *Forbes*, May 31, 2019.

Yakowicz, Will. "NXIVM 'Crime Boss' Keith Raniere Convicted, Faces Possible Life Sentence." *Forbes*, June 11, 2019.

Yakowicz, Will. "NX IVM 'Sex Cult' Leader Posed as a Mentor for Women, But Was a Predatory 'Crime Boss,' Prosecutors Say." *Forbes*, June 11, 2019.

Yakowicz, Will. "NXIVM Trial Witness: We Hacked Billionaire Edgar Bronfman Sr.'s Email." *Forbes*, May 29, 2019.

Yakowicz, Will. "When We Exposed Keith Raniere, The Leader Of The NXIVM 'Sex Cult.'" *Forbes*, May 15, 2019.

2. SAUL NEWTON AND THE SULLIVANIANS

Conason, J. And McGarrahan. "Escape from Utopia." *The Village Voice*, April 22, 1986.

Hoban, Phoebe. Psycho Drama: "The Chilling Story of How the Sullivanian Cult Turned a Utopian Dream into a Nightmare." *New York*, June 19, 1989.

Lambert, Bruce. "Saul Newton, 85, Psychotherapist And Leader of Commune, Dies." *New York Times*, December 23, 1991.

Offenhartz, Jake. "Inside the Rise & Fall Of A 1970s Upper West Side Cult." gothamist. com, September 21, 2016. https://gothamist.com/arts-entertainment/ inside-the-rise-fall-of-a-1970s-upper-west-side-cult

Ridley, Jane. "How a Psychosexual "Cult" Tried to Tear Apart My Family." *New York Post*, November 24, 2018.

Span, Paula. "Cult or Therapy Parents at War." *Washington Post*, July 27, 1988.

3. MAGDALENA SOLÍS, THE HIGH PRIESTESS OF BLOOD

Casale, Steven. "Magdalena Solís: The Blood Drinking High Priestess of Mexico." *The Lineup*, March 11, 2015. https://the-line-up.com/ magdalena-solis-high-priestess-of-mexico

Magdalena Soliís. "Murderpedia." https://murderpedia.org/female.S/s/ solis-magdalena.htm

Magdalena Solís. TrueTv's Crime Library. Archived 2013-10-19 at the Wayback Machine. Accessed July 17, 2008.

4. BHAGWAN SHREE RAJNEESH AND THE RAJNEESHEES

Bonnar, Myles and Brocklehurst, Steven. "The Scot Who Was the Sex Guru's Bodyguard." *BBC Scotland News*, June 4, 2018. https://www.bbc.com/news/uk-scotland-44300915#:~:text=Hugh%20Milne%2C%20from%20Edinburgh%2C%20 spent,him%20to%20do%20hard%20labour.

Perry, Douglas. "What Happened to the Rajneeshees' Oregon Paradise? Photos Show Decay, Rebirth." *Oregonian*, March 25, 2018.

The Oregon History Project. Bhagwan Shree Rajneesh, 2018. https:// oregonhistoryproject.org/articles/biographies/bhagwan-shree-rajneesh-biography/#.XnDfukN7lBy

"Wild Wild Country," Netflix Documentary. https://www.netflix.com/title/80145240

Wollaston, Sam. "'Calling It a Cult is Degrading'": Wild Wild Country's Ma Anand Sheela on Her Time as Bhagwan's Lieutenant." *Guardian*, June 25, 2018.

Wollaston, Sam. "Growing up in the Wild Wild Country Cult: 'You Heard People Having Sex All the Time, Like Baboons.'" *Guardian*, April 24, 2018.

Zaitz, Les. "As Ma Anand Sheela's Play to Involve Gov. Vic Atiyeh Fizzles, She
Expands Her 'Dirty Tricks' to Burning a County Office"—Part 5 of 5.
Oregonian, April 14, 2011.

Zaitz, Les. "Rajneeshee Leaders Take Revenge on The Dalles' with Poison, Homeless"—
Part 3 of 5. *Oregonian*, April 14, 2011.

Zaitz, Les. "Rajneeshees' Utopian Dreams Collapse as Talks Turn to Murder"—
Part 5 of 5. *Oregonian*, April 14, 2011.

Zaitz, Les. "Thwarted Rajneeshee Leaders Attack Enemies, Neighbors with Poison"—
Part 2 of 5. *Oregonian*, April 14, 2011.

Zaitz, Les. "25 Years After Rajneeshee Commune Collapsed, Truth Spills Out"—
Part 1 of 5. *Oregonian*, April 14, 2011.

5. JOSEPH DI MAMBRO, LUC JOURET, AND THE ORDER OF THE SOLAR TEMPLE

Barkun, Michael. "An Apocalyptic Vision Finds a Logical, Tragic End: Religion: Solar
Temple Members Foresaw Environmental Doom as the Post–Cold War End."
Los Angeles Times, October 12, 1994.

Cowell, Alan. "Body Found in Swiss Chalet Identified as No. 2 Cult Leader."
New York Times, October 9, 1994.

Cowell, Alan. "Swiss Say Some Sect Members Found in Fires Were Murdered."
New York Times, October 9, 1994.

Farnsworth, Clyde H. "Canada Seeks Money Trail Of Secret Cult." *New York Times*,
October 16, 1994.

Farnsworth, Clyde. "Quebec Fire Kills 2; Linked to Cult in Switzerland."
New York Times, October 6, 1994.

Farnsworth Clyde H. "Quebec Police Say Baby Was Target of Cult." *New York Times*,
November 20, 1994.

Hunter, Brad. "Solar Temple Massacre: Mystery Endures 25 years Later. "*Toronto Sun*,
October 5, 2019.

Kraft, Scott. "Deaths of 16 Cult Members Appear to Be Acts of Murder, Suicide,
Investigators Say." *Los Angeles Times*, December 25, 1995.

Niebhur, Gustav. "Leader of the Sect: 'New Age' Warped by Apocalyptic Visions."
   New York Times, October 7, 1994.

Niebhur, Gustav. "Victims in Mass Deaths Linked to Magical Sects." *New York Times*,
   October 6, 1994.

"The 1994 Solar Temple Cult Deaths in Switzerland." October 5, 2014. SwissInfo.ch
   2014. https://www.swissinfo.ch/eng/series-of-killings_the-1994-solar-temple-
   cult-deaths-in-switzerland/40878686

"On This Day1994: Cult members die in 'mass suicide.'" *BBC* 1994, http://news.bbc.
   co.uk/onthisday/hi/dates/stories/october/5/newsid_3933000/3933957.stm

Riding, Alan. "48 in Sect Are Killed in Grisly Ritual in Switzerland." *New York Times*,
   October 6, 1994.

Riding, Alan. "A Preacher With a Dark Side Led Cultists to Swiss Chalets."
   New York Times, October 9, 1994.

Riding, Alan. "Swiss Say They've Identified Body of Solar Temple Leader."
   New York Times, October 14, 1994.

6. JIM JONES AND THE PEOPLES TEMPLE

Gibson, Caitlin. "40 Years Ago, This Journalist Survived the Jonestown Massacre.
   He Warns It Could Happen Again." *Washington Post*, November 18, 2018.

Jonestown: "The Life and Death of Peoples Temple." Public Broadcasting System,
   2007. https://www.pbs.org/wgbh/americanexperience/films/jonestown/

Marks, Andrea. "Jim Jones and the Lessons of Jonestown: Ignoring the Warning Signs
   of a Dangerous Demagogue Can Be Deadly." *Rolling Stone*, November 5, 2018.

Minutaglio, Rose. "First Look: Jim Jones's Surviving Sons Speak Out in New
   Documentary About the Jonestown Massacre." *Esquire*, September 18, 2018.

Portwood, Jerry. "See Jim Jones' Surviving Sons Speak About Jonestown Murder-
   Suicide in New Doc: Former Members of the Peoples Temple Mark 40th
   anniversary of the Largest Murder-Suicide in American History with New
   Special." *Rolling Stone*, September 28, 2018.

Poster, Alexander. "Jonestown Teaches Us That No On Person Can Solve Our
   Problems." *Washington Post*, November 18, 2018.

Valiente, Alexa and Monica Delarosa. "40 Years After the Jonestown Massacre: Jim Jones' Surviving Sons on What They Think of Their Father, the Peoples Temple Today." ABC News 2018, https://abcnews.go.com/US/40-years-jonestown-massacre-jim-jones-surviving-sons/story?id=57997006

7. JAMES ARTHUR RAY

"After Sweat Lodge Deaths, Fewer Tourists with Spiritual Needs." *New York Times*, October 19, 2010.

Archibold, Randal C. "Guru Indicted in 3 Deaths at Arizona Sweat Lodge." *New York Times*, February 3, 2010.

Archibold, Randal C. "Sweat Lodge Deaths Not Criminal, Guru's Lawyer Says." *New York Times*, January 13, 2010.

Archibold, Randal C. and Joseph Berger. "Sweat Lodge Leader Is Indicted in Deaths." *New York Times*, February 4, 2010.

"Doctors Feared Mass Suicide After Deadly 'Sweat Lodge,' Survivor Says." *CNN*, March 17, 2011. https://www.cnn.com/2011/CRIME/03/16/arizona.sweat.lodge.trial/index.html.

Dougherty, John. "Arizona: Self-Help Expert Contests Police Statements." *New York Times*, October 12, 2009.

Dougherty, John. "Deaths at Sweat Lodge Bring Soul-Searching." *New York Times*, October 11, 2009.

Dougherty, John. "For Some Seeking Rebirth, Sweat Lodge Was End." *New York Times*, October 21, 2009.

Dougherty, John. "New Details About Deaths in Sweat Lodge Are Revealed." *New York Times*, December 29, 2009.

Dougherty, John and Gregory Roth. "Questions About 'Sweat Lodge' Rite Where 2 Died." *New York Times*, October 10, 2009.

Goodwin, Christopher. "At the Temple of James Arthur Ray." *Guardian*, July 8, 2011.

Hudson, John. "The People Who Bought James Arthur Ray's Shtick: The Self-Help Guru Had Many Fans on His Way to the Top." *Atlantic Monthly*, June 23, 2011.

"James Ray's Mother Describes Him as Misportrayed." *CNN* March 29, 2011. https://
www.cnn.com/2011/CRIME/03/29/arizona.ray.mother/index.html

Karas, Beth and Ashley Hayes. "Self-Help Author Stands Trial in Sweat Lodge Deaths."
CNN March 1, 2011. https://www.cnn.com/2011/CRIME/03/01/arizona.
sweat.lodge.deaths/index.html

Lacey, Marc. "New Age Guru Guilty in Sweat Lodge Deaths." *New York Times*,
June 22, 2011.

Lovett, Ian. "Guru Sentenced to Prison in Sweat Lodge Deaths." *New York Times*,
November 18, 2011.

O'Connor, Anahad. "2 Die and 16 Are Sickened at Spa in Arizona." *New York Times*,
October 9, 2009.

O'Neill, Ann. "Inside the Sweat Lodge: Witnesses Describe a Ritual Gone Wrong."
CNN March 14, 2011. https://www.cnn.com/2011/CRIME/03/14/ray.sweat.
lodge.witnesses/index.html

"Sweat Lodge Leader Sentenced to Two Years in Prison." *CNN* November 18, 2011.
https://www.cnn.com/2011/11/18/justice/arizona-sweat-lodge-sentencing/
index.html

"'Sweat Lodge' Survivor Says Ray Dismissed Plea, Didn't Check Victim." *CNN*, March
7, 2011. https://www.cnn.com/2011/CRIME/03/04/arizona.sweat.lodge.
deaths/index.html

"Trial in Sweat Lodge Deaths Begins. New York Times." *New York Times*, March 1, 2011.

"US motivational speaker arrested over sweat lodge deaths." *Guardian*, February 4, 2010.

8. SHOKO ASAHARA AND AUM SHINRIKYO

"Japan Executes Sarin Gas Attack Cult Leader Shoko Asahara and Six Members."
Guardian, July 5, 2018.

Kaneko, Maya and Cory Baird. "Japanese Have Mixed Opinions on Execution of Aum
Leader Shoko Asahara and Six Accomplices." *Japan Times*, July 6, 2018.

Kristof, Nicholas D. "Japanese Cult Leaders Sought in Huge Police Manhunt."
New York Times, April 14, 1995.

Kirstof, Nicholas D. "Japanese Police Find Body of a Lawyer Believed Killed by Cult."
New York Times, October 31, 1995

Kristof, Nicholas D. "May 14-20: Cause for Reassurance; Japan Arrests Leader Of
Doomsday Cult In Subway Gas Attack." *New York Times*, May 21, 1995.

Kristof, Nicholas D. "Terror in Tokyo: The Overview. Japanese Police Find Chemicals
and Gas Masks at Sect's Offices." *New York Times*, March 23, 1995.

Krirstof Nicholas D. And Sheryl Wudunn. "A Guru's Journey—The Seer Among the
Blind: Japanese Sect Leader's Rise." *New York Times*, March 26, 1995.

Pollack, Andrew. "Japanese Police Find Body of a Lawyer Believed Killed by Cult."
New York Times, September 7, 1995.

Pollack, Andrew. "Roundup in Japan. Japanese Sect May Struggle To Get By Without
Its Leader." *New York Times*, May 17, 1995.

Spaeth, Anthony. "Shoko Asahara: Engineer of Doom." *Time*, June 12, 1995

Wudunn, Sheryl. "For Ex-Cult Members in Japan, a Hard, Slow Recovery."
New York Times, June 5, 1995.

Wudunn, Sheryl. "Japanese Critics Say Schools Pushed Best and Brightest Into Sect's
Arms." *New York Times*, May 22, 1995.

Yoshida, Reji and Murakami Sakura. "Aum Shinrikyo Guru Shoko Asahara and Six
Other Cult Members Hanged for Murders." *Japan Times*, July 6, 2018.

9. THE FALL RIVER CULT

Bagni, Adam. "Fall River Woman Convicted in Satanic Cult Killing Asks for
Parole." turnto10.com, March 28, 2017. https://turnto10.com/news/local/
fall-river-woman-convicted-in-satanic-killings-asks-for-parole

"The Fall Rivers Cult." behindtheveil07.wordpress.com, July 12, 2018. https://
behindtheveil07.wordpress.com/2018/07/12/the-fall-rivers-cult/

Folco, Marc. "Looking Back: Murder, in Satan's Name." southcoasttoday.com,
October 6, 2013. https://www.southcoasttoday.com/article/20131006/
LIFE/310060305

Laskey, Mark. "Sex, Satanism And Sacrificial Slaughter: The Fall River Cult Murders, 1979-80." cultnation.com, September 6, 2016. https://cvltnation.com/sex-satanism-sacrificial-slaughter-fall-river-cult-murders-1979-80/

Wedge, David. "GOP Cries Ethics Foul on Suzanne Bump." *Boston Herald*, October 30, 2010.

Wedge, David. "Suzanne Bump Defends Office's Hiring of Paroled Killer." *Boston Herald*, October 29, 2010.

"Woman Convicted of 1980 Satanic Cult Murder Up for Parole." turnto10.com, March 27, 2017. https://turnto10.com/news/local/woman-convicted-of-1980-satanic-cult-murder-up-for-parole

10. CHARLES MANSON AND THE FAMILY

Carter, Chelsea J. and Hamasaki, Sonya. "Manson Murder Mystery: LAPD Hopes Decades-Old Tapes Hold Clues." https://www.cnn.com/2013/03/26/justice/california-manson-tapes/index.html

CNN Staff. "Gov. Brown Nixes Release of Former Manson Follower." https://www.cnn.com/2013/03/01/justice/california-manson-follower/index.html

Corwin, Miles. "Charles Manson, Mastermind of 1969 Murders, Dies at 83." *Los Angeles Times*, November 20, 2017.

Fox, Margalit. "Charles Manson Dies at 83; Wild-Eyed Leader of a Murderous Crew." *New York Times*, November 20, 2017.

Full Coverage: "The Manson Murders—50 Years Later." *Los Angeles Times*, July 26, 2019.

Henry, Erica and Carter, Chelsea J. "Charles Manson Follower Accused of Trying to Smuggle Phone to Cult Leader." https://www.cnn.com/2013/03/26/justice/california-manson-phone/index.html

Klaus, Olivia. "My Life After Manson." *New York Times*, August 4, 2014.

La Ganga, Maria L. and Himmelsbach-Weinstein, Erik. "Charles Manson's Murderous Imprint on L.A. Endures as Other Killers Have Come and Gone." *Los Angeles Times*, July 28, 2019.

Manson, Charles (as told to Nuell Emmons). *Manson In His Own Words by Charles Manson*. New York: Grove Press, 1986.

Martinez, Michael and Lah, Kyung. "California Governor Weighs Parole for Charles Manson Follower." https://www.cnn.com/2013/02/01/justice/california-parole-manson-follower/index.html

Medina, Jennifer. "California Today: Charles Manson's Grip on Los Angeles." *New York Times*, November 20, 1957.

Padnani, Amisha. "What Became of the Manson Family?" *New York Times*, November 21, 2017.

Serratore, Angela. "What You Need to Know About the Manson Family Murders." *Smithsonian*, July 25, 2019.

Stack, Liam. "Charles Manson, Unhinged Pop Culture Figure." *New York Times*, November 20, 1917.

11. ADOLFO CONSTANZO AND THE MATOMOROS HUMAN SACRIFICE CULT

Applebome, Peter. "13th Victim Is Found on Ranch Where Drugs and Occult Mixed." *New York Times*, April 14, 1989.

Applebome, Peter. "Drugs, Death and the Occult Meet In Grisly Inquiry at Mexico Border." *New York Times*, April 13, 1989.

Bovsun, Marva. "Spring Break Turns to Horror as Mexican Druglord Kills University of Texas Student in Sicko Human Sacrifice Voodoo Ritual." *New York Daily News*, March 15, 2015.

"Cult Chief's Death Suspect as Fake." *New York Times*, May 9, 1989.

"Leader in Cult Slayings Ordered Own Death, Two Companions Say." *New York Times*, May 8, 1989.

"Leader of Drug Cult Is Reported Killed." *New York Times*, May 7, 1989.

Schiler, Dane. "Woman Called Priestess of Satanic Cult Says She's Changed/Inmate Has Served 15 Years in Prison in Mexico for Ritual Sacrifices of 13 People." *San Antonio News Express*, March 28, 2004.

Vindell, Tony. "Aldrete, 4 Others, Sentenced in Killings." *Brownsville Herald*, May 4, 2009.

12. MARSHALL APPLEWHITE AND HEAVEN'S GATE

Ayres Jr., B. Drummond. "Families Learning of 39 Cultists Who Died Willingly."
New York Times, March 29, 1997.

Bearak, Barry. "Eyes on Glory: Pied Pipers of Heaven's Gate." New York Times,
April 28, 1997.

Brooke, James. "For Ex-Wife of Leader, No Wish for the Limelight." New York Times,
April 1, 1997.

Brooke, James. "Former Cultists Warn of Believers Now Adrift." New York Times,
April 2, 1997.

Bruni, Frank. "Leader Believed in Space Aliens and Apocalypse." New York Times,
March 28, 1997.

Bruni, Frank. "Odyssey of Regimentation Carried Cult Over Decades." New York Times,
March 29, 1997.

Chua-Eaon, Howard. "Imprisoned by His Own Passions: Marshall Herff Applewhite."
Time, April 7, 1997.

Corliss, Richard. "A Star Trek into the X-Files." Time, April 7, 1997.

Gleick, Elizabeth. "The Marker We've Been . . . Waiting For." Time, April 7, 1997.

Hafford, Michael. "Heaven's Gate 20 Years Later: 10 Things You Didn't Know."
Rolling Stone, March 24, 2017.

"Las Vegas Man Following Heaven's Gate Cult Beliefs Kills Self." Las Vegas Sun,
May 6, 1997.

Purdum, Todd S. "Videotapes Left by 39 Who Died Described Cult's Suicide Goal."
New York Times, March 28, 1997.

Steinberg, Jacques. "From Religious Childhood To Reins of a U.F.O. Cult."
New York Times, March 29, 1997.

Quittner, Josh. "Life and Death on the Web." Time, April 7, 1997.

Rogers, Kaleigh. "A Suicide Cult's Surviving Members Still Maintain Its 90s Website."
Vice, October 27, 2016. https://www.vice.com/en_us/article/aeky35/
a-suicide-cults-surviving-members-still-maintain-its-90s-website

Scott, Cathy. "Las Vegas Family Devastated by Loss of Cult Participant." Las Vegas Sun,
April 1, 1997.

Wambaugh, Joseph. "Meanwhile, Back at the Ranch . . ." *Time*, April 7, 1997.

Yuko, Elizabeth. "American Cult: 5 Spiritual Groups That Went Too Far." *Rolling Stone*, September 12, 2017.

13. CHRIS KORDA AND THE CHURCH OF EUTHANASIA

Bromley, David G. And Izaak Spiers. "Church of Euthanasia." Wrldrels.org 2018. https://wrldrels.org/2018/09/15/14893/ Chris Korda "The Church of Euthanasia Archives" at GOSWELL ROAD, Paris. Mousse Magazine, 2019. http://moussemagazine.it/chris-korda-church-euthanasia-archives-goswell-road-paris-2019/

Davis, Simon. "'Save the Planet, Kill Yourself': The Contentious History of the Church of Euthanasia." *Vice* October 23, 2015. https://www.vice.com/en_us/article/bnppam/save-the-planet-kill-yourself-the-contentious-history-of-the-church-of-euthanasia-1022

"'Save the Planet, Kill Yourself'"—An Interview. DigBoston.com, October 14, 2015. https://digboston.com/save-the-planet-kill-yourself-an-interview/

14. DAVID KORESH AND THE BRANCH DAVIDIANS

Barcella, Lou. "The Waco Siege: Six Little-Known Facts." History.com, April 13, 2018. https://www.history.com/news/waco-siege-what-happened-little-known-facts

Benson, Eric. "At Bible Study with David Koresh's Last Followers." *Texas Monthly*, March 26, 2018.

Benson, Eric. "The FBI Agent That Can't Stop Thinking About Waco." *Texas Monthly*, April 2018.

Benson, Eric. "The Reporter That Waco Destroyed Has No Regrets." *Texas Monthly*, March 29, 2018.

Boyer, Peter J. "The Children of Waco." *New Yorker*, May 15, 1995.

Chan, Melissa. "The Real Story Behind the Waco Siege: Who Were David Koresh and the Branch Davidians?" *Time*, January 24, 2018.

Childress, Sarah. "10 Things You May Not Know About Waco." *PBS Frontline*,
February 28, 2018. https://www.pbs.org/wgbh/frontline/article/10-things-you-may-not-know-about-waco/

Gladwell, Malcolm. "Sacred and Profane." New Yorker, March 24, 2014.

15. DAVID BERG AND THE CHILDREN OF GOD

Brocklehurst, Steven. "Children of God Cult Was 'Hell on Earth.'" *BBC Scotland News*,
June 27, 2018. https://www.bbc.com/news/uk-scotland-44613932

Bruney, Gabrielle. "Joaquin Phoenix and Rose McGowan Spent Their Early Years in a
Religious Cult. Then it Became Infamous." *Esquire*, October 5, 2019.

Farrell, Mike. "The Siblings Who Escaped the Children of God Cult." *BBC
Scotland News*, October 3, 2019. https://www.bbc.com/news/uk-scotland-49813941

Graham, Kate. "'I Grew Up in a Sex Cult': Surviving the Children of God Abuse."
Marie Claire, May 2018.

Nolasco, Stephanie. "Former Children of God Member Details Life in the
Apocalyptic Sex Cult That Lured Hollywood Celebs. *Fox News*,
June 13, 2018. https://www.foxnews.com/entertainment/former-children-of-god-member-details-life-in-the-apocalyptic-sex-cult-that-lured-hollywood-celebs

Tewa, Sophia. "Life After a sex cult: 'If I'm Not a Member of This Religion Any More,
Then Who Am I?'" *Guardian*, March 11, 2017. https://www.theguardian.com/world/2017/mar/11/children-of-god-church-sex-cult-texas-mexico-fbi

16. BOB MATHEWS AND THE ORDER

Flynn, Kevin and Gary Gerhardt. *The Silent Brotherhood: Inside America's Racist
Underground*. New York: Free Press, 1989.

Jimison, Robert. "How the FBI Smashed White Supremacist Group The Order."
CNN.com, August 21, 2018. https://www.cnn.com/2017/08/17/us/fbi-spying-white-supremacists-declassified/index.html

McClary Daryl C. "Robert Jay Mathews, Founder of the White-Supremacist Group The Order, Is Killed During an FBI Siege on Whidbey Island on December 8, 1984." historylink.org December 6, 2006. https://www.historylink.org/File/7921

Singular, Stephen. *Talked to Death: The Life and Murder of Alan Berg.* Sag Harbor, NY: Beech Tree Books, 1987.

17. JEONG-MYEONG-SEOK AND PROVIDENCE

Groom, Nelson. "'Your White Skin Arouses Me'": Inside the Sinister Hitler-Loving Korean Sex Cult Luring Young Australian Girls into Being 'Spiritual Brides' for a Serial Rapist—but Members Strongly Deny the Claims." *Daily Mail,* May 19, 2016.

Morgans, Julian. "A Cult Expert Explains What's New in Cults for 2018." *Vice,* May 27, 2018. https://www.vice.com/en_us/article/59j3m8/a-cult-expert-explains-his-role-in-helping-create-far-cry-5

Power, John. "How a South Korean Cult Tried and Failed to Sue This Australian Professor." *Vice,* December 31, 2014. https://www.vice.com/en_au/article/gq9wxy/how-a-south-korean-cult-tried-and-failed-to-sue-an-australian-school-teacher-for-defamation

"S. Korea Cult Leader Jailed for Sex." crimes.abc.net.au/news. August 12, 2008. https://mobile.abc.net.au/news/2008-08-12/s-korea-cult-leader-jailed-for-sex-crimes/473842?pfm=sm&pfmredir=sm

"Sex, Cults and the Bizarre World of Providence Leader Jeong Myeong-seok." *ABC News Australia,* December 12, 2017. https://www.abc.net.au/news/2017-12-11/the-bizarre-world-of-providence-cult-and-its-leader-jms/9224564

"South Korean religious sect leader jailed for rape." Reuters, August 12, 2008. https://www.reuters.com/article/us-korea-sect/south-korean-religious-sect-leader-jailed-for-rape-idUSSEO9345720080812

18. WARREN JEFFS AND THE FLDS

"Convicted Polygamist Leader Warren Jeffs Hospitalized in Tyler." *Dallas Morning News*, August 29, 2011.

Editorial: "Warren Jeffs' Conviction Ends a Sordid Tale of Perversion." *Dallas Morning News*, August 12, 2011.

"It Took Texas to Bring Polygamist Sect Leader Warren Jeffs to Justice." *Dallas Morning News*, August 13, 2011.

O'Neill, Anne. "Feds Deal Double Blow to FLDS, the Sect Led by the Jeffs Brothers." *CNN*, March 8, 2016. https://www.cnn.com/2016/03/07/us/flds-justice-department-warren-jeffs/index.html

O'Neill, Ann. "FLDS Prophet Warren Jeffs Reorganizing Sect from Prison, Feds Say." *CNN*, August 8, 2016. https://www.cnn.com/2016/08/08/us/flds-warren-jeffs/index.html

O'Neill, Ann. "Witnesses: Scallops for the Bishop, Toast for the Kids." *CNN*, April 6, 2016, https://www.cnn.com/2016/04/05/us/flds-secrets-warren-jeffs/index.html

O'Neill, Anne. "The turncoat: 'Thug Willie' Spills Secrets of FLDS and Its 'Prophet.'" *CNN* February 27, 2016. https://www.cnn.com/2016/02/25/us/jessop-flds-warren-jeffs-short-creek/index.html

Perkins, Nancy. "'Uncle Fred Arranged Marriage,'" Sister Says at Jeffs Trial. *Deseret News*, September 18, 2007.

Perkins, Nancy. "Warren Jeffs resigns as leader of the FLDS Church." *Deseret News*, December 5, 2007.

Perkins, Nancy. "Witness Recounts 'Complete Despair,' Betrayal in Testimony Against Polygamist Leader Jeffs." *Deseret News*, September 14, 2007.

Perkins, Nancy and Ben Winslow. "Prison Bound: Warren Jeffs Sentenced to 2 Terms of 5 to Life; He Plans Appeal." *Deseret News*, November 21, 2007.

Singular, Stephen. *When Men Become Gods: Mormon Polygamist Warren Jeffs, His Cult of Fear, and the Women Who Fought Back*. New York: St. Martin's Press, 2008.

Statement from Elissa Wall, Prosecution Witness in Warren Jeffs Trial. *Deseret News*, September 25, 2007.

Tomaso, Bruce. "Imprisoned Polygamist Leader Warren Jeffs Is Hospitalized in Critical Condition." *Dallas Morning News*, August 29, 2011.

Tomaso, Bruce. "Polygamist Warren Jeffs, Accused of Sex with Children, Objects in Court by Shouting, 'This Sayeth the Lord, Cease!'" *Dallas Morning News*, August 3, 2011.

Tomaso, Bruce. "Warren Jeffs, Polygamist and Child Rapist, is Expected to Live." *Dallas Morning News*, August 30, 2011.

Wagner, Dennis." Jeffs Gets Life; Sect's Future in Question." *Arizona Republic*, August 10, 2011.

Weissert, Will. "Warren Jeffs Convicted of Child Sex Assault." *Arizona Republic*, August 10, 2011.

Winslow, Ben. "FLDS Sect May Splinter Now That Jeffs Is in Prison." *Deseret News*, December 2, 2007.

Winslow, Ben. "'I Am Not the Prophet,'" Says Note by Jeffs. *Deseret News*, April 5, 2007.

Winslow, Ben. "Jeffs Tried to Kill Self, Papers Say: Unsealed Evaluation Says he Tried to Hang Self in Cell." *Deseret News*, November 7, 2007.

Winslow, Ben. "Warren Jeffs' Accuser No Longer Anonymous." *Deseret News*, September 21,

Winslow, Ben and Nancy Perkins. "Jury Finds Jeffs Guilty." *Deseret News*, September 25, 2007.

Winslow, Ben and Nancy Perkins. "Released Video Shows Emotional Jeffs in Jail." *Deseret News*, November 8, 2007.

Winslow, Ben and Nancy Perkins. "Warren Jeffs Sentenced to 2 Five to Life Terms for Child-Bride Marriage." *Deseret News*, November 20, 2007.

19. THE COLUMBINE MASS SHOOTING CULT

Barnett, Jackson, Saja Hindi, and Kieran Nicholson. "'Massive Manhunt' Underway for Florida Woman 'Infatuated with Columbine' Now Armed with Shotgun in Colorado: Sol Pais, 18, Purchased a Shotgun and Ammunition in Colorado After Arriving from Miami, Officials Say." *Denver Post*, April 16, 2019.

Brothers, Amy. "Bearing Witness Podcast, Part 3: How the Conversation Has Changed in the 20 Years Since Columbine." *Denver Post*, April 19, 2019.

Brothers, Amy. "Bearing Witness Podcast, Part 2: The Search for 'Why' in the Aftermath of Columbine." *Denver Post*, April 18, 2019.

Brothers, Amy, Katie Rausch, and Kyle Newman. "Bearing Witness Podcast, Part 1: Looking Back at the Day of the Columbine High School Shooting." *Denver Post*, April 17, 2019.

Chappell, Bill and Sasha Ingber. "'This Is Not Who We Are,' Colorado Officials Say After Deadly School Shooting." *NPR*, May 8, 2019. https://www.npr.org/2019/05/08/721474989/this-is-not-who-we-are-colorado-officials-say-after-deadly-school-shooting

Daley, John. "Colorado Authorities Probe School Shooting Not Far From Columbine." *NPR*, May 8, 2019. https://www.npr.org/2019/05/08/721350564/colorado-authorities-probe-school-shooting-not-far-from-columbine

Editorial: "20 Years After Columbine, Colorado Gripped by Fear and Sorrow." *Denver Post*, April 19, 2019.

Fernandez, Manny, Julie Turkewitz, and Jeff Bidgood. "For 'Columbiners,' School Shootings Have a Deadly Allure." *New York Times*, May 30, 2018.

Gehring, Kurt. "20 years after Columbine Shooting, Little Has Been Accomplished on Gun Control: America's Deeply Rooted Gun Culture Has Made for a Partisan Stalemate on Dealing with Gun Violence." *Denver Post*, April 14, 2019.

Gibbs, Nancy and Timothy Roche. "The Columbine Tapes: In Five Secret Videos They Recorded Before the Massacre, the Killers Reveal Their Hatreds—and Their Lust for Fame." *Time*, December 20, 1999.

Goode, Eric. "The Things We Know About School Shooters." *New York Times*, February 15, 2018.

Hernandez, Elizabeth. "Columbine Community Gathers for Tearful, Hopeful Ceremony: Survivors of the Shooting, Alumni, Current Students and Impacted Families Came to Clement Park Saturday for the 20th Anniversary of the Columbine High School Shooting." *Denver Post*, April 20, 2019.

"How The Columbine Massacre Shaped Survivors' Lives 20 Years Later." *NPR*, April 20, 2019. https://www.npr.org/2019/04/20/715393905/how-the-columbine-massacre-shaped-survivors-lives-20-years-later

James, Susan Donaldson. "Columbine Shootings 10 Years Later: Students, Teacher Still Haunted by Post-Traumatic Stress." *ABC News*, April 9, 2009. https://abcnews.go.com/Health/story?id=7300782&page=1

James, Susan Donaldson. "Psychology of Virginia Tech, Columbine Killers Still Baffles Experts." *ABC News*, April 15, 2009. https://abcnews.go.com/Health/MindMoodNews/story?id=7345607&page=1

James, Susan Donaldson. "Surviving Columbine: What We Got Wrong." *ABC News*, April 17, 2020.https://abcnews.go.com/Health/MindMoodNews/story?id=7363898&page=1

Kennedy, Merrit and James Doubek. "FBI Says Armed Woman Obsessed With Columbine Apparently Killed Herself In Denver Area." *NPR*, April 17, 2019. https://www.npr.org/2019/04/17/714205353/denver-area-schools-closed-as-authorities-search-for-armed-and-dangerous-woman

Kohler, Judith. "On Eve of Columbine's 20th Anniversary, Hundreds Turn Out for Solemn Vigil: Vigil One of Several Events Marking the Anniversary of the School Shootings." *Denver Post*, April 19, 2019.

"List: Colorado School Shootings Since Columbine: The STEM School Shooting Is the Fourth Since April 20, 1999." *Denver Post*, May 7, 2019.

Maslin, Sarah. "19 Years After Columbine, Students Again Say 'Enough' on Gun Violence." *New York Times*, April 20, 2018.

Minor, Nathaniel and Andrea Dukakis. "How Effective Are School Lockdown Drills?" *NPR*, April 19, 2019. https://www.npr.org/2019/04/19/715193493/how-effective-are-school-lockdown-drills

Nista, Monica. "Teen Accused of Planning Columbine-Like Attack in Orange Co., N.Y." *ABC News*, October 20, 2009. https://abcnews.go.com/WN/teen-charged-planning-columbine-attack-orange-ny/story?id=8875075

Ontiveroz, Aaron. "Columbine Families, Survivors Reflect on Hope and Healing 20 Years After One of Colorado's Darkest Days." *Denver Post*, April 20, 2019.

Patterson, Leigh. "20 Years After The Columbine Shooting, Students And Staff Reflect On What Happened." *NPR*, April 19, 2019. https://www.npr.org/2019/04/19/715266719/20-years-after-the-columbine-shooting-students-and-staff-reflect-on-what-happene

Thomas, Pierre, Mike Levine, Jack Cloherty, and Jack Date. "Columbine Shootings' Grim Legacy: More Than 50 School Attacks, Plots." *ABC News*, October 7, 2014. https://abcnews.go.com/US/columbine-shootings-grim-legacy-50-school-attacks-plots/story?id=26007119

Turkewitz, Julie. Columbine, Virginia Tech, Sandy Hook. "How 3 Communities Honor Their Dead. The Process of Creating a Permanent Memorial to the Victims of a Mass Shooting is Often Riddle with Emotion and Conflict." *New York Times*, April 20, 2018.

"Twenty Years Later, A Look At Columbine, Then And Now." *NPR*, April 18, 2019. https://www.npr.org/2019/04/18/714788633/twenty-years-later-a-look-at-columbine-then-and-now

Wingerter, Meg and David Migoya. "Since Columbine, Colorado Schools See Increase in Lockdowns As Students Report More Possible Threats: While School Lockdowns Are Increasing Across the State, Most Incidents Aren't Direct Threats to Schools." *Denver Post*, April 16, 2019.

IMAGE CREDITS

INDEX

ABOUT THE AUTHOR

Stephen Singular's work has appeared in *New York* magazine, *Psychology Today*, *Inside Sports*, *The New York Times Magazine*, and *Rolling Stone*. A two-time *New York Times* bestselling author, he's written twenty-five non-fiction books, many about high-profile crimes. His wife, Joyce Jacques-Singular, has assisted him with many of these titles and co-wrote the two most recent ones. Through her research, editorial suggestions, and creative input, she was a critical part of *Killer Cults*. Singular's other books include social criticism and business and sports biographies. He's appeared on "Good Morning, America," "The Today Show," CNN's "Larry King Live" and "Anderson Cooper 360," FOX-TV, MSNBC, TRU-TV, ESPN, CNBC, and many other media outlets. Five of his books have been turned into films, television movies, or documentaries. For more information, please visit www.stephensingular.com.